THE MORVILLE YEAR

KATHERINE SWIFT lives at the Dower House, Morville Hall, in Shropshire. She worked as a rare-book librarian in Oxford and Dublin before becoming a full-time gardener and writer in 1988. She was for four years gardening columnist of *The Times*, and has written widely in the gardening press, including an acclaimed series on the gardens and landscapes of Orkney for *Hortus*. She is the author of *Pergolas, Arbours and Arches: Their History and How to Make Them* (with Paul Edwards and Jessica Smith), *Jim Partridge* (with Alison Britton) and *The Morville Hours*.

BY THE SAME AUTHOR

Jim Partridge (with Alison Britton)

Pergolas, Arbours and Arches:
Their History and How to Make Them
(with Paul Edwards and Jessica Smith)

Preserving Our Printed Heritage:
The Long Room Project at Trinity College Dublin
(with Anthony Cains)

The Morville Hours

THE MORVILLE YEAR

Katherine Swift

BLOOMSBURY

LONDON · BERLIN · NEW YORK · SYDNEY

First published in Great Britain 2011
This paperback edition published 2012

Copyright © Katherine Swift 2011

Illustrations copyright © Dawn Burford 2011
Photographs copyright © Jane Sebire 2011
Maps by Reginald Piggott

Katherine Swift has asserted her right to be identified as the author of this work

All articles first published in *The Times*/nisyndication.com

Bloomsbury Publishing Plc
50 Bedford Square
London WC1B 3DP

www.bloomsbury.com

Bloomsbury Publishing, London, New York and Berlin

A CIP catalogue record for this book is available from the British Library

ISBN 978 1 4088 2213 5

10 9 8 7 6 5 4 3 2 1

Typeset by Hewer Text UK Ltd, Edinburgh
Printed in Great Britain by Clays Limited, St Ives plc

for Mirabel Osler

Contents

Maps   x

Introduction   xv

Spring

March   3
    Lilies in the Snow – Pilgrimage – Changing Your Mind
    – Primroses – Horehound & Hyssop – What's in a
    Name? – Black & Gold – Easter Gardens

April   23
    'Sing all a green willow' – Falling in Love Again – Plum
    Blossom – Weeding & Seeding – Geological Map – It's
    True . . . – Fritillaries – *In Dreams Begin Responsibilities*
    – Old Walls

May   47
    Blackthorn Winter – Blue & Green – *Carpe Diem*
    – Wakefield Tulips – The Lesson of the Master –
    Sundials – Morville Flower Festival – Rabbit-proof Fence

Summer

June   71
    Just Looking – Foxgloves – *Endeavour* – Transitions
    – Not a Bed of Roses – Peonies – Eyes Wide Shut
    – Midsummer's Day

July 91
All Change – Lupins – Losing Control – In Siberia
– Leaving Home – Cottage Yellows – Gillyflowers
– July Gap – Other People's Gardens

August 115
Dog Days – Rain – Black & White – Summer Pruning
– Sour Grapes – Rapunzel, Rapunzel – Bees on the
Lavender – Autumn Raspberries – Dewpoint

Autumn

September 141
Seen from a Train – After Dark – Two Elegant Ladies
– How Does Your Garden Go? – *All Passion Spent*
– 'What is that wonderful tree?' – Old Potts Way
Traffic Island – Yew Clipping

October 165
Eat Your Greens – The Poetics of Space – The Colour
Red – Choosing Tulips – Bread & Roses – The
Eponymous Lord Derby – Taking Stock – 'Do you
remember an inn, Miranda?'

November 189
Little Sparta – After the Storm – An American
President – Autumn Colour – Queen Olga's Snowdrop
– The Patient Mulberry – Ghost Story – Frost Warning

Winter

December 211
Inside Out, Outside In – The Art of Looking –
Metamorphoses – 'And what will the robin do then,
poor thing?' – Mistletoe – Christmas Tales – Paper-clips
& Diaries – Christmas Eve

January 233

    Midwinter Bonfires – Chiltern Seeds – Weathervanes
    – In Praise of Winter – Glamour – A Little Vase of
    Flowers – Traveller's Joy – A Different Perspective
    – Tax Return

February 257

    Candlemas Day – *Madonna of the Pinks* – Make
    Yourself at Home – February – A Winter's Tale –
    Springwatch – Treasure – *Et In Arcadia Ego*
    – Welcoming the Wilderness

and Spring again . . .

March 281

    A Windy Day – It Must Be Spring – Beginning Again
    – Cats & Cardoons – Simple Pleasures

Appendix

Recipes 297

Addresses 303

Acknowledgements 305

Index 307

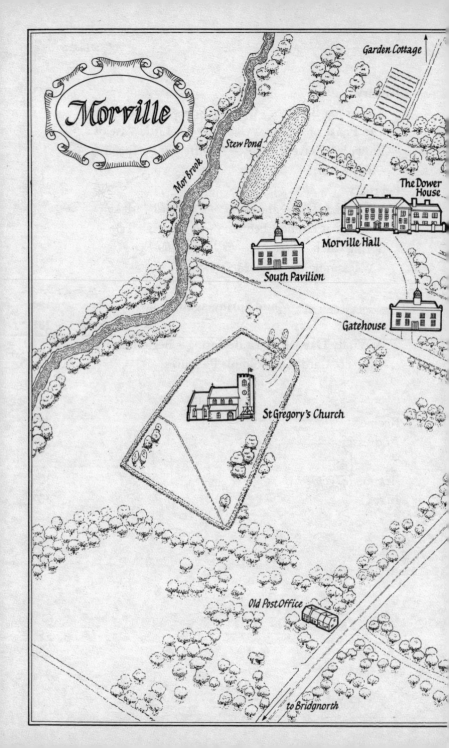

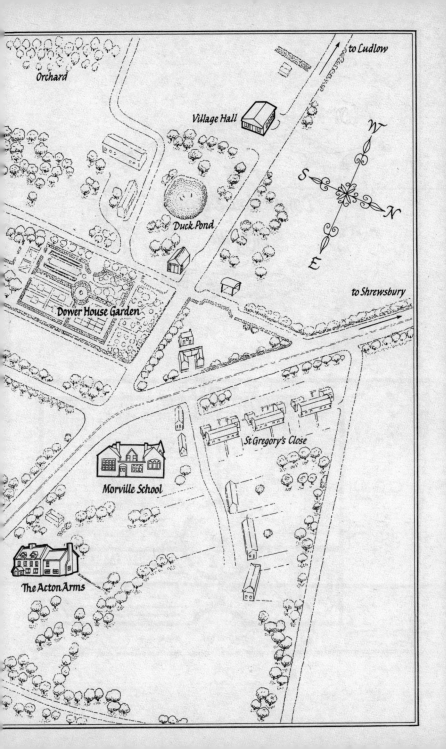

The
Dower House Garden
Morville

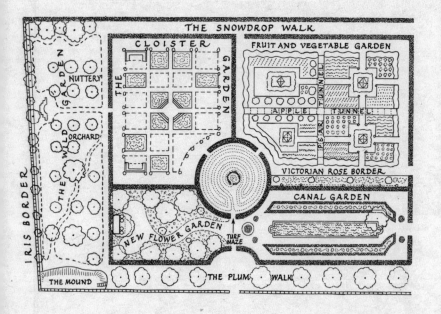

THE SNOWDROP WALK

CLOISTER GARDEN

THE GARDEN

NUTTERY

THE WILD GARDEN

ORCHARD

IRIS BORDER

FRUIT AND VEGETABLE GARDEN

APPLE TUNNEL

PEAR TUNNEL

VICTORIAN ROSE BORDER

CANAL GARDEN

NEW FLOWER GARDEN

TURF MAZE

THE MOUND

THE PLUM WALK

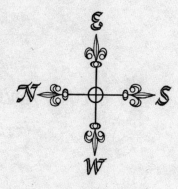

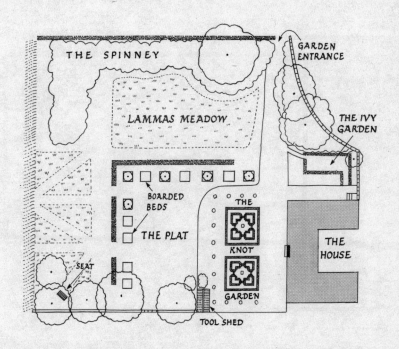

THE SPINNEY

LAMMAS MEADOW

GARDEN
ENTRANCE

THE IVY
GARDEN

BOARDED
BEDS

THE PLAT

SEAT

THE

KNOT

GARDEN

THE
HOUSE

TOOL SHED

Introduction

From the December of 2001 to the July of 2005 I wrote a weekly column about gardening for the Saturday edition of *The Times* newspaper. For a dozen or so years before that, I had been keeping a diary about the making of the garden at Morville in Shropshire, where I had come to live in 1988. The columns seem to have taken the place of the diaries (certainly I wrote no more diaries after 2001), and are thus a record of what I was doing and thinking each week in my own garden, together with the books I might have been reading, occasional trips I might have made to see plays or exhibitions in London and elsewhere, and forays into other people's gardens, all of which provided stimulus and ideas for the garden I was making at home.

The idea behind the garden was to try (by means of a series of gardens-within-a-garden) to tell the history of the house and its setting and, incidentally, of English gardening as it unfolded over a period of a thousand years or so. When I began the research that would underpin the garden, I found that every plant had a story – who first grew it or collected it from the wild, gave it a name or painted its picture, wrote a poem about it or used it to cure some ailment? Every one came trailing clouds of glory. Many of these preoccupations are reflected in the columns: there is much here about the plant-hunters and the histories of individual flowers, from a handful of the old 'florists' flowers' (tulips, auriculas, pinks, anemones, gold-laced polyanthus, hyacinths) to fruit trees (pears, plums, apples, quinces), herbs medicinal and culinary, old vegetables like cardoons, cottage garden flowers like peonies and (especially) old roses – which between them formed the backbone of the garden – as well as a lot about lilies and agapanthus (which I fell for in a big way). In the columns, I go to see Raphael's *Madonna of the Pinks* and admire William Nicholson's painting of dandelions. I take up bee-keeping and buy a motorbike. There is a long-running debate with myself about wildness and self-seeding in the garden, and the extent to which, even within a formal garden, one can step back and let Nature take a hand; 'Losing Control' is one of several such gleeful episodes.

By 2001 the broad outline of the garden and much of the planting was in place, but there was plenty of tinkering going on as I continued to collect plants, to arrange and rearrange them, and to see what would 'do' and what would not in my red Shropshire soil. The columns thus record my own deliberations and discoveries at the time they were being made, the gathering of information and the weighing of pros and cons as – largely by trial and often by error – I made my own decisions about plants and planting, pruning and maintenance, the siting of a garden seat or the choice of a colour scheme. But whatever the weekly subject, one constant theme was the weather, the turning of the seasons: that sense of being out of doors, vigilant for those tiny signs (and sudden reversals) – first dewfall of autumn, perhaps, or threat of late frost in spring – that signal big changes in the life of the garden and its occupants. In the world of the columns, those inhabitants included not only me and my plants, but peacock butterflies and hawk moths, blackbirds and robins, foxes and rabbits, bumble-bees and – to the dismay of some readers and the delight of others – my tribe of cats. (The account of Grace making an elegant beeline for a blackbird's nest ('It Must Be Spring') provoked howls of outrage – the single biggest post-bag the column ever received; my neighbour Bridget's cat Blackberry, on the other hand – a devilishly successful hunter of rabbits – acquired his own fan club.)

The idea of 'close looking', the attentive chronicling of plants and flowers in the garden at all stages of their growth, in all weathers, not simply when in flower, runs through the columns, a constant exhortation to the reader (but above all to myself) to 'look: really *look*; tomorrow may be too late' ('*Carpe Diem*'). I see now that this close looking, and the linked theme of *carpe diem* ('seize the day'), is the mainspring not only of many of the columns – 'Just Looking' is another example – but of all my writing, generating not simply the urge to record but the need for precision, the search for exactly the right word. I am conscious that this often led (and leads) to strings of adjectives (a journalistic solecism) and often, when plainer words failed, to simile and metaphor (a frequent target for *The Times* sub-editors). But I am unapologetic. The aim was always to capture, as precisely as possible, the fleeting nature of a particular day, a particular cast of the weather, a particular plant: a moment in my life.

The writing of the columns also ran concurrently with the writing of *The Morville Hours*, a project begun in 1993 and worked at intermittently for the next fifteen years until it finally saw publication in 2008. That book told the story of how I came to Morville and began to make the garden, interwoven with the stories of the many other people (present day as well as long past) who had lived at Morville and whose lives ran parallel with mine. Some of the themes of *The Morville Hours* are also thus reflected in the columns (a fascination with the peculiarities of calendars and other methods of measuring time; the procession of saints' days and other feasts of the liturgical calendar which make up the church year), though the columns are generally more practical in tone and content, often providing me with a way of dealing with a problem or an idea more directly than was possible within the pattern of the book, from which they came to be both an escape and a relief.

The addressee of the columns is frequently a conversational 'you', not in any prescriptive sense, but with the sort of fellow feeling that might have been conveyed in an earlier age by 'one'. Writing the column came to be like writing a weekly letter to a circle of gardening friends – friends who, I felt, would sympathise with my all too frequent failures, laugh at my follies and join in my occasional triumphs, understanding what a switchback ride of highs and lows making a garden is.

I had always written about my gardens, and whether the columns supplanted the diaries or not, there was never any question of ceasing to record in some form or other my life in the garden. What had begun in 1970 as bare chronology – lists of jobs to do and jobs done (or more often un-done) each week in my first garden on the outskirts of Oxford – had by 2001 become a detailed record of thoughts and feelings and observations. The writing had become a way of thinking aloud, a way of answering that perennial question, 'What if?', conjuring a new garden or a new part of the garden into existence by means of words on the page. That process is described in one of the earliest columns reprinted here ('In Praise of Winter'), which tells the story of how in 1989, my first winter at Morville, 'I read and dreamed and cross-referred and made lists', writing the guidebook to a garden which did not yet exist: 'by March my imaginary garden was so real that I could walk about in it and smell the flowers'. Reading, writing and gardening remain for me indissoluble, the garden not simply the physical place where I spend most of my days, but a mental space built out of thoughts and emotions, associations and memories – mine and other people's.

The urge among gardeners to record their daily doings seems very strong. While I was writing for *The Times* the paper held a garden-writing competition jointly sponsored by the quarterly gardening magazine *Hortus*; we received more than seven hundred entries. Reading them was a delight. Almost everyone chose to write about not great or famous gardens but ordinary, everyday gardens, especially their own. There was one overriding theme: the extent to which memory provides the warp and weft of our gardening lives. Here were parents and grandparents digging for victory, lawns given over to potatoes, flower-beds surrendered to hump-backed Anderson shelters camouflaged with trailing nasturtiums; here were gardens once full of cars and boats and motorcycles, 'filling all the back gardens with a wonderful young man's roar', now quiet again as children grew up and left home; here were gardens left behind, given up, surrendered, but never forgotten.

The book I eventually wrote about making my own garden, *The Morville Hours*, dealt extensively with episodes from my childhood, stories of my parents' own upbringings during the Depression of the 1930s, and especially with the gardens I remember my father making as we moved house from place to place – a theme continued in that book's forthcoming sequel, provisionally entitled *A Rose for Morville* – so I have chosen not to reprint here columns which deal with some of those same issues.

The 105 columns (and occasional feature) selected here are the original versions, and are thus frequently longer than the versions which appeared in *The Times*. The exigencies of writing for a weekly newspaper meant that, especially in my early days on the paper, the columns were often trimmed and occasionally hard-pruned by sub-editors to fit a space which varied from week to week. Later on, the columns settled down to a steady eight hundred words apiece. Apart from the removal of some out-of-date references to suppliers or prices or garden opening times, they are printed here as originally written, and in much the same order, month by month, with the exception of an occasional interpolation or rearrangement for the sake of continuity or clarity. Where it is felt that addresses or further information might be helpful, these are included in the appendix at the back of the book. Inevitably some subjects came up every year, and so some columns have been shortened to avoid repetition. I have dated each column, to give the context where this may not be immediately apparent, such as the arrival of the first photographs beamed back by the Huygens space probe from the surface of Titan, Saturn's largest moon, in January 2005 (which prompted one column's reflections on lichens), or the transit of Venus in June 2004 (the starting point for a column about Cook's circumnavigation of the globe), or the election later that year of an American president (prompting a re-examination of Thomas Jefferson in the unaccustomed role of gardener). If there is a common theme, it is that gardening is about so much more than just gardens.

Katherine Swift
Morville, 14 January 2010

SPRING

March

March comes in with an adder's head
and goes out with a peacock's tail

Gold-laced polyanthus

Lilies in the Snow

We're on the cusp of spring, havering back and forth between spring and winter. Some days are as balmy as April; others still feel like the middle of winter. In Bridgnorth, our nearest town, the gardens are bright with yellow daffodils and purple aubretia, the lawns green and trim. But not up here. It still looks (and feels) like winter – drifts of snowdrops, unkempt grass, not a daffodil in sight.

And my mood, too, swings between periods of mad energy and elation on the one hand, and days when I can hardly bear to stir out of the house. The other day I found two huge cardboard boxes on the doorstep: a consignment of plants and bulbs ordered from the wholesalers in a fit of enthusiasm a week or two ago. And now I can hardly remember what I ordered. Or why. What on earth was I planning to do with all those red-hot pokers? Those dahlias? Those lilies?

The lilies are *Lilium longiflorum* from Japan, the most elegant and refined of all lilies, with long narrow white trumpets washed outside with palest green, and a scent as delicate as sweet box on a cold January day. I had dreamed of filling a dozen large terracotta pots with them to surround the little Ivy Garden. The thought of the lilies cheers me up. So I take them and the pots and some bags of John Innes No. 2 into the open-sided trap-shed to pot them up out of the wind. They are stem-rooting lilies, and the secret is to plant them low down in the pot (three to a ten-inch pot). You put a good layer of crocks and three or four inches of compost beneath, then just cover the bulbs with a pinch of sand and a little more compost, leaving five inches or so of empty pot above. Then gradually earth them up as the stem lengthens. But they can be tender, so I'll put them in a cold frame when I've finished, and throw an old blanket over them on cold nights.

As I work, I glance up from time to time. The wind seems to have dropped. Then suddenly, with hardly any warning, there's a blizzard steaming down the valley opposite, roaring with a sound like an express train, the grainy whiteness of it outlined against the dark hillside behind, while where I stand only an occasional flake slowly spirals down in the still air. It's like a monstrous flock of starlings coming in to roost: the noise, the numbers so densely packed, the swirling mass of them. And then just as suddenly it's gone. Later, when I drive down to Ludlow, I can see in the distance that the snow has settled on the peak of the Titterstone Clee, transforming it for an afternoon into a Japanese woodcut of Mount Fuji.

9 March 2002

Pilgrimage

For the medieval Englishman, a pilgrimage to St David's was considered so onerous that it counted as the spiritual equivalent to half a pilgrimage to distant Rome itself. Transport may have improved since then, but reaching the far western tip of Wales can still feel like a satisfyingly long and even arduous journey. Last week the snow was still lying in the fields as I headed out of Herefordshire and into Wales: I was on a pilgrimage of my own, in search of the elusive Tenby daffodil.

The Tenby daffodil (*Narcissus obvallaris*) is unique to Pembrokeshire. Its origins are a mystery: some say that it was brought by monks or perhaps by Flemish workers; others have traced it to a wild population in the Montes de Toledo of Spain; still others maintain that it is a hybrid of garden origin which arose by chance in Wales itself. Remnants of a once much larger population can still be found in old gardens and hedge bottoms. Vast quantities of the bulbs were dug up out of the fields and sold during the nineteenth century, and more were ploughed and sprayed out by modern farming methods in the mid-twentieth. It was then extensively replanted in gardens and by roadsides in a new wave of enthusiasm thirty years later. It is probably impossible now to say where or whether or when the Tenby daffodil ever grew wild.

In Tenby itself the parks and planters are awash with daffodils of all sorts at this time of year, including the Tenby daffodil. But I wanted to see them, if not in the wild, at least in great sheets and swathes the way they used to grow. I went to enquire at St John's Church in Tenby, up against the walls of the old town, where the parishioners were holding their annual Festival of Daffodils for St David's Day, with fluttering Welsh flags and ladies outside selling Welsh cakes hot from the griddle, and inside, tied to each pew, bunches of daffodils, each with the name of a loved one remembered on that day. 'Try Manorbier,' one of the ladies said.

I knew Manorbier, with its gloomy Norman castle overlooking the sea, the birthplace of Giraldus Cambrensis (one of the first chroniclers of the deeds of Merlin). I had already scoured the lanes, looking for daffodils. But it was here, following a chain of clues, that I at last found my Tenby daffodils. Nick Bean and his wife Pat specialise in growing miniature daffodils as cut flowers, and they have been building up stocks of Tenby daffodils for the past twenty years. Their friend Monica took me up to one of the small fields they cultivate almost within earshot of the sea, and there they were, Tenby daffodils in their hundreds of thousands, running across the field like liquid sunshine in the melting snow.

The Tenby daffodil is a perfect miniature of the traditional yellow trumpet daffodil. The crisp neat little flowers are hardly more than two inches across, bright sunshine-yellow, against noticeably grey leaves. It is stiff and sturdy, with strong straight stems perhaps twelve inches tall, not at all like the wild daffodils which Wordsworth described 'fluttering and dancing in the breeze' on the shores of Ullswater in the Lake District. Wordsworth's daffodils were *N. pseudonarcissus*, the delicate nodding little Lent Lily, which has an altogether more secretive and tremulous air, with slender, slightly arching stalks, and long narrow trumpets with paler, slightly twisted, outer petals. Both are excellent bulbs for naturalising in grass.

Wordsworth's poem was based upon an actual incident, a walk which the poet took with his sister Dorothy to Gowbarrow Park one windy Maundy Thursday in 1802. But – reflecting Wordsworth's view of poetry as 'the spontaneous overflow of powerful feelings recollected in tranquillity' – the poem was not written until two years later, when Wordsworth was recalling the pleasure that the memory of finding the daffodils continued to give him over the years. The poem lacks the immediacy of Dorothy's journal entry, written on that windy day in 1802: it is Dorothy who captures the real feeling of that wild walk over the hills, and how the daffodils 'tossed and reeled and danced and seemed as if they verily laughed with the wind that blew upon them over the lake . . . ever glancing ever changing.' If the Tenby daffodil is like liquid sunshine, the *pseudonarcissus* is a personification of the March wind itself.

I had one final question. In Shakespeare's *Henry V*, Captain Fluellen wears a leek in his hat on St David's Day. Is the daffodil the true emblem of Wales, or is it the leek? Apparently in Welsh the two names are very similar: '*cenhinen*' is Welsh for leek, '*cenhinen Bedr*' ('Peter's leek') for daffodil. It seems that Shakespeare was only teasing: it's the daffodil, of course.

13 March 2004

Changing Your Mind

It's every gardener's privilege to change their mind. And everyone's duty to admit when they were wrong. We are not all blessed with second sight, and sometimes it can be difficult to envisage how a shape or a colour will look until you see it in the flesh. It took me three attempts to get the shape of my Canal right. It's a narrow water feature halfway between a pool and a rill, running down the middle of a long thin formal bit of the garden. I call it my Canal; my friend Jeremy, more down to earth – he's an archaeologist – calls it my 'long pond'. But whatever its name, the shape at one end was patently wrong. Changing it meant asking the dear man who had done the stonework partly to demolish it and start again. But what could I say? I'd just got it wrong.

We once moved a ten-year-old mulberry tree here, too, which took six of us to carry. Most trees and shrubs can be moved when dormant if you take a few elementary precautions. Better that than endure that irritating niggle every time you walk up the garden.

Plants can be very forgiving. There are some huge climbing roses here now in their third home. I bought four bushes of the crimson multiflora rambler *Rosa* 'Russelliana', thinking they would look wonderful draped over the entrance to the apple tunnel with the white flowers and sealing-wax stems of the evergreen rambler *Rosa* 'Adélaïde d'Orléans'. But draping is just what 'Russelliana' will not do – it is stiff and strong – and in any case I decided later on that I wanted to have all white roses in that part of the garden. So I found the 'Russellianas' a home in the Cloister Garden, where they ramped away splendidly over two wooden trellis arbours, mixed this time with *Rosa* x *alba* 'Semi plena'. The problem there was their date. I was trying to reproduce the effect of the arbours seen in many medieval paintings and miniatures where double red and double white climbing roses frame a Madonna and Child or a pair of all-too-secular lovers. But there is no tall double red climbing rose of the right date. It's one of those horticultural mysteries: was the effect produced by multiple grafts? Was it a symbol, poetic licence? Or has the rose just disappeared from cultivation? I substituted the 'Russellianas'. But they wouldn't do: every time I looked at them they screamed 'nineteenth century' at me, betraying their origin by getting black spot (which no self-respecting medieval *gallica* would ever dream of doing).

So last year I moved them again. My long-suffering 'Russellianas' are now planted against the far south-facing wall at the bottom of the Wild Garden, partnered with newly planted pale purple and lilac wisteria, and drifts of pale sky-blue irises. The crimson roses, the tumbling wisteria, the clear cool colours of the irises – it sounds lovely. But you never know . . .

For established wisterias, now is your last chance to prune. My wisterias are only young, and I'm still training them out on horizontal wires in the hope that they will clothe the whole wall from top to bottom. The trick is not to let them run up vertically, otherwise they will only flower at the top. Established wisterias are usually pruned twice a year, once in late August, and then again in February. In August all the whippy new growth is shortened to five or six buds. Then in February the shoots are shortened still further, cutting them back hard to no more than two buds. The point of this is to insure against the flower buds being pecked out by bullfinches or damaged by frost.

For my wisteria wall I chose varieties of all three common wisterias in order to lengthen the season of flowering – W. *floribunda, W. sinensis* and W. x *formosa* – plus the silky white scented W. *venusta* as a highlight in the middle. Then I added standards of white W. *sinensis* at either end, for a touch of frivolity. After all, gardening is meant to be fun, isn't it? And if it doesn't work I can always change my mind.

2 March 2002

[*I did: the standard wisterias were later moved to the Fruit and Vegetable Garden, and were replaced in the Wild Garden by six pollarded silver-leaved* Salix alba *'Sericea' (see 'Taking Stock').*]

Primroses

Everything in the landscape is always older than you think. The ridges rumpling the hillside opposite my garden, like a billowy green eiderdown, are the remains of medieval ridge and furrow – the open field system of agriculture which predated the present eighteenth-century enclosed fields. The terrace below them which seems to stop abruptly halfway along may have been gouged out by a glacier millions of years ago. The track which curves across the valley floor to my left is almost certainly pre-Norman and may well be more ancient than that. And on this side of the valley, sweeping away to the right, is a long flat grassy platform, a seventeenth-century garden terrace, cut into the steep slope beneath a twentieth-century vineyard.

In a few weeks the cowslips (*Primula veris*) will be out on the sunny open south-facing slope above the grass terrace, primroses (*Primula vulgaris*) in the damper heavier ground below it, where the bank is shaded by trees and runs down towards the brook. And I'm told that there are oxlips in the woods opposite. These must be what are known as 'false oxlips' (*Primula veris* x *vulgaris*), which are naturally occurring variable hybrids often found where the two species grow close together. True oxlips (*Primula elatior*) have pale flowers like small primroses, held in drooping bunches all on one side of slender cowslip-like stalks. They are very rare indeed now, virtually confined to the counties of Cambridgeshire, Suffolk and Essex, where they are indicators of ancient woodland. So if they do indeed grow in our woods (I've never found them) it would mean the woodland here is much older than anyone ever thought.

It's always instructive to think about natural habitats when siting things in one's own garden. I grew a few cowslips from seed the other year and planted them in impoverished turf in the poor soil of a sunny bit of the Cloister Garden, aiming at a *mille fleurs* effect like a medieval tapestry, with little clumps of thrift and wild pinks. Although the other things gradually died out, the cowslips self-seeded prolifically, studding the turf in April and May with spikes of bright yellow – and here and there a red one, the result of cross-pollination with some red cowslips I planted elsewhere in the garden. Red cowslips occur naturally in some wild populations and may have been one of the ancestors of the modern polyanthus.

I have more difficulty growing primroses (especially the garden doubles which are notoriously difficult to keep), but I think I may now have found just the spot where the wild ones will be happy and seed themselves around without further mollycoddling from me: up in the Nuttery, where the canopy of the hazels has gradually closed overhead and suppressed the taller grasses.

Primroses and cowslips are fascinating plants. They throw up a large number of highly attractive mutant forms such as the jack-in-the-green, where the terminal lobes of the calyx continue to grow as leafy appendages, making a little ruff of leaves around the flower, and the hose-in-hose, where the calyx is transformed into a second corolla, giving the impression of one flower sitting inside another. Then there is the jackanapes with a striped calyx – a mixture of petal and leaf; the gallygaskins with an enlarged ribbed calyx; and even double and triple mutations such as the jackanapes-on-horseback. Elizabethan and Jacobean gardeners loved them all.

Before the great influx of exciting new plants from Turkey and Persia in the seventeenth century, gardeners depended for novelty upon finding chance mutations of common native flowers like these. The science behind such mutations is now more clearly understood. It is known, for example, that many of the mutated genes in anomolous forms of primrose are dominant (which is why these plants have survived for so long). Start your very own seed strain with seed from Barnhaven Primroses, guaranteed to yield a high proportion of such forms.

30 March 2002

Horehound & Hyssop

It's been a terrible winter for 'flu. My mother, my husband, my next-door neighbour Bridget, Reg the butcher, Mark the milkman, Nick who brings us logs – just about everyone seems to have had it. My husband in fact had it twice, poor man, with bronchitis afterwards for good measure, which left him with a nagging cough. So I went up into the garden the other day to look for some horehound for him, to make an infusion. I was relieved to see that one or two plants had survived the recent bad weather and were still leafy enough to yield a few sprigs (this is not ideal, of course: the best way is to pick the flowering tops in early summer and dry them). But I can see that I shall have to sow more this year. It's one of those plants I simply couldn't do without.

White horehound (*Marrubium vulgare*) has been known since Roman times as an excellent remedy for chesty coughs. I sympathise with those old Romans, posted up to Hadrian's Wall in their short skirts: no wonder they got coughs and colds. A tea made from the leaves tastes reassuringly nasty but is one of those old cottage remedies that really does seem to work. You can make it palatable (just about) by disguising the bitterness with lemon and honey. Simply pour on boiling water. I often combine horehound with hyssop (*Hyssopus officinalis*) – equally bitter, but wonderful for the sinus troubles that often accompany a cough.

Horehound is a perennial which grows wild in this country, especially in the lighter soils of Norfolk and Suffolk, and is easily raised from seed, though my experience is that it has long tap roots and resents disturbance, so sow it *in situ* or transplant early. It is about a foot high, with square stems and small densely white-felted leaves and whorls of tiny white flowers, not unlike a deadnettle. I grow it with purple sage and catmint beneath some pink 'Königin von Dänemark' roses.

Hyssop is a low evergreen woody plant, best kept clipped, which comes in pink, blue or white. I like the blue form best, and I grow it as a low hedge round a bed of yellow-flowered woad in the Cloister Garden, next to some old white Alba roses.

Last week I finally got down to pruning the roses. I sometimes suspect that one of the chief reasons why people don't grow more roses is that they are alarmed by the prospect of pruning them, which is a pity. My rule is that there is no rule. On the one hand, all old roses have their own unique characters and habits of growth (and are likely to grow differently in different parts of the country and in different situations), so they all need to be treated as individuals in any case. And on the other, it all depends on what you want to do with them. Many big shrub roses can be pruned into a conventional shape, but can equally well be treated as short climbers or pegged down as ground cover, or even cut really hard like hybrid teas. I've seen a big moss rose like 'William Lobb' treated in all these ways, and they all work. It's comforting to remember that pruning roses is just like having your hair cut: if you don't like the result, console yourself with the thought that it will grow again and you can have another go next year.

Pegging down is one of my favourite ways with taller roses. Bend down any strong new shoots coming up from the base and hold them in place with pegs and string, or with hooks of wire (this is a good use for all those wire coat-hangers from the dry cleaners which clutter up your wardrobe). Bending the stems has the effect of making the rose flower all along the stems, instead of just at the top. You can bend them right down to the ground, or you can tie them into a wooden support around the bush – both will make a pretty arched shape. If they are long enough, you can fan the stems out along the ground through other plants or through roses of a contrasting colour. I grow a couple of big climbers like this: pale pink and white 'Baltimore Belle', pegged down through beds of deep crimson Portland roses. Cut out all the old flowered stems each year, and tie the new ones in.

As for timing, I try to finish the rambling roses before Christmas (it's easier then, when they are totally dormant, because it means you can yank away with impunity, without damaging the emergent buds) but I'm never in a hurry to prune the other roses, as so often new shoots can be damaged by late frosts. And although snipping and shaping is a lovely job for a nice day in late winter, most roses won't mind a bit if you don't prune them every year – or indeed at all.

8 March 2003

What's in a Name?

What's in a name? Romance, adventure, derring-do? There are some things I swear I could grow just for the name alone. Take 'Lord Anson's Pea', for instance. Admiral Lord Anson is best known for two things: getting spectacularly lost off the coast of Chile in 1741, and for the blue perennial sweet pea named after him. Anson had been despatched to the Philippines via Cape Horn in 1741 to capture the Manila galleon, a Spanish treasure ship which each year crossed the Pacific from Mexico. But, blown off course by storms when rounding the Horn, Anson found himself unable to re-establish his correct longitude, and helplessly zigzagged up the South American coast for two excruciating weeks while his crew dropped dead of scurvy around him. He ultimately lost more than half of his five hundred men. Nevertheless, Anson went on to capture the Manila galleon, and returned to London in triumph with the treasure and with the seeds of the sweet pea, which the cook on board Anson's ship the *Centurion* had found growing near the Strait of Magellan on the return journey.

Turning disaster into triumph – and pausing to do a little bota-nising on the way back – seems a particularly British form of heroism. The debacle was one of the two great maritime disasters which spurred the search for a correct method of determining longitude – eventually achieved by clockmaker John Harrison, as told in Dava Sobel's 1996 bestseller *Longitude*. (The other was the wreck of Sir Clowdisley Shovell's fleet off the Scillies in 1707, with the loss of two thousand lives.)

For very many years the true 'Lord Anson's Pea', *Lathyrus nervosus*, was very difficult to come by, and it was often confused with two other blue peas, *L. magellanicus* and *L. sativus*. But now all seems clear at last, and both seed and plants of *L. nervosus* are available from Thompson & Morgan. *L. nervosus* is a vigorous climber (six to ten feet), with round-oval greyish heavily veined leaves (hence the name), and clusters of soft mauve-blue flowers which – unusually in an everlasting pea – are sweetly scented. Although it is hardy it dislikes the winter wet, so if drainage is a problem, grow it in a pot or protect the roots with a sheet of glass in winter. I'm going to grow mine through a yellow climbing rose at the foot of a warm wall in the Ivy Garden.

1 March 2003

Black & Gold

What *was* it he reminded me of, Blackberry, the cat next door, turning on me the searchlight glare of his black-and-yellow eyes? On his best behaviour, front feet neatly together, impeccable in his black coat. There he sits in the back kitchen, not a hair out of place, eyes fixed on mine. He has recently taken to joining my cats for breakfast, and – weakly – I feed him: not so much to encourage him, but to reward him for not beating them up. They are all sitting together now, waiting for their food; I secretly hope this rapprochement will continue outside in the garden.

But for days I have been tantalised by those eyes of his. What *do* they remind me of? Unlike the pupils of Grace's eyes – sly, slanting, opal-green cat's eyes, rarely more than lazily half-open – Blackberry's eyes are two perfect concentric circles of black and gold, staring fixedly at me. Like something half-glimpsed disappearing around a corner, I sometimes think I have it, only to discover no, that's not quite it at all. The bright round eye of the blackbird who follows me about as I weed the garden, his head cocked as he searches for worms? The filigreed gold of the key to the tiny black japanned box which sits on the mantlepiece in my study? The braid of half-remembered school uniforms? Even the black and gold strip of Wolverhampton Wanderers, our beleaguered local team, battling it out against relegation? (I pass their egg-yolk yellow stadium every time I drive to the railway station.) But no.

And then I have it: gold-laced polyanthus.

Surely they are not out yet? But I go and look, and they are. Gazing up at me from a litter of winter-brown oak leaves and wayward trails of ivy: tiny, neat, utterly improbable, sandwiched between the sprawling trusses of rose-flushed *Helleborus* x *sternii* and a samphire-green thicket of *Helleborus foetidus* – so perfect that they might have been hammered out of black metal and gold wire, or stitched with gold thread on black velvet, each black petal outlined with a narrow rim of gold which dips in the middle, seeming to divide the five petals into ten gilded loops around a central yellow eye, gazing up at me with their pinprick pupils of filament and anther.

The gold-laced polyanthus is, as the doyenne of plant historians the late Ruth Duthie once said, a very English flower. It was one of the eight 'florist's flowers', grown by amateur breeders and exhibited at their shows or 'florists' feasts' in the late eighteenth and early nineteenth centuries, but it never seems to have been popular on the Continent, and even in this country it seems to have had a shorter reign than most. It was on the decline by the 1880s and by the Second World War it was reputed to be almost as defunct as George IV himself – the name of one of the most famous of the old varieties. In recent years, however, it has made a comeback. Seed-raised plants are now relatively easy to find: mine came from a market stall beneath the arches of Bridgnorth's seventeenth-century town hall.

Its ancestry is a mystery. The word 'polyanthus' was originally used to denote any multi-headed flower. What we now know as a polyanthus is of garden origin, and seems to have arisen in the second half of the seventeenth century. The fact that the flower-heads of a polyanthus consist of several separate florets held as a group at the top of a single stalk (like a cowslip) but the florets open wide and flat like the flowers of a primrose has led some experts to suggest the false oxlip – a cross between the two – as one ancestor. But where the dark colouring of the gold-laced poly-anthus came from remains a mystery. Possibly it owes something to 'Tradescant's Turkie-purple Primrose' (*Primula vulgaris*, ssp. *sibthorpii*), introduced into English gardens at about the same time from the Near East.

There are silver-laced sorts as well as gold-laced, and flowers with a dark red or chocolate-brown background, but none to my mind has the cachet of the black and gold. For all their strangeness, they are tough and easy to grow. They can be grown in pots, but the best plants are raised in open ground, ideally in a north-facing bed where they get the benefit of early morning sun without having to endure a long day's grilling in the heat. A decent heavy-ish soil seems to suit them. Divide the plants up every year after flowering to maintain vigour, and replant them with the addition of some garden compost or old manure and some sharp sand.

27 March 2004

Easter Gardens

After the long damp winter, the garden here is dripping with moss: great frondy swathes of bright green feather moss, smothering the concrete coal-bunker and threatening to engulf the tottering stacks of spare auricula pots; neat little cushions of screw moss on top of the walls; velvety cord moss (*Funaria hygrometrica*) on the hoggin paths; more feather moss on the limestone of the mock 'ruin' in the Wild Garden.

I remember gathering moss as a child for the miniature gardens we used to make at church on Holy Saturday. There was always a little hill, with three crosses on top of it for Calvary, and a cave beneath for the tomb, with the stone rolled away to show that it was empty. We used moss for the green 'grass', and we used to push flowerheads into it – especially primroses, I remember – to make the flowers for the garden where on Easter Sunday morning Mary Magdalene mistook the risen Christ for the gardener.

Moss is lovely stuff: it seems a pity that in the European gardening tradition it is all too often looked upon as an enemy to be eradicated. In Japan, whole gardens are devoted to it. Moss naturally grows abundantly in the moist climate around Kyoto – one of the ancient capitals of Japan – and it is here that the most famous moss garden of all was created, at the fourteenth-century Saiho-ji Buddhist temple. In place of the raked gravel of the later 'dry' gardens of Zen Buddhism, at Saiho-ji (also known as Kokedera, or the Moss Temple) it is moss which undulates over the ground, beneath the trees, swirling round rocks and lapping the shore of the little lake – lush, green, silent, and utterly tranquil.

There are moss gardens too on the Pacific north-west coast of America, which has a similar climate to Kyoto. In this country too, you have the best chance of making a moss garden if you live on the north-west side of the country. Mosses have no defence against drought, so a moss garden needs to be sited somewhere moist and shady, and preferably north-facing. The terrain should be slightly uneven, in order to get that gently swelling, swirling effect. A site under trees looks good – mossy tree roots are a classic ingredient of this style – but you will have to pick up every fallen leaf in autumn, otherwise the moss will discolour and eventually die. You also need to decide how you are going to view your moss garden: moss will not stand the tramp of feet, so it is best to provide some stepping stones through it, or to view it from a separate path at one side.

There are eleven thousand species of moss worldwide. At Saiho-ji alone there are more than one hundred. Many species are available commercially in Japan, giving Japanese gardeners a wide range of colours and textures to experiment with, such as the fine needle-like leaves of the hairycap (*Polytrichum commune*), and the feathery texture of the fern moss (*Thuidium delicatulum*). In this country you will have to collect mosses from the wild (with the landowner's permission, of course) or transfer them from another part of the garden. Or you could use a substitute such as *Sagina subulata* (known as Pearlwort or Irish moss), together with its golden counterpart *S. subulata* var. *glabrata* 'Aurea', both of which are listed in *The RHS Plant Finder*.

Pearlwort bears minute white flowers in summer. True mosses are flowerless. They propagate themselves by means of spores, like ferns. The one that invades poorly drained lawns is apparently the rough-stalked feather moss (*Brachythecium rutabulum*). My lawns are full of it. Keen gardeners rake the moss out and use it to line their hanging baskets. But I rather like the cushioned feel of it as I walk round the garden at this time of year. And I know

that the moss will retreat once I start to cut the grass regularly
again in spring – cutting stimulates the grass, which then out-
competes the moss (though it is important not to cut the grass too
short, as this has the opposite effect of weakening the grass and
encouraging the moss).

Besides, the birds love it. All through the recent cold spell I
have been throwing down boxes of apples for them from the fruit
store – great big dumpling-like Lord Derbys, as yellow as butter-
cups, getting past their best now – and the birds are repaying me
by scratching the moss out of the lawn to line their nests.

Before being permitted to enter the moss garden at Saiho-ji,
visitors are required to spend time chanting from the Buddhist
sutras and preparing themselves spiritually for the experience they
are about to undergo. It makes me look at my mossy grass with
new eyes.

26 March 2005

April

*The Willow will buy a horse before
the Oak will pay for his saddle*

Crown imperial

'Sing all a green willow'

I find the sight of slender young willows sprouting new leaves at this time of year uniquely cheering. They seem for me the epitome of spring – better than daffodils, better than Easter eggs. In medieval times they were used to decorate churches on Palm Sunday in place of real palm – in short supply in medieval England, I imagine – and they have the same sort of triumphant feeling. According to John Maplett, writing in 1567, the willow gets its Latin name *Salix* from '*saliendo*, for his swift skipping and comming [*sic*] up'. And it's true: willow cuttings root in the blink of an eyelid.

So it is a surprise that willow has such melancholy connotations. Wearing a garland of green willow used to be the sign of a rejected lover, and fans of 1970s electric-folk group Steeleye Span will no doubt remember Maddy Prior's version of the English folk song 'All around my hat I will wear the green willow', which reached number three in the British charts in December 1975. The link between willows and broken hearts goes back at least as far as the sixteenth century, to John Heywood's lament for lost love, 'A Ballad of the Green Willow', which has the refrain

> All a green willow, willow;
> All a green willow is my garland;

and to Desdemona's haunting little song on the night of her death:

> Sing willow, willow, willow:
> Sing all a green willow must be my garland.

A willow 'aslant a brook' is also the place where poor Ophelia goes to drown herself. Nice, then, to find the whole thing sent up in the person of W. S. Gilbert's suicidal tomtit in *The Mikado*:

> 'Is it weakness of intellect, birdie?' I cried,
> 'Or a rather tough worm in your little inside?'
> With a shake of his poor little head, he replied,
> 'Oh, willow, titwillow, titwillow.'

There's something very satisfying about woven willow structures in the garden. They are the perfect combination of nature and art. Woven willow fences made *in situ* (rather than bought ready-made as panels) can be individually tailored to follow the contours of your garden, folding themselves round existing features or boldly striking out in a crinkle-crankle. The height too can vary, swooping down to reveal a view you don't want to lose or up to block out the neighbour's garage. And as wind protection they are hard to beat, filtering the wind – unlike a solid wall, which blocks the wind, setting up damaging turbulence on the other side. A woven willow fence can even incorporate features like a delicious woven arbour or a single seat, wrapping you around like the keel of an upturned boat.

Both arbours and fences can also be made out of living willow, and this shouldn't be beyond the competence of any keen gardener. As a rule of thumb, you should plant the new unrooted rods before Easter – at any rate before they start to leaf up. Plant the rods in pairs, diagonally, and weave them into a diamond-paned trellis pattern. Then cut the sides twice a year with a hedge-trimmer, exactly as you would a hedge.

The old techniques of coppicing (cutting the old growth right down to the ground each year) and pollarding (growing the willow as a tree with a single stem which is annually cut back at a height of six feet or so) mean that willows can be accommodated even in the smallest gardens. And very many have brilliantly coloured shoots in winter, too. When I started the garden here, I planted several different sorts of ornamental willows, now producing a useful crop of long pliable shoots. I use the bright orange twigs of *Salix alba* ssp. *vitellina* 'Britzensis' to make woven edgings around some of the beds in the medieval part of the garden. And this week I pollarded the row of *Salix alba* var. *sericea*, a variety which has narrow grey leaves and something of the look of a young olive tree; it goes well with the grey-green leaves and Mediterranean feel of the irises in my sunny south-facing border, but is hardy and is therefore a much more practical proposition than the olive in colder counties. I will use these twigs to weave supports for peonies and Michaelmas daisies. The smaller, more delicate twigs of the violet willows (*Salix daphnoides*) I use to braid around the wigwams of canes, to give extra support to the sweet peas. And I have even been trying my hand at a bit of living willow-weaving: last year I plaited together nine cuttings of *Salix acutifolia* 'Blue Streak', making a single thick woven trunk. Curious rather than beautiful, I think, but redeemed by its enormous fluffy pussy willows and the promise of a crop of dark purple twigs for weaving, later on.

2 April 2005

Falling in Love Again

What is it that makes people fall in love with one flower and not another? One old friend (whom I have known for thirty years and never suspected of being a gardener at all) confessed recently to a passion for chrysanthemums. Another, in every other respect so elegant and so sophisticated, admitted to adoring big pink fuschias, the bigger and blowsier the better. Not that I have anything against chysanthemums or fuschias – simply that they don't do it for me. Like falling in love, these things are beyond one's control.

And it can happen anywhere, anytime. Last weekend I was buying flowers for my mother in our local florist's shop in Much Wenlock. I usually buy the same safe things – alstromerias, carnations, lilies – all the things which enjoy the same sort of hothouse atmosphere as she does, and can be guaranteed not to wilt under the duress of central heating.

It was then that I saw them, across the room: bunches of pale, pale anemones, silver-white, with a wash of dusky pink on the backs of their petals and the largest boss of sooty black stamens I had ever seen, as thick and luxuriant as the richest, deepest velvet. They were absolutely ravishing. Where did they come from, what was their name, how could I get some, how could I *grow* some? I had to have them.

But then – oh calamity! – I caught sight of the ranunculus. Not the plain red or yellow or orange globes that one usually sees – gorgeous though they are, with their gleaming satin petals, as regular as the immaculately folded wrappings of a turban – but white, with a cool greenish cast at the throat of each petal and the merest hint of a pink picotee edge around the top, camellia-like in their perfection.

The Canal Garden in spring

The Turf Maze (*above*)
Camassias line a path through the Wild Garden in spring (*below*)

Tulips in the Canal Garden: clockwise from top left, 'Apricot Parrot', 'Black Parrot', *Tulipa acuminata*, 'Generaal de Wet'

The Apple Tunnel in May (*overleaf*)

A bed of leeks and strawberries in the Fruit and Vegetable Garden

The Auricula Theatre by the kitchen steps

The path through the Nuttery in spring, looking back into the Cloister Garden

How could I be so fickle? To be struck once by such a *coup de foudre* was bad enough, but twice in an afternoon? Both anemones and ranunculus have stirred strong passions before. They were two more of the original 'florist's flowers' – meaning not that they were sold in florists' shops but that in the seventeenth and eighteenth centuries they were shown in competition (as tulips and carnations also were, and as chrysanthemums and dahlias still are today), giving rise to passionate rivalries. Two species of anemones were involved: *A. coronaria* (known as the poppy anemone) and *A. pavonina* (known as the star anemone, from its more pointed petals). The most prized forms were doubles, especially those known as plush anemones, which had not only extra petals (or, more properly, tepals, since petals and sepals are undifferentiated in anemones), but also a central boss of fine velvety threads, known as 'plush'.

A. coronaria has narrow, deeply divided, feathery leaves, and is the familiar cut flower of today's florists' shops. It comes in shades of crimson, purple and blue, as well as white. This is the species from which the modern de Caen (single) and St Brigid (semi-double) strains are derived. *A. pavonina* is rather less well known today. It has broader, tough, less-divided leaves, and comes in a wide range of softer shades such as lilac and mauve. Until my recent love affair with the white ones, my favourite garden anemones were *A.* x *fulgens* (a brilliant red hybrid of *A. pavonina*) and the tall, moisture-loving *A. rivularis*, which has blue stamens and white flowers washed on the reverse with gun-metal blue.

The florists' ranunculus *(R. asiaticus)* must have been a splendid beast. There were yellow ones striped with scarlet, white ones edged with rose or dark purple, orange ones speckled with red – a multitude of glorious colour combinations and patterns, all apparently caused by the action of a virus. By the middle of the nineteenth century the ranunculus had gone out of fashion and the fancy sorts had all disappeared.

In the British Isles the ranunculus is not hardy, and is usually grown from tubers planted out each May. These produce plain unvirused flowers. But it is possible to grow your own from seed, selecting and growing on any which show interesting variations. And there is a promising new seed strain of ranunculus, the Bloomingdale strain, which does appear to throw a few picotee-edged sorts (available in this country from Chiltern Seeds).

5 April 2003

Plum Blossom

It's good to have an excuse to stand and stare. The Japanese celebrate the coming of the cherry blossom with special cherry blossom parties. But why wait for the cherries? Plums anticipate them by six weeks or more. First comes *Prunus cerasifera*, the myrobalan or cherry plum, which blooms in February or early March, with its airy haze of tiny white flowers frosting the hedges like a snow flurry. The form most commonly seen in towns is the purple-leaved 'Pissardii' or 'Atropurpurea', which I think is a pity. The ordinary green-leaved form is lovely and fresh as part of a mixed hedge, or you can clip it into shapes. These were known in medieval times as 'estrades' – the whimsical cake-stand-shaped trees seen in the background of some medieval paintings. They make a cheerful alternative to traditional sombre evergreen topiary.

Myrobalan is often mistaken for sloe (*Prunus spinosa*) but it's easy to tell the two apart. The sloe flowers a whole month later, at the beginning of April, and on bare wood, giving rise to its common name of blackthorn. It's a beautiful thing, very under-used in gardens. It's good as an alternative to hawthorn for a hedge, and not only the blossom but also the blue-black fruit is highly ornamental (and an excuse, if you need one, to make sloe gin). The double form (*Prunus spinosa* 'Plena') is well worth seeking out as a pretty and unusual standard.

Then, in order of flowering, comes the damson (derived from the wild bullace, *Prunus institia*) and the garden plum, *Prunus domestica*, believed to descend from a cross between the sloe and the myrobalan. I made a plum and damson walk along the west side of the garden here – standard trees, all of different varieties, planted as one-year-old whips. My natural inclination elsewhere in the garden is for symmetry, matched specimens, trained fruit, etc., but I love the comicality of this mismatched row of plums, each with its own distinctive personality: 'Warwickshire Drooper' with long arching boughs flowering right down to the tips of its young red-brown wood; leggy 'Guthrie's Late Gage'; tall, narrow, upright 'Comte d'Althan's Gage', with something of the military about its bearing; neat and shapely 'Early Transparent'; little 'Kirke's Blue' struggling a bit out in the open; the flattened, crowded, almost contorted crown of 'Reine Claude'; and 'Shropshire Damson' at the far end, with all the elegance and vigour of the natural wildling. And the fruit is as varied in colour and shape as the trees themselves.

At Morville I am in the heart of damson-growing country. In the north-west of England, from Cheshire and Shropshire up to Cumberland and Westmorland, every cottage garden had its damson tree, and the hedgerows here are still full of them. The fruit was used in dyeing, and was shipped off in baskets to the cotton and woollen mills of Lancashire and Yorkshire – though not as one might imagine to produce a dark purple colour but, oddly, khaki instead. Old damson trees make a dramatic presence in any garden, not only in spring but in autumn too, with their golden leaves and swarms of tiny blue-black fruit. Even leafless in winter they have charm, with their black angular trunks and lopsided crowns shattered by winter storms. They are notoriously brittle: the doctors hereabouts knew when it was damson-picking time from the number of broken bones treated.

There are few things in the garden which please me so much as these simple white flowers of spring: white damson blossom against a pewter sky, white sheets bellying out on the washing-line, a rainbow, the caw of jackdaws nesting.

13 April 2002

Weeding and Seeding

I like weeding. I like the finished effect, of course: the garden all neat and tidy, the plants like small green mounds surrounded by dug earth. I even like the process: the close-up focus, shuffling along on hands and knees; sitting back on your heels to rest an aching back, having a look around, sniffing the air. So much of what is happening in the borders at this time of year goes on at ground level that it's rather a pleasure to be getting up close and personal with it all.

Up to a point. I know perfectly well that my benign mood will evaporate very rapidly when I have to face perennial weeds like the couch grass and ground elder elsewhere in the garden or, come to that, annual weeds like groundsel and bittercress if I haven't caught them before they start to fling their seed everywhere. And I find it hard to suppress a knee-jerk reaction when I see the shining green leaves and bright yellow flowers of celandines all down the back of the long rose border, clashing with the subtle rose-pinks and slate-purples of my hellebores in front. But I try to keep a sense of proportion: as long as I can corral the ground elder into the wilder parts of the garden, I'm happy to call a truce. Later on, I know that its white froth of flowers will make a pretty enough understorey in my little spinney, lighting up what is quite a dark spot in summer. And in my garden's wet heavy soil celandines are endemic: I would never be able to eradicate them entirely; and do they really do any harm? The best I can do is to try to curb their worst excesses. And soon they will disappear underground again in any case.

In late April and early May my garden is about as tidy as it ever gets, with the straight stems of the tulips standing ramrod stiff to attention, and the soil around them neatly weeded. Nature abhors a vacuum. Every time the soil is disturbed by weeding a fresh crop of weed seeds is exposed to the light – the trigger for germination – and all the lovely bare earth I have just exposed will rapidly be colonised by a fresh crop of weeds unless I now get a move on and cover the ground with mulch. In this sense, weeding can just be making a rod for one's own back. In many of the less formal parts of my garden I prefer to let prolific self-seeders like foxgloves, campanulas, columbines and sweet rocket cover the ground instead, crowding out all but the biggest weeds, which can then be hand-pulled. I rely on self-seeding like this to keep lots of cottage garden flowers going (all my *Nigella* and *Lychnis* too are self-sown, as well as the verbascums and the white musk mallows). So after one careful weeding at the start of the season, I tend to let the weeds and the self-seeders battle it out. And usually it is the self-seeders who win.

There can be unexpected bonuses to this: something huge and thrillingly out of scale like a verbascum or a foxglove right at the front of a border where I never would have dared; colours combined with a verve that I entirely lack; plants which arrive and depart of their own accord, like the double scarlet poppy which wandered into my garden from somewhere else and then wandered out again a few seasons later, or the double white feverfew which became one of the mainstays of my garden in midsummer.

Letting your plants cross and self-seed can produce unexpectedly beautiful variants, too. The ordinary sorts of single *Aquilegia vulgaris* – the sort we used to call Granny's bonnets – have nodding bell-like flowers with backward-pointing spurs and a centrepiece rolled into a sort of hollow honeycomb. But introduce the cottage garden types to a few plants of something more select, such as *A. vulgaris* var. *stellata* 'Nora Barlow' – a green and ginger and white double spurless clematis-flowered form (also available from seed) – plus a couple of white doubles, put away the hoe, and you'll be amazed what they get up to. Every year I go on a pilgrimage around the garden, turning up the heads of their progeny to look inside, finding little square pleated ones like tiny box accordions, big double bicoloured ones, starry flat clematis-flowered ones, spurless double dahlia-flowered ones – all in every shade and combination from deep purple and almost black through blue to rose-pink and white.

The Latin name comes from '*aquila*', meaning an eagle, presumably in reference to the spurs. Columbine, their gentler English name, comes from the Old French word for a dove – the eagle's prey. A curious dichotomy; but whichever name you choose, there is something airborne about these sweet and flighty flowers as they dance in the winds of May.

16 April 2005

Geological Map

Mile for mile, Britain has some of the most varied scenery in the world. Take a look at a geological map and you will see what I mean. A railway journey from London to Carlisle takes you scything across more than a dozen different geological divisions, all strung out in long narrow strips like slices of bacon falling from an old-fashioned bacon-slicer, each running north-east to south-west, cross country, and tied in a glorious knot at the bottom somewhere on the south coast.

I dream about this map. I plan journeys along the limestone from Whitby through Louth and Lincoln, via the Cotswolds and Bath, to Lyme Regis and Portland Bill. Or following the chalk and flint from Wells-next-the-Sea across Norfolk and Suffolk to the Chilterns, the North Downs, Romney Marsh and Dungeness. Or heading on beyond Carlisle to the schists and gneisses and basalts of the Highlands. I dream of the gardens I would visit: gardens on granite and slate, on limestone and chalk, gardens on clay, gardens on sand, island gardens and gardens marooned on the high moors, gardens from the far north to the subtropical south. Gardens where people grow meconopsis and trilliums, gentians and mountain avens, orchids and eucryphias – all the things I don't or can't. And gardeners who cope with salt-laden gales or frost in June or under twenty inches of rain a year.

One day I will do it. But it is hard to get away when you have a garden of your own. How could I bear to miss the hyacinths, the tulips, the roses, the agapanthus? Who would deadhead the sweet peas or water the lilies? My pyschotherapist friend Mary calls this 'separation anxiety'. This spring I had entertained a fond fantasy of visiting gardens in the Scilly Isles, abandoned when I realised how much work was still to be done before the garden opened for the season. Ten tons of gravel blocking the drive less than two weeks before. The Canal still half-drained of water and all the coping stones off with less than a week to go. The new plan of the garden drawn only days beforehand and the computer which was to scan it into the new garden brochure still protesting up until the very last minute. As it was, the paint on the newly refurbished signs was still wet when they were put out by the roadside, and the Wild Garden was still full of stinging nettles, but we opened on time. Just. As the Duke of Wellington said of Waterloo, it was a damn close-run thing.

Easter is traditionally the time when garden visiting – that great British pastime – gets under way. Every year the two 'Yellow Books', *Gardens of England and Wales Open for Charity* and *Gardens of Scotland,* get thicker and thicker, with new gardens – both gardens which are newly made and older gardens opening for charity for the first time – added every year, from remote Kerrachar, a new garden on the far north-west coast of Scotland reachable only by a twenty-five-minute boat ride from Kylesku, north of Ullapool, to the famous Tresco Abbey in the Isles of Scilly. They both sound wonderful. One day I'll get there. When I retire. Possibly.

19 April 2003

It's True . . .

It's true: 'Rambling Rector' really does ramble, and 'Paul's Himalayan Musk' really does climb mountains. I planted these two roses four or five years ago between a rock and a hard place – the situation could hardly have been less favourable – at either side of the entrance to the garden, between an enormous old yew tree on the one hand and an equally enormous old prostrate juniper on the other. I fondly imagined that the roses would quickly shin up into the two trees and transform a dark and dreary spot into a rosy bower. They did not. Out of the poor dry soil beneath the trees they produced a single shoot apiece which disappeared up into the gloomy canopy. After a year or two I forgot about them, and imagined them dead.

Until the other day, when squinting up into the sun in search of one of the cats I saw an unmistakable garland of bright green young leaves trailing down from the top of the yew tree: the 'Himalayan Musk'. And looped across between the two trees was 'Rambling Rector', festooning the entrance exactly as I had imagined it.

It's a good thing that I had for the moment put down my loppers. I had been doing a bit of last-minute rose-pruning – it's easier to see the dead wood when the rose trees are coming into leaf – and I had already got a bit scissor-happy, unthinkingly lopping off a couple of low-slung branches from a ten-year-old walnut tree at the other end of the garden, whose cut branches immediately began to drip like a tap – clear, colourless, almost tasteless liquid – and continued to drip reproachfully all afternoon. But how much worse to have lopped off the apparently dead stems of those two heroic roses.

The cold frames are bursting with the great green strap-like leaves of the agapanthus which have overwintered in the cellar. I grow them in big black plastic pots which can be sunk into the ground when it is time to move them to their final flowering positions. These are mainly the hardy deciduous agapanthus, which are the ones I find easiest to manage. They would do quite well planted in the ground, but our soil is cold and heavy, and I'm unwilling to risk them. And this way I can use them in succession to the pots of black and white tulips which fill the same spots under the apple and pear tunnels earlier in the season.

But I'm getting addicted: every year I find myself ordering more.

I started with a dozen mid-blue, mid-season *A. campanulatus*, together with four white ones. Then I started adding deeper tones and later-flowering varieties: 'Blue Moon' and 'Bressingham Blue', 'Clarence House' and 'Donau'. And then I fell for the subtle colours of 'Blue Steel', 'Lilac Time' and 'Silver Mist', and for the sulky beauty of *A. inapertus* ssp. *pendulus*, with its long pendulous inky-blue flowers.

I've long since run out of precious space in the cold frames. The big pots of scarlet *Lobelia cardinalis* for the boarded beds in the Plat have been turned out to fend for themselves. A dozen pots of white *Nicotiana sylvestris* for brightening up the Rose Border later in the summer are camping out on the kitchen floor. The orange nasturtiums and the single marigolds for bedding out in the *plates-bandes* may have to take their chances *in situ* this year. But the agapanthus are worth every inch.

27 April 2002

Fritillaries

Think of it: to dine upon violet leaves. What a life! Violet leaves are the larval food plant of the pearl-bordered fritillary and the equally poetically named silver-washed fritillary. I see them as Roman exquisites, lounging toga-clad on their couches, nibbling larks' tongues, or as maidens from an Alma-Tadema painting, trailing their pale fingers in rose-scented pools. Stinging nettles may be good enough for tortoiseshells and red admirals and peacocks, but not for the fritillaries, the epicures of the butterfly world.

I discovered this as I was leafing through my butterfly books, trying to find out why the botanical genus *Fritillaria* shares its name with a group of butterflies. *Fritillus* is Latin for 'dice box' (or perhaps for the chequered board on which dice games were played), and what the flowers and the butterflies have in common is a similar sort of diapered pattern composed of tiny alternating squares of two contrasting colours or textures, like an old-fashioned damask tablecloth.

The butterflies are exquisite creatures, with wings the colour of oak leaves in winter: bright copper, divided by darker veins into a chequerboard of velvety brown and amber. You see the same tessellated effect on the petals of the most common European fritillary, *F. meleagris* (native throughout much of northern Europe, including Britain), but carried out in tones of pale mulberry and sultry purple.

The flower's common name, the snake's head fritillary, refers to the way the flower stem uncoils as it rises, carrying the curious wedge-shaped unopened flower bent at the neck, as if it were a cobra rearing up to strike. The sinister name seems to suit it. The Elizabethan herbalist Gerard called it the 'Ginny hen flower', after the diapered black-and-white feathers of the guinea fowl, but this is altogether too innocuous a name for such a splendidly malevolent-looking plant. It grows in damp meadows and self-seeds happily in my garden in quite long grass. It is naturally variable, throwing up a range of light and dark forms, with even the occasional white one. You can buy white snake's head fritillaries (at an inflated price) from bulb catalogues, but I find them rather disappointing, for they are quite without the patterning of the ordinary ones.

The diapered effect is also apparent on sumptuous Middle Eastern species of fritillary, such as *F. davisii* and *F. crassifolia* ssp. *kurdica* – even darker than *F. meleagris*, with streaks of green – or *F. graeca*, which is green diapered with deep chocolate brown. Sultry and sulky, these are plants with attitude. But most of the Middle Eastern fritillaries need perfect drainage and the protection of a cold frame to keep off the wet. They're lovely, but life's too short. Try the little European *F. pyrenaica* instead, with dainty black-purple bells scrolling up at the bottom to reveal jade-green interiors: it is tolerant of a far wider range of conditions.

The two non-native fritillaries which do best out of doors for me are *F. imperialis* and *F. persica*. They are both stately plants (up to a few feet or more in height) and can make substantial clumps. Neither has the lovely chequerboard pattern of the smaller sorts, but *F. persica* has the same sort of sulky colour, with tall spires of dark pendent bells above broad grey leaves. It prefers a sunny, well-drained spot. *F. imperialis* will tolerate damper soil than *F. persica*, but it is a good idea to plant both with the hollow-crowned bulbs on their sides to keep out the worst of the wet.

The English name for *F. imperialis* is the crown imperial, familiar from every seventeenth-century Dutch flower painting. It has a ruff of large orange or yellow bells at the top of each stem, with a tuft of leaves emerging above, for all the world like a miniature palm tree. The sorts most prized in the seventeenth century had leaves with silver or gold edges, or were the sorts known as crown-on-crown, with a double row of bells, one above the other. All these are still available. I like the burnt orange sorts best, which have petals patterned with a network of gorgeous bronze veins, like the veins on its namesake the butterfly's wings.

The crown imperial may not have the colour or the diapered pattern of some of the other fritillaries, but it has another secret: tilt up one of the bells and look inside. At the base of each petal is a large nectary, brimming with silver liquid like a dewdrop about to fall. They are known collectively as 'Mary's tears', in reference to the crucifixion of Christ. It is also said that the reason the crown imperial hangs its head is because it was the only flower not to bow down as Christ passed on the way to Calvary. I wonder whether its foxy stink was given to it as a penance as well. Some people find it unpleasant, but I like it. It's an exciting sort of smell, pulsing with pheromones: it's the smell of spring.

17 April 2004

In Dreams Begin Responsibilities

Even before I read it I was haunted by the title of Delmore Schwartz's collection of stories, *In Dreams Begin Responsibilities*. I can't exactly put my finger on why. The strange inverted syntax of it appealed to me, but so did the surreal notion of being held responsible for the content of one's dreams. Titles, it seems, have a life of their own. Why I should associate it with auriculas is less hard to fathom.

I have always adored show auriculas, despite never having had anywhere proper to put them. As a consequence, over the years I have had – and guiltily lost – rather more auriculas than I care to remember. With their brilliantly enamelled colours and perfect rings of white 'paste', they are not really plants for the garden at all. They need to be seen up close, at eye level, rather than down on the ground. Then there is their wonderfully musky scent, which is dissipated in an ordinary garden setting. And the fact that both the paste and the powdery white 'meal' or *farina* (the Latin for flour) which covers the leaves can be ruined by rain or careless watering.

There are other sorts of auriculas more amenable to life outdoors: alpine auriculas, without the paste and the *farina*, less susceptible to being spoiled by rain; border auriculas, an altogether hardier and more miscellaneous race, which includes the lovely old 'Dusty Miller' types with their heavily powdered leaves. But for me they lack the mystique of the show auriculas: the 'selfs' with their intense red, blue, yellow or dark cocoa-coloured flowers; the strange, otherworldly 'edged' flowers with their black body colour, ring of white paste, and green, grey or white edges. I could never quite rid myself of the addiction.

All auriculas are fussy creatures: they dislike our warm wet winters and overcast skies. They miss the dry cold and the bright light of the mountains. In winter they are best kept under glass, in an unheated greenhouse or a cold frame, with as much ventilation as you can give them. In summer, after flowering, they need to be kept cool and shady and rather on the dry side: it is a good idea to sink them, pots and all, in a cool north-facing border, if you have one. But what they really need to show them off in April, in their moment of glory, is an auricula theatre.

And at last I have one. In the eighteenth and nineteenth centuries auricula theatres were quite grand affairs, lined with black velvet or mirrors to accentuate the effect of the flowers. Mine is in comparison very modest, adapted from a set of surplus bookselves with a mock-classical base and pediment made from an old picture frame. But painted grey, and put in place near the back door where I can see the flowers every time I come in or out, it is just the ticket. The flowers are arranged on the upper shelves, with spare clay pots on the lower ones, and the whole thing is open at the back so that there is plenty of ventilation. It faces north, and with careful attention to watering I find that the auriculas do splendidly there. And then, after flowering, they can be plunged into the cool soil at its base to dream away the summer months in safety. End of guilty conscience.

Here in the village we are all busy with preparations for the annual Morville Flower Festival next month: Ian working in his vineyard, Chris and Sara painting their newly restored revolving summerhouse, Barry and Joy doing some last-minute pruning in their very elegant courtyard garden. Theirs is a modern take on the parterre, with clipped hedges of variegated euonymus instead of dwarf box, and a glorious *Rosa banksiae* which is always one of the highlights of the festival. Barry planted the *banksiae* on a south-facing wall seven years ago. It now clothes an area fifteen feet high by twenty-three-feet broad with a thicket of bright green thornless shoots which in late April and early May are absolutely smothered from top to bottom with tiny primrose-yellow flowers. Although winters are getting milder all the time, this rose is still not reliably hardy in many parts of the country. But Barry has a secret weapon. The rose grows above the vent where the duct from his tumbler-drier exits the wall of the house: it has its own central-heating system.

23 April 2005

Old Walls

You don't really notice them most of the time. Old walls, built of massive red sandstone masonry, propping up later buildings or underpinning the sides of the rocky outcrop upon which the town is built. They crop up in the most unexpected of places, rising out of the rock in peoples' cellars or diving down under their gardens. These are the remains of the old town walls and fortifications of Bridgnorth, repeatedly built up and thrown down again as the tide of politics washed to and fro across this part of Shropshire for the best part of seven hundred years.

Politics in those days was conducted by the sword. The lady Aethelflaed, Lady of the Mercians, fortified the site against the Danes in 912. Robert de Bellême re-fortified it against the Norman King Henry, who then came and knocked it down again in 1102. Colonel Billingsly held it for King Charles during the Civil War, until the Parliamentarians came and blew up the castle in 1646. The castle keep still leans at an angle of seventeen degrees – three times more than the Leaning Tower of Pisa.

But at this time of year you can't miss the old wall above John James's garden: it is ablaze with wallflowers. They have seeded themselves into the cracks in the masonry – vivid splashes of rust-red and gold against the dark red sandstone. The wall is what remains of the thirteenth-century castle barbican; it now underpins the foundations of the modern red-brick Post Office garage. According to John, one of the postmen threw some seeds out of the Post Office window some years ago to brighten up a patch of spare ground squeezed between the new garage and the nineteenth-century Grecian-style Baptist church, and the wallflowers have kept themselves going ever since, migrating into nooks and crannies in the masonry, doing just what wallflowers have been doing for hundreds of years.

Red and yellow single wallflowers like those on John's wall (formerly classified as *Cheiranthus,* and now listed under *Erysimum cheiri*) grow wild around the Mediterranean. They were known in this country by the time of the Normans, if not before. Parkinson, writing in 1629, described the single sorts as 'growing upon old wals [*sic*] of Churches, and other houses in many places of England, and also among rubbish and stones'. The double sorts, such as the double gold 'Harpur Crewe' and double rust-red 'Bloody Warrior', are much more temperamental, but they are worth persevering with. Both may well date from the sixteenth century, and are deliciously perfumed.

Modern strains of bedding wallflowers are hybrids between *E. cheiri* and various other species of *Erysimum*, extending the colour range into cream, pale yellow, rose-pink, maroon and orange, as well as the traditional reds and yellows. One of the nicest mixtures, with a range of soft intermediate shades, is the old 'Persian Carpet' strain, still available from Chiltern Seeds. This is worth growing in drifts on its own, not simply as an understorey for tulips. Chiltern Seeds also have a strain of double-flowered bedding wallflowers, which are very rare nowadays – not fully double like 'Harpur Crewe' or 'Bloody Warrior', which can only be propagated by cuttings, but with a few more petals than the ordinary types, and tall enough for cutting (two feet rather than fifteen inches or less). Or if you want to colour-coordinate your bedding, you can buy seed of single named colours from most seed merchants.

Bedding wallflowers are usually grown as biennials, but they are in fact short-lived perennials. If, after flowering, you shear them over instead of discarding them, they should provide you with another crop of flowers in the autumn, which will last through into winter. The so-called 'perennial wallflowers', such as 'Bowles' Mauve' and 'Wenlock Beauty' (which has the fascinating habit of bearing flowers of different colours at the same time), are mainly hybrids involving Spanish and North African species, and are perennial in my experience only if you give them good drainage and a warm spot. But they are big, handsome, sub-shrubby plants nevertheless. Best for fragrance – if you can bear its searing orange colour – is *E.* x *allionii*, the Siberian wallflower, which despite its Russian name was raised by an English nurseryman, John Marshall, in 1847.

But best of all I love the wild, self-seeded wallflowers, like the ones on John's wall: survivors – tough, wayward, and when you take the trouble to really look at them, spectacularly beautiful – not simply rust-red or gold, but gold veined with red, or gold with red reverses to the petals, or red stripes on a gold background. They put a whole different complexion on being called a wall-flower. Not an insult at all, but a badge of honour.

30 April 2005

May

As many mists in March,
So many frosts in May

Tulips

Blackthorn Winter

Treacherous days. My neighbour John the farmer came to fetch me up the hill the other evening to admire the carpet of wild primroses in the old stone-pit. This is the pit from which the stone for both our houses may have come, quarried from just under the brow of the hill as it sweeps round to join the Brown Clee. It had been a beautiful day, warm and sunny, one of several fine dry days in succession. But as we stood on the top of the hill, with our shadows stretching out like giants over the farms and villages below, we felt the temperature start to drop. We hurried down – John to see to his cattle, me to put the tops back on my frames and swaddle the lilies in fleece. The next morning we had to break the ice on the buckets.

The 'blackthorn winter' had arrived. This is a period of intense cold following a mild spell, which often accompanies the flowering of the blackthorn (*Prunus spinosa*). This was in turn followed by a week or more of temperatures which would not have been out of place at midsummer. I went down to Ludlow to buy paint for the auricula theatre, and the town had the air of August Bank Holiday rather than Easter. We basked in the sun and I fetched the orange trees out from their winter quarters in the house to stand on the gravel around the Knots.

Then the temperature dropped again, this time accompanied by a bitter north-east wind which whirled the pear blossom from the trees and naked chicks from their nests. Back went the orange trees into the house, and I mowed the grass in a blizzard of white, with mittens on my fingers and hat pulled down over my eyebrows, the petals crusting the tops of the yew hedges like snow.

It is not only humans who suffer from this see-saw of the weather. In the warm days before Easter I was joyfully (but briefly) reunited with my bees. All four hives seemed to have come successfully through the winter. Even the bad-tempered colony which had been relegated to my friend Natalie's 'sin bin' in a remote corner of one of her fields was quietly getting on with its own business – which at this time of year means gorging on the nectar from the oilseed rape. When I opened the hive I could see that the combs were already dripping with liquid honey. But now that the weather has changed, the bees will be unable to fly and will be mured up in the hives, fomenting mischief. At least they will have something to eat and won't starve, but I doubt their temper will improve. And in the meantime I shan't be getting any honey.

This set me thinking about other means of sweetening our food. Honey was of course the universal sweetener before the introduction of beet sugar and cane sugar, but both of these have surprisingly long histories in this country. Sugar cane (*Saccharum officinarum*) came originally from India, and was imported as loaf sugar into Europe via Venice as early as the twelfth century. Our own King Edward I, who ruled at the end of the thirteenth century, spent £1600 in a single year on sugar and spices. Sugar cane was planted in Spain by the Moors, and taken to Brazil and the West Indies by Spanish and Portuguese explorers in the fifteenth and sixteenth centuries. And as the sugar plantations spread, sugar came down in price and consumption rocketed, especially with the fashion for sweetened drinks like coffee and later tea in the eighteenth century.

We have Napoleon to thank for promoting sugar beet, but it might just as well have been carrots. Experiments were being conducted in Silesia as early as the middle 1700s for extracting sugar from various sweet roots, but it was not until the British blockaded France, and prevented (among other things) sugar from the West Indies reaching Napoleon's armies, that production was given the necessary boost.

Our only indigenous sweetener is sweet cicely (*Myrrhis odorata*), which grows wild in many parts of the country. It is a pretty, anise-tasting plant, with soft, bright green, ferny leaves and umbels of white flowers. Its leaves used to be added to stewed fruit to reduce the amount of sugar needed. There is a tradition that sweet cicely bloomed on old Christmas Eve (5 January) and, like the Glastonbury thorn, was one of the plants people turned to after the reform of the calendar in 1752, to see whether they would obey God or the government in the time of their flowering.

It certainly feels like January at the moment.

3 May 2003

Blue & Green

I've just seen my first bluebells of the season on a wooded hillside not far from the sea in Pembrokeshire. It's a sight to take your breath away – literally, as when you wade out into cold sea water and one wave, bigger than the others, suddenly catches you unaware smack in the midriff. It's the unexpectedness of them, glimpsed through distant trees. But there *is* also something of cool blue water about the colour and movement of bluebells : the way they flow in little eddies and swirls, lapping at the trunks of the trees; the way they collect in the hollows and overflow down the hillside, at first in little rivulets and then in whole cascades; the way their slender stems respond to the slightest breeze, shivering across the floor of the valley like ripples spreading across the surface of a pool.

But how to describe the colour? It is deep but clear, with a lovely transparency about it, a shimmer as if wet with dew or spring rain. Just for once I think Vita Sackville-West was wrong when she described bluebells as 'spreading across the woods in clouds of low and horizontal smoke [recalling] the smoke of autumn bonfires, only clinging to the ground instead of mounting through the trees, drifting slowly across the russet branches' (*Country Notes*, 1939). She's got the movement and the shape exactly right, but smoke is warm and opaque, and makes us think of autumn, whereas bluebells are all clarity and freshness and belong to the spring.

Gerard Manley Hopkins in his diary for 1871 caught both the colour and its clarity and the movement perfectly: for him blue-bells were 'falls of sky-colour washing the brows and slacks of the ground with vein-blue'. I like 'vein-blue', with its feeling of transparency and fluid movement, the blue blood flowing beneath the semi-transparent veil of white skin at throat or wrist. I like 'falls' too, as if the bluebells were fragments of fallen sky. But for me, that day, the bluebells belonged to both the sea and the sky – a cool rain-washed sky reflected in the blue sea of a Pembro-keshire spring.

In the garden, I like the blue of bluebells with the acid green of euphorbias. My favourites are *E. characias*, a native of the western Mediterranean, and *E. amygdaloides* var. *robbiae*, a variant of our own native wood spurge. Both are evergreen, and both spread themselves around – an amiable trait, within reason – *robbiae* by means of underground stolons, and *characias* by seed. But whereas *robbiae*, with its broad glossy dark green leaves and spikes of lime green, enjoys dry shade, the taller, slimmer *characias* with its narrower blue-grey leaves is a sun-worshipper. I have them both on opposite sides of a small walled area near the house where one side sulks in perpetual gloom and the other side bakes in full sun.

The bluebells growing with them are the Spanish sorts (*Hyacinthoides hispanica*) rather than the native wild British ones (*H. non-scripta*). It seems to be something of a gardening solecism nowadays to confess to growing Spanish bluebells (their habit of crossing with and crowding out the native ones in the wild has made them very unpopular), but they do have their uses. They seem to be much less demanding than the native ones, and are equally at home with both my euphorbias, in full sun or total shade. Just don't let them escape into the wild.

Flowering later than the European bluebells is the camassia, sometimes known as the American bluebell. Camassias thrive in similar conditions to our own bluebells, but are altogether more statuesque in appearance. *C. leichtlinii* can be as much as three feet in height. *C. quamash* (syn. *C. esculenta*) is smaller, and slightly later flowering. Both naturalise well in grass. A good lime-green companion for them is alexanders (*Smyrnium olisatrum*), also known as black lovage, from the shape of its leaves. Alexanders grows wild in damp places, especially by the sea. It's like a shorter, earlier-flowering version of angelica (*Angelica archangelica*), with similar large spherical heads composed of masses of tiny green flowers. It was used in salads and as a pot-herb in medieval times, but is perhaps best blanched and eaten as a vegetable like celery. I suspect it is a bit too pungent for most modern tastes, but if you like the hot taste of watercress and rocket, try alexanders for something different – it'll blow your socks off.

10 May 2003

Carpe Diem

Suddenly everything seems to be racing away too fast. The first orange tulips in the far border are lolling open to show the blue stain at their throats, pollen-smudged, while their May-flowering sisters – only yesterday in green bud – are pushing up to replace them, all lemon and gold. The tide of plum blossom – the myrobalan (*Prunus cerasifera* or cherry plum), then the sloe (*P. spinosa*), then the damson, then the plums themselves; waves of whiteness lapping at the edges of the garden all through March and April – has already receded and given way to the creamy curds of pear blossom. And now across the Church Meadow I can see the first froth of wild cherry. I want it all to stop, to slow down. I want more time. I want time to look.

Carpe diem. It's a theme familiar from the ancients. Horace said as much in the first century BC. Time is running: seize the day, trust not to tomorrow. Restoration rakes used it to urge maidens into bed before their youth and beauty faded: 'Gather ye rosebuds while ye may,' said Robert Herrick. Or as Marvell said to his coy mistress, 'The grave's a fine and private place / But none, I think, do there embrace.' Stop and look, really *look*. Tomorrow may be too late.

Most of us know the opening words of Housman's poem about the wild cherry, 'Loveliest of trees, the cherry now / Is hung with bloom along the bough', but how often do we remember how it goes on?

> Now, of my three-score years and ten,
> Twenty will not come again,
> And take from seventy springs a score,
> It only leaves me fifty more.

And since to look at things in bloom
Fifty springs are little room,
About the woodlands I will go
To see the cherry hung with snow.

Cherry trees have always been synonymous with the brevity of life, not only because of the fleeting nature of their blossom, but because of the short season for their fruit. The sight of them, like the taste of the wild fruit, can be bitter-sweet. As Chaucer said, 'This world is but a cherry fair'. So I don't know about you, but this weekend I'm downing tools and going off on my motorbike to look at the cherries.

Housman's wild cherry was the gean (*Prunus avium*), the first of the cherries to flower. It is the most graceful of all the cherry trees – a little big for some gardens, perhaps (sixty feet or more), but with a natural elegance denied to the dumpier oriental sorts. It is the ancestor of all our sweet garden cherries, known here since at least Roman times. Quantities of cherry stones have been found at Roman sites such as the legionary fort at Caersws in North Wales, and near Roman waterfront areas in London, suggesting that they were brought up-river to London by boat from Kent. The name comes from the Old French '*guine*' ('*guigne*' in modern French), meaning a sweet cherry. In the west country it is called the mazzard, a name which is perhaps related to its other lovely country name, merry, from French '*merise*', a wild cherry.

The transitoriness of its blossom is part of the charm. But if you want to try to prolong the effect, you could add some of the other native or naturalised cherries to flower in succession. They are all white. The double form (*P. avium* 'Plena') flowers slightly later, in early May. Its flowers last longer, because they are sterile, and the tree itself is a little smaller (up to about forty feet). The morellos, the sour cherries, are much smaller: they are derived from *Prunus cerasus*, another wild hedgerow species. They flower next, and are happy in the most unpromising of positions – I have them here trained on a north wall. Then comes *Prunus cerasus* 'Rhexii', the old double form of the sour cherry, which has been grown in gardens since the sixteenth century. It makes a small tree with a rounded lollipop head – very double, very white. I grow it in the Cloister Garden here, surrounded by a tiny meadow of cowslips. And last of all comes *Prunus padus*, the bird cherry, a native of the northern counties of Britain, with long drooping fragrant racemes, like a sort of delicate white lilac.

On the other hand, you could plant another gean. Or better still, plant an avenue of them. A grove of them, a whole wood of them. For a few brief days in early May they would take your breath away. They wouldn't last long, but what a glorious sight they would be! As Marvell says, at the end of his poem,

> Thus, though we cannot make our Sun
> Stand still, yet we will make him run.

1 May 2004

Wakefield Tulips

There are some things money just can't buy. Love, proverbially, is one of them. Peace of mind, possibly, is another. But a 'rectified' English florists' tulip is certainly one. These are the sorts of tulips which drove men mad in the 1630s, when fortunes could be made or lost on the strength of a single bulb.

Plain un-virused English florists' tulips (known as 'breeders') come in smouldering tones of khaki, plum and slate. A 'rectified' or 'broken' tulip is one which has been infected with the tulip mosaic virus which causes the tulip's coloration to run up into the fine veins around the petals' edges, intensifying the colour and (in the best blooms) making a perfectly regular pattern of pencil-fine 'feathers' and 'flames' on a ground colour of pure white or egg-yolk yellow. The colours are extraordinary: peat-brown, rich mahogany or bright chestnut on a yellow ground, and shades of wine-purple, grape-black or Beaujolais Nouveau-pink on a white ground.

The virus is highly contagious and its effect on other tulips can be both unpredictable and dramatic. Plain 'Blue Parrot', for example, in my garden was transformed into a ravishing thing of dark lilac stripes on a crystal-white ground. But the virus tends to weaken them and can kill some things (such as lilies) stone dead. Partly for this reason, and partly as a result of changing fashions, the bulbs have not been grown commercially for many years. The only way the bulbs change hands nowadays is between members of the Wakefield and North of England Tulip Society, who every October can apply to the society to be given one or two of the society's precious stock of bulbs. It is thanks to the society that over the years I have gradually built up a collection of my own.

A good 'break' – a virused tulip which has the fine regular markings which meet the society's high standard – is much sought after. Every 'rectified' bulb breaks in a different way, and only perhaps one or two in fifty will be good enough to enter the society's annual show. The total number of show-quality bulbs in existence at any one time is probably no more than five hundred, including both plain 'breeders' and 'broken' tulips. And in an early season the number on display at the annual show in Wakefield may be far fewer. But flowers like these are worth the trip.

At the Wakefield Show (usually on the second or third Saturday in May) the flowers are displayed in the traditional way, in brown beer-bottles. This is a survival of the old florists' feasts (when the shows were held in public houses and accompanied by a slap-up dinner), but also because a beer bottle makes the ideal container for a single bloom, permitting each flower – each petal – to be individually examined and appreciated.

It's a good habit to cultivate in the garden, too, this habit of close looking. Have you ever really looked at a horse chestnut, for example? I mean, really stared one in the face? Many old horse chestnuts have great down-sweeping branches which can reach almost to the ground, and when I lived in the Botanic Garden at Dartry in Dublin I used to cycle through them at eye-level every evening on my way home from work in the library at Trinity College. I was reminded of this the other day down in our church-yard here in Shropshire where the recent storms had brought down whole spires of horse chestnut blossoms. The florets are white and palest lemon, flushing rose pink in the centres with age, and with long white lolling stamens like lascivious tongues. The edges of the petals are all crinkled and frilled like white silk Fortuny-pleated dresses or the delicately crumpled tissue paper which the eight-eenth-century Irish gardener Mrs Delaney used to make her exquisite collage portrait of them (preserved in the British Library together with her other flower collages, and quite my favourite picture postcard). Sometimes it takes the eye of an artist to make you really *see* something for the first time.

11 May 2002

The Lesson of the Master

'I want to be alone,' as Greta Garbo is supposed to have said. She should have tried visiting an English garden in the rain. I wonder at the English being so put off by a little dampness: I would have thought rain was our natural element. One day last week I found myself at Buscot Park in Oxfordshire and had the whole garden virtually to myself, apart from a visiting Japanese couple. What could be more delightful than warm spring rain? Smells seem intensified, trees and grass glow with a hundred different greens, and the feeling of having it all to oneself, of a mild intrepidity, is simply reinforced by the overarching canopy of the umbrella.

I had come to see Harold Peto's water garden, built in 1904 for the 1st Lord Faringdon. Dutifully I followed the signs round the side of the house and across the terrace at the back. Signs in gardens can be vexatious. 'Lavatories' this way, 'Tea Room' that, 'Walled Garden' through here. Necessary, but unromantic. They puncture the illusion that you are discovering a garden for yourself, that you have perhaps strayed in here by chance. Sometimes you want just to wander, without the map which so carefully details the points of interest, without the guidebook which tells you what to think. Imagine coming unexpectedly upon the laburnum tunnel at Bodnant, quite unprepared for that rolling surf-wave of sparkling colour. Or turning a corner in the garden at Levens, and suddenly finding the topiary shapes looming above you like the assembled beasts in *Where the Wild Things Are*.

But sometimes the signs lead you to exactly where you want to be, to the exact vantage point from which a master of his art wants you to see his creation – in this case, at the head of a stone staircase plunging steeply down through a cleft in the surrounding trees, from the manicured lawn of the terrace above to the water garden below, with a distant glimpse of the lake beyond. Context, here, is everything: you feel it in the contrast between the extreme formality – even severity – of the water garden itself, with its long sequence of classically inspired pools and stone-edged canals, its ramparts of clipped green box and columns of slim evergreens like black flames, set against the naturalness of the surrounding woodland (at this time of year all bluebells and lady's lace and the straight slim boles of the trees with their canopies just coming into leaf; in autumn a tapestry of reds and yellows, with coloured leaves drifting down on to the stonework and patterning the surface of the water). You feel it too in the way the grandeur of the setting – a wide scoop of hillside and noble expanse of lake, complete with domed garden temple on the far side of the water – is contrasted with the intimacy of the narrow green corridor of grass and the sequence of little lawns which flank the various elements of the water garden; and in the way the feeling of enclosure, emphasised by the height of the trees and the narrowness of the cleft between, gives way to the mild grey expanse of sky-reflecting, bird-skimming lake at the end. There is control of pace and mood, too, in the way the swoop of the hillside and the drama of that first sight gradually smooth out into the quieter pleasures of the water garden below, with each step of the chain of pools and canals gradually lengthening, each smoother and quieter than the one before, until the water merges imperceptibly at last with the greyness of the lake and the sky. Photographs don't really do it justice: you can admire the detail, but it's the mood that counts. And the rain of course helps.

15 May 2004

Sundials

Shadow is a medium which, like water, can be shaped and directed. Think of a big urn as a container for shade – its outside pattern a texture that catches the shadow like a veil snagged on a rough surface, its cavernous inside full to the brim with darkness. Think of a high hedge with sides sculpted into architectural pillars and recesses, the light and shade alternating across it like tide patterns on a wet sandy beach. Think of a pergola with the shadow of its cross timbers barring the path before your feet – the feel of sun and shade, warmth and coolness, alternating on the surface of your skin as you walk.

You can play with it, enjoy it, create artistic effects with it – and learn from it. A sundial lets you do all four at once. I once made a sundial in my garden using a tall straight young tree planted in the middle of the concentric circles of the Turf Maze. For the whole of one long Midsummer's Day I listened out for the striking of the church clock across the meadow, and every hour I marked the position of the tree's shadow with a series of wooden pegs hammered in around the edge of the maze. It was a delight – to make, to look at, to use. And easy to correct for British Summer Time, by simply moving the markers. But as the year went on, the shadow of the tree got more and more out of step with the striking of the church clock.

What was happening?

Sundials measure time as it is, whereas watches (and the church clock) measure time as we would like it to be. I now know that the difference between my sundial and the church clock can be accounted for by the fact that not every day is of equal length: noon on 26 December is actually twenty-four hours, zero minutes and twenty-nine seconds away from noon on Christmas Day; and noon on 15 September is only twenty-three hours, fifty-nine minutes and thirty-nine seconds away from noon on the following day. Over the months this can accumulate to a sizeable discrepancy. Then there's the fact that noon at Morville is actually ten minutes later than noon reckoned by Greenwich Mean Time. (To calculate local noon, when the sun is actually overhead, you add four minutes for every degree west of Greenwich.) Before the coming of the railways everywhere had its own time, and church clocks were corrected from sundials, not vice versa.

I like this difference. The garden is a magical place, out of time. I take my watch off on the days I am in the garden. But it was discrepancies such as these which led people like Hilaire Belloc to poke fun at the supposed unreliability of sundials, as in his mock motto:

> I am a sundial, and I make a botch
> Of what is done far better by a watch.

It is perfectly possible to have a sundial which tells the 'right' time: it's just a matter of fine-tuning it to the precise place where it is to be set up.

There are many different sorts of sundials to choose from. In addition to the conventional horizontal dial you can have a vertical dial for mounting on the side of a house, or something you can walk into like the human sundial at Ryton Organic Gardens, near Coventry, where you use your own body to tell the time. Or you could opt for one of David Harber's stunning modern designs on display at the Chelsea Flower Show each year, which harness the elements of both sunlight and water. Or – for total accuracy – you could choose one of John Gunning's exquisite brass Heliochronometers.

Sundials have always presented artists, craftsmen and calligraphers with opportunities to show off their skills. They have never gone out of fashion, and have outlasted both the waterclock and the hourglass. I expect they will outlast the atomic clock too.

19 May 2002

[*Did I ever manage to correct my own sundial in the maze? No. The tree eventually grew too big and leafy, and later succumbed to Dutch elm disease.* Tempus fugit, *as the motto says.*]

Morville Flower Festival

I wake to the sound of Ian hammering stakes into the ground: red direction markers, 'Car Park' signs, 'To the Gardens', 'Refreshments'. Overnight a white marquee has sprouted in the churchyard like a giant mushroom. Bunting flutters in the wind. It's the opening day of the Morville Flower Festival.

All last week the gardeners of Morville have been watering and weeding; the flower-arranging ladies have been busy with their creations in the church; cakes have been baked; the maypole erected; the vintage car and the ponies polished to a gleam. Now there's a sort of hush as we wait for the first visitors to arrive.

There are no gold medals or swords of honour to be won here, just the hope that everyone will have a good time – and that we will raise enough money to build a loo and a kitchen for the nine-hundred-year-old village church. In the twenty years since the festival started, the church has been re-roofed and its tower repaired. Next on the agenda is the restoration of the bells, silent for fifty years, and the repair of the stonework in the nave.

The flower display this year is daringly modern: abstract designs by the ladies of the Stimulus Design Group, all angles and anthuriums and knarled pieces of wood. Two ladies come out of the church, en route for the tea tent. 'Well, I was shocked. But then I began to find them really rather exciting.'

Soon there's a knot of people buying plants from the plant stall – one up on Chelsea. But then Chelsea doesn't have to cope with a herd of cattle galloping through the gardens only days before the show opens, or a mainstay of its tea tent called away to supervise the crime scene of a murder. At least this time the bees haven't swarmed. Bestseller on the plant stall this year is *Leucojum aestivum*, the summer snowflake. I scoop up *Dahlia* 'Tally Ho' to add to my collection of red dahlias.

Just time for a quick tour of the gardens: the twenty-foot *Rosa banksiae* on Barry's south-facing wall is just on the point of blooming, and by Monday should be smothered in tiny double yellow flowers; Mary's *Magnolia stellata* is holding on; Sara's amelanchers are just reaching perfection; Pat's red 'Apeldoorn' tulips are a blaze of colour in an otherwise green and white spring. Everything is a month late. But never has there been such a spring for blossom: sloe, plum, pear and cherry, as thick as clotted cream, every tree and hedge blooming all at once as if their lives depended upon it.

Then it's back to my own garden to welcome the visitors who are beginning to filter through from Pat's next door. We do a brisk trade in honey and horticultural advice: 'When did you put your oranges out?' 'Do you dig your tulips up every year?' 'Why are some of your cowslips red?' People stop to gaze at the snakeshead fritillaries, to sit on the stone bench in the Temple, to peer at a plant label. There are people strolling down the pear tunnel, children running round the Turf Maze.

In the church, Alison the organist is playing favourite hymns on request for fifty pence a time. By now the tea tent is heaving.

There are fiery vegetable samosas among the sandwiches and cakes. It's going to be a success. But will the weather hold?

The last morning dawns clear and bright. Stallholders start arriving to set up their tables and tents. The children from the school come to practise their maypole dance. There are reports of hail in Wenlock, five miles to the west, and a downpour in Bridgnorth, three miles to the east. But at Morville the sun shines. At 2 p.m. the town crier arrives in his tricorn hat and claret-and-gold greatcoat to open the fête. There's a tombola and welly-wanging, swingboats and pony rides. The trad jazz band strikes up a tune.

I meet a stout matron who camped here as a Brownie forty years ago, now bringing back her children and grandchildren; people who knew my garden when it was still a field, and who come back year after year just to see how it's getting on; new friends who are just getting to know the garden; old friends not seen often enough, swooped on with delight. And then at last as the shadows lengthen it's all over. The notices are put away, the money counted, the tables and chairs returned to the village hall. We can all put our feet up. Until next time.

20 May 2006

Rabbit-proof Fence

It was like a scene straight out of Beatrix Potter, with me cast in the role of Mr McGregor. I had got up at five – something buzzing around in my head that I wanted to get down on paper – and while the kettle boiled I went down to open the front door for a sniff of early morning air. And there they were: two young rabbits skidding around the corner of the tool-shed and up into the Vegetable Garden like a couple of kids on mountain bikes.

Don't get me wrong: I bear them no ill will. Actually I'm rather fond of them. When it was reported that there was myxomatosis on the outskirts of the village, the prospect filled me with horror. They haven't (so far) eaten the roses or the clematis or the peonies, the things I really care about. And I don't mind a bit them and their siblings and their aunts and uncles and cousins cropping my rather shaggy grass to the fine consistency of something more nearly approaching lawn. By general consensus they seem to have adopted the Turf Maze in the centre of the garden as their parliament and meeting place. And a jolly good job they are doing of keeping it tidy, too. I only wish they would stay there.

Unfortunately they also have a taste for cowslips (which explains why my little cowslip meadow didn't flower this year: all the flowerheads had been neatly nibbled off) and aquilegias (especially my favourite grey-leaved double white ones, which must be tastier than the ordinary sorts), but I can live with that. I do, however, fear that it may be the thin end of the wedge. I fear for my sweet peas, raised in February on the kitchen window-sill and still not planted out. I fear for my tender beans and little peas. Until I can solve the rabbit problem, I can't see any point in starting the Vegetable Garden at all. I imagine myself, McGregor-like, in dressing-gown and wellington boots, shaking my fist at their retreating white rumps as I examine the damage to the 'Lollo Rosso' and 'Cavolo Nero'.

But worse, much worse, they have been digging up my neighbour Sara's immaculate lawn and munching their way through my neighbour Pat's prized artemisias. Something has to be done. Together we have already jointly fenced every gap in our common defences. Bar one: the access across the front of my house, which functions as a sort of village street – the short cut to the church in one direction, and to our joint bonfire yard, car park and dustbin area in the other. It's also where the delivery vans pull up, and it's handy on occasions to be able to drive a car across, to deliver heavy items to the front door. However, some years ago I turned the adjacent area into an Elizabethan-style knot garden, with lots of elegant period woodwork. So the problem is to construct an Elizabethan rabbit-proof fence, one which my neighbours will not fall over in the dark, which is dismountable for occasional vehicular access, and which we can all easily negotiate several times a day with laden wheelbarrows, gas cylinders, armfuls of shopping and all the rest of the traffic which passes to and fro through here.

I think the answer may be a moat. Rabbits were originally introduced into this country by the Normans as a valuable addition to the diet, and, as such, great efforts were made to keep them *in*, rather than to keep them *out*. Their owners built warrens for them, specially constructed with a moat or water-filled ditch around the perimeter, to stop them sloping off and getting eaten by someone else. One of the fields on the outskirts of the village here is still called the Cunnery, which is the old word for a rabbit warren (from 'coney', the old word for a rabbit). There's already an open storm-drain across the bottom of our shared drive, near my house. I wonder whether I can widen this, and somehow keep it filled with water? Perhaps with a drawbridge over it which I could pull up at dusk . . . ?

31 May 2003

SUMMER

June

*A swarm of bees in June
is worth a silver spoon*

Rosa *'New Dawn'* (*& bumble bee*)

Just Looking

'Just looking.' Do you remember that phrase, the shopper's defence against intrusive shop assistants (in the days when shops *had* shop assistants)? Sometimes I think we work too hard in our gardens. It's important to take time just to look.

I was due to go off pounding up the motorway again – to see a bulb merchant, a sculpture park, a man about a dog – when some friends arrived to see my garden. Already tired and harassed, I pointed them in the right direction, promising to catch up with them before I left. When I found them, they were standing under the pear tunnel, with the first rose petals drifting down on to the grass around them and the green spearheads of agapanthus already plump and swelling. It seemed to be spring last time I looked. How could the time have gone so fast?

I cancelled the trip. The next few days were spent pottering about, alone in my garden, just looking. It was achingly beautiful – that brief moment when the garden is poised between late spring and high summer. No black spot yet, no leaves yellowing from future droughts. Everything green and succulent and growing. And I nearly missed it.

As it happened, it turned out to be rather an exciting week. The National Trust had decided to install lightning conductors here (my computers and all my neighbours' having already been blasted by one recent lightning strike) and all week there have been men working on the roofs. One day, when they were working on the tallest of the chimneys, they saw a large swarm of bees heading towards them. I didn't dare confess that they were probably mine. But this was no time to try to explain that a swarm of bees is usually placid and totally uninterested in human beings, having stuffed themselves with honey in preparation for their journey. With a loud clang the men dropped their ladders and sprinted across the roofs to safety.

The bees having taken up residence on the chimney stack, and seeming in no hurry to go off and find more permanent accommodation, the men went off to spend the rest of the day at another nearby National Trust property. But the problem there was long-eared bats – not to be disturbed at any cost. So now the men are mooching about with nothing to do, and we shall have to rely instead on our colony of houseleeks, *Sempervivum tectorum*. Together with the stonecrop, *Sedum acre* (which shares with the houseleek the delightful vernacular name of 'welcome-home-husband-though-never-so-drunk'), it encrusts our garage and many a cottage roof around here with its flat rosettes of spiny leaves. Anciently dedicated to Jupiter or Thor (whose name gives us the first syllable of thunder), it is said to ward off lightning and thunderbolts. And if all else fails, the juice of its fleshy green leaves is said to make a soothing ointment for burns.

29 June 2002

Foxgloves

Can you improve on perfection? Wild foxgloves, everywhere: self-seeding themselves through the Rose Border, where they add grace and elegance to the blocky shapes of the roses; in the margins of the Vegetable Garden, where they add height and colour before the vegetables have had time to make their mark; even invading the formal *plates-bandes* (the box-edged beds in the Canal Garden), where they mask the dying foliage of the bulbs, making a transition to the summer bedding of nasturtiums and marigolds. I can never have too many of them.

I love the way wild foxgloves have their bells all on one side, as if straining to catch the last notes of some far-off tune – I don't think the huge 'Excelsior Hybrids' with flowers all around their seven-foot-tall stems are any improvement at all. And I like the secret way the wild foxglove's bells hang down, so that what goes on between bee and flower is conducted in private, and you have to lift the flower and peer inside to see its delicately spotted throat – I don't want flowers that stick out brazenly at me, revealing their secrets too easily. And why breed shorter ones? Surely the foxglove's tall elegant spires are an essential part of its appeal. The 'Foxy Group' with its bluntly horizontal flowers and short stature fails to charm me on all counts.

And what about spots? Can you have too many? The markings of the 'Giant Spotted Group' look to me as if someone has had an accident refilling the ink cartridge of their computer. Or too few? I love the pure white form, *Digitalis purpurea* 'Albiflora', but its spotless unspotted throat strikes me as sad and somehow unsatisfactory, like a rose without scent.

No, the common or garden wild foxglove with its tall spires and spotted throat, its colours drifting from deep rose to palest pink to white, is just perfect as far as I'm concerned. I started with white ones, grown from seed, and then after a year or two allowed a few of the coloured seedlings to remain. (That way you can get exactly the mixture of shades you want; it's much harder the other way round.) It's easy to rogue out unwanted coloured seedlings because they have a dark flush staining the midrib of the leaves in the basal rosette; the white ones are a downy grey.

If you want fashionable apricot and brown shades, try some of the other species. *D. ferruginea* was introduced into this country from southern Europe in 1753. Like our own native *D. purpurea*, it is a biennial, self-seeding with abandon where it is happy. Its name means 'rusty', and that's exactly the sort of colour it is, with a rosette of dark green pleated leaves and tall, very narrow, dramatic spikes of tiny rusty-brown florets. *D. lanata* (called the 'woolly' foxglove because of the silvery hairs on its stems and sepals) is a perennial, with smaller rounder florets than *D. purpurea*, veined and netted greenish-brown over white, like miniature orchids or little Venus fly-traps. And then there's the lovely soft creamy yellow *D. grandiflora*, another perennial, also from eastern Europe, grown here as long ago as 1595. This one is shorter and stockier, less graceful than the others, but has large florets scalloped and flicked out at the edges like a yellow campanula. I love them all.

8 June 2002

Endeavour

How young they all were! The naturalist Joseph Banks, future founder member of the Royal Horticultural Society, twenty-four; the artist Sydney Parkinson, engaged by Banks to record their botanical findings, twenty-three; the ship's master, Robert Molyneux, twenty-two. Daniel Solander, the Swedish naturalist and pupil of Linnaeus, was the old man of the party at thirty-five. Even Cook was only forty.

And *Endeavour* herself: a converted Whitby-built collier, chosen

Climbing rose 'Leverkusen'

Early morning in June

Roses in the Wild Garden: clockwise from top left, *Rosa roxburghii*, Rose 'Violacea', *Rosa forrestiana*, *Rosa* x *richardii*

Beehives in the Wild Garden (*overleaf*)

Part of the yew cloister, which gives its name to the Cloister Garden

Roses in the Fruit and Vegetable Garden: clockwise from top left, 'Gruss an Aachen', 'Blairii Number Two', 'Königin von Dänemark', 'Charles de Mills'

The Cloister Garden in summer

because she was broad and shallow in the draught and easy to re-float if she ran aground, rescued from hauling coals between Tyne and Thames. Converted, she accommodated a crew of seventy-one, plus twelve marines and Banks's party of eleven – ninety-four in all – by the insertion of a new deck into her hold which reduced the headroom in places to a scant four feet six inches.

It was quite a shock to come over the hill and see her again dwarfing the town as she must have done that day in 1768: a forest of spars and timbers against the grey stone and the red-tiled roofs, her mainmast higher than the highest chimney-pot. This was the bark *Endeavour*, a sea-going full-scale plank-by-plank reconstruction of the three-master in which Captain James Cook and Sir Joseph Banks circumnavigated the world in the years 1768 to 1771, riding at anchor among Whitby's trawlers and dredgers as incongruously as a fairground swan among steam engines and fire trucks.

The original *Endeavour* sailed from Plymouth for Tahiti on 26 August 1768. Her ostensible mission was to observe the transit of Venus which the astronomer Edmond Halley had predicted would take place on 3 January 1769. Knowing that he would not live to see it, Halley had calculated that the distance from Earth to the sun – and hence the distance from the sun to each of the other planets (and hence the size of the entire solar system) – could be quantified if observers stationed at different parts of the globe timed the transit of Venus as it moved across the face of the sun.

This was to be the task of the astronomer Charles Green, who was appointed by the Royal Society. Cook had a different agenda: to find or finally to disprove the existence of a huge land mass in the southern hemisphere, balancing that on the other side of the world. Banks was a wealthy young naturalist in search of new plant species. He took with him a library of reference books,

including Linnaeus's revolutionary new system of plant nomenclature *Species Plantarum* (published in 1753) to help him
systematise his findings.

To stand in the Great Cabin of the *Endeavour* is an extraordinary feeling, like being in the nose-cone of a rocket – all that power
and energy and concentrated intelligence, about to be launched
into the unknown. They all shared a passion for knowledge, and
they were prepared to die for it. Of Banks's party of eleven, two
of the field assistants died in Tierra del Fuego. The artist Alexander Buchan died in Tahiti. Charles Green, Herman Spöring
(Banks's secretary) and Sydney Parkinson all died of fever on the
voyage home, together with Molyneux (the ship's master) and
thirty-five other members of the crew.

The expedition yielded over 30,000 plant specimens collected
from New Zealand and the eastern seaboard of Australia, representing over 3,600 species of which around 1,400 were then new
to science. Banks himself lived on to become what was, in effect,
the first director of the Royal Gardens at Kew, and became
hugely influential. Under his direction plant collectors were sent
out for the first time to south and west Africa, to Australia, to
China, and to the north-west coast of Canada with Vancouver's
expedition, shaping not just our gardens today but horticulture
the world over.

So think of Banks and his heroic companions when you look
up into the sky next week. On Tuesday 8 June, Venus once again
passes in front of the sun. Because Earth and Venus do not orbit
the Sun in the same plane, transits only occur at long intervals,
and in pairs: in 1761 and 1769 (the transit observed by the crew
of the *Endeavour*), in 1874 and 1882, and now in 2004 and 2008.
It won't happen again for another 105 years.

5 June 2004

Transitions

'Eglantine': the very word conjures up an English summer. Shake-speare, Shelley, Pre-Raphaelite paintings – the eglantine is there, with its soft pink petals and candid white eye, breathing out its faint apple-breath. Titania's bower in *A Midsummer Night's Dream* was 'over-canopied with luscious woodbine, / With sweet musk roses, and with eglantine'. Eglantine is part of the dream landscape in Shelley's 'The Question', with 'green cow-bind and the moonlight-coloured may'. Queen Elizabeth I adopted it as one of her personal emblems.

This is *Rosa rubiginosa*, formerly *R. eglanteria*. Its other English name is the sweet briar. It is native to the whole of the British Isles, though commonest south of the Wash, where it seems to favour the chalk. It has stiff bright green little leaves which smell of apples, especially after rain. Graham Stuart Thomas recommended plant-ing it on a south or west boundary, so that summer's prevailing south-west winds would waft the scent over the garden. Or you could plant it as a hedge alongside a path or drive, so that you can rub a leaf or two in your fingers as you pass. Clipped, it will form a dense and impenetrable hedge. Left to its own devices, it can reach eight to ten feet, and as much across. It is also armed with stout thorns. Surely this was the briar through which the Prince fought his way to reach Sleeping Beauty?

Elizabeth I used the eglantine as an image of her tough native Englishness in the face of the Spanish threat, in much the same way that her grandfather Henry VII used the Tudor rose at the end of the Wars of the Roses as a symbol of reconcilation. Her portraits, clothes and jewellery (such as the Phoenix Jewel in the British Museum, where she appears in profile, surrounded by a wreath of roses) frequently incorporate eglantines, and the praises of contemporary poets are liberally sprinkled with them too. In a masque performed in her honour at Theobalds in 1591, one character observes of the eglantine that, 'The deeper it is rooted in the ground, the sweeter it smelleth in the flower, making it ever so green that the sun of Spain at the hottest cannot parch it' – a reference to Elizabeth's defeat of the Spanish invasion fleet three years earlier.

There is also an interesting Scottish connection. There are a dozen or so hybrid eglantines – generally with larger flowers or a few more petals – which bear the names of heroines from the novels of Sir Walter Scott: Catherine Seyton, for example (soft pink with prominent gold stamens), appears in *The Abbot*, Edith Bellenden (rose-pink) in *Old Mortality*, Flora McIvor (deep pink with a white eye) in *Waverley*, and Meg Merrilies (bright crimson semi-double) in *Guy Mannering*. Collectively they are known as the Penzance sweet briars, after the name of their raiser, Lord Penzance. He was a judge in the Court of Probate and Divorce, and took to rose-breeding in 1872 after a lifetime on the bench. They are all splendidly healthy roses, with the curious exception of the two he named after himself and his wife (both with a hint of coppery yellow), which tend to be subject to black spot. A Rumpolesque comment on the state of his own marriage?

Not all the hybrid eglantines have the same deliciously scented foliage as the species, though the ones listed above do. I have a little collection of them growing in a tunnel arbour along one side of my Wild Garden. I love the dappled shade of it, and the scattering of crimson petals on the floor. The tunnel is made of bent hazel poles, and is given an extra sense of occasion by the fact that it runs along the top of a raised walk, like a viewing platform. I enjoy the touch of artificiality which the eglantines provide, with their more vivid colouring framing the waving sea of long grass and the mounds of paler, more discreet wild roses below. They provide a transition from the cultivated part of the garden to the Wild Garden, gently changing the mood.

Transitions in the garden can be tricky. Sometimes you want people to come round a corner and exclaim, 'Oh, how lovely!' – to take them by surprise. But sometimes you want to provide a gentler transition, for people to linger – to give them little glimpses of what is to come. And a tunnel arbour like this is just the thing: less formal than a pergola, quicker and easier to make, certainly cheaper, and with its own quirky irregularity.

A final word about nomenclature. David Austin's English rose called 'Eglantyne' (note the different spelling) is a double-flowered garden shrub rose, a pretty rose in its own right, but named after Eglantyne Jebb, founder of the Save the Children Fund. It has nothing to do with either *R. rubiginosa* or Lord Penzance and his sweet briars.

19 June 2004

Not a Bed of Roses

Gardens may be good for the soul, as my colleague Anthony Grayling wrote recently, but gardening – to use an appropriately horticultural metaphor – is not always a bed of roses. Sometimes there's more of the hair shirt about it than the primrose path. This year I've got downy mildew, powdery mildew and rust. I've got whitefly and greenfly, and I'm sure I would have blackfly too if I had got my broad beans sown in time. I've had tulip fire and hellebore leaf spot, and now I'm braced for ordeal by lily beetle. There are cleavers up to my knees and nettles up to my neck, carpets of bittercress and shepherd's purse, and weeds I don't even have a name for.

Is it possible to have a garden and a life? I went away for a couple of weekends and got back to find unwatered pots, parched lawns, and weeds everywhere. It was an odd sort of a week – a week of contrasting perspectives and clashing emotions, in which I joyfully escaped from the garden only to curse my folly when I returned; thundered up the crowded motorway to see new sights, and then lost an hour mesmerised by a single flower in my own garden.

It was already late evening when I got back. Muttering, I dragged out the hoses and started watering. Better to give things a long cool overnight drink than wait until morning, I thought. Must have been mad to go away: turn your back and now look at it. Back and forth I went, further and further out into the garden, eventually beyond even the reach of the hose, out into the Wild Garden, filling watering-cans from the tap near the road. Back and forth I trudged, the sound of the water crashing into the cans echoing the cacophony of my thoughts.

Finally, the watering done, I turned the tap off. There was a sudden silence. The road was empty of traffic. Not a car, not a pedestrian, not a sound. Not even a breath of wind. Clouds of cow parsley, taller than me, stood on either side of the path, ghostly in the light of the streetlamp. My senses were flooded with the sweet nutty smell of them, their falling petals drifting into my hair. Gazing into them was like looking up at the Milky Way on a starry night. And slowly all the panic and the irritation and the exhaustion drained away.

I don't know how long I stood there, but the next thing I knew was the church clock striking 11.30 and a voice calling out as I returned to the house, 'Have you gone quite mad?' No, just the opposite. I had been getting my head together.

Gardeners have always known this phenomenon. Now it's official. Experts cited in a new publication, *A Plant a Day Keeps the Doctor Away*, recommend a twenty-minute daily exposure to plants to maintain health and well-being – a sort of Recommended Daily Allowance of greenery, just like eating your five pieces of fruit or taking your Recommended Daily Allowances of vitamins and minerals. One study cited by the report claims that a couple of hours in the garden each day can reduce coronary heart disease and other chronic illnesses. In older people, gardening also keeps mental abilities sharp and wards off depression. In hospital, having something green to look at will speed your recovery and make you less susceptible to post-operative pain. And in the workplace it reduces stress and makes the boss easier to bear. It is even claimed that the greener and more natural a girl's view from home, the better she scores on tests of concentration, impulse inhibition and delayed gratification: in other words, according to Plant*for*Life (a partly EU-funded initiative aimed at raising awareness of plants and the role that they can play in enhancing people's quality of life), self-discipline – which, according to them, is a predictor of delinquency, drug abuse, poor school grades, and teenage pregnancy. Good heavens! I think on the strength of this we should get gardens on the National Health Service.

12 June 2004

Peonies

Flowers are never just flowers. Not just a shape or a colour, however lovely. They come trailing clouds of glory: the person who first saw them, used them, loved them; the romance of the place they come from – some remote steppe in Siberia, perhaps, or some rocky mountainside in Greece. They remind us of the civilisations which prized them, of the artists who painted them and the materials in which they worked: not just oil-paint and watercolour, but silk and damask and marquetry, lacquer and fine bone china. Who could grow *Paeonia rockii*, for instance, incomparably beautiful though its flowers are – huge, fragile, paper-white, each petal with a blotch of deepest maroon at its base – without also being aware of Reginald Farrer's breathless description of first glimpsing it growing wild on the side of a deep gorge in south-west China; and knowing that the plant was then lost again until 1926 when the American plant collector Joseph Rock found it growing in the garden of a Tibetan monastery in Gansu? Who could pick *Paeonia* 'Renkaku' out of a catalogue without being influenced by the poetry of its name, which means 'flight of cranes'? Could anyone grow peonies at all without in their mind's eye seeing those ruffled petals and bold dissected leaves painted on the side of a Chinese porcelain bowl or on a Japanese scroll-painting?

Hybrid tree peonies, grouped under the name *P. suffruticosa*, have always been the most glamorous of all peonies, evoking the splendour of the Empress Wu Zetian's court in seventh-century China, when a single plant could be sold for a hundred ounces of gold. But herbaceous peonies too are rich in images and associations. And they do not all come from the East.

P. mascula and *P. officinalis* are European species, with almost equally long histories which go back to the ancient Greeks. The name *Paeonia* is from the same root as a 'paean' of praise, both being derived from the name Paeon, physician to the gods, who in Greek mythology used peony roots to cure a wound given to Pluto by Hercules. (Paeon became identified with Apollo as God of Healing, and hymns addressed to him were known as paeans.)

Both *P. mascula* and *P. officinalis* were used in medicine right up to the seventeenth century – hence the name *officinalis*, which always denotes a medicinal use. *Mascula* speaks for itelf: *P. mascula* and *P. officinalis* were long considered to be the male and female of the same species. But you collected peony roots at your peril for, like the mandrake, the peony was popularly supposed to emit a brain-shattering shriek if uprooted.

I wonder whether this superstition has anything to do with the old myth that herbaceous peonies cannot be moved? For myth it is: the fact that peonies once transplanted may prove shy to flower has much more to do with people planting them too deep. Newly planted herbaceous peonies rarely flower in their first year, but they will not flower at all if their crowns are buried more than about two inches below the surface. However, it is true that once established they will flower happily undisturbed for fifty years or more, with none of that biennial lifting and dividing which so many other herbaceous plants demand.

Peonies are not native to this country, though the single red *P. mascula* is naturalised on the island of Steep Holm in the Bristol Channel, where it is very possibly a relic of the herb garden of the Augustinian priory founded there in the twelfth century. Possibly the colony is even older: tradition has it that in the sixth century, during the Saxon invasions, the historian Gildas took refuge on Steep Holm and wrote his 'complaining book' there, *Liber Querulus De Excidio Britanniae* (literally, *The Book of Complaint about the Fall of Britain*). Certainly peonies were known in this country in Anglo-Saxon times.

In iconographical terms, European peonies are all gold leaf and sumptuous crimson flowers. In the very celebrated painting known as *The Garden of Paradise*, painted in about 1410 by an unknown master from the Upper Rhine, a clump of peonies takes centre stage at the feet of the Blessed Virgin; in Martin Schongauer's serene *Madonna and Child* of 1473, another peony blooms at her right hand. In both instances, the peonies are grown in turf. This is still an excellent way to grow the European species, as they are shorter than *P. lactiflora* (the other main group of herbaceous garden peonies) and rarely need support.

P. lactiflora itself was introduced into this country from China at the end of the eighteenth century. Its name means 'milk flower'. In contrast to the European species, the opulent *P. lactiflora* hybrids are pale, lax and heavy-headed – more John Singer Sargent portraits of affluent Edwardian ladies than medieval paintings of the Blessed Virgin – but (unlike the largely scentless European species) blessed with the most divine scent.

4 June 2005

Eyes Wide Shut

At this time of year I swear I could navigate my way around my garden blindfold, by sense of smell alone. Sometimes on a midsummer's night – perhaps after working late, or after returning from a long car journey, opening the car door and taking great sniffs of air – I do just that, stepping out into the garden in the warm darkness, feeling my way by sound and smell. First, the crushed garlic smell of the ramsons, their leaves bruised under my heel as I pass – *Allium ursinum*, growing wild in the cool shade by the back door – followed by the odd, foetid smell of the yellow Turk's-cap lily (*Lilium pyrenaicum*) in the Kitchen Border, almost invisible by day among the mass of yellow-green euphorbias.

Then the hot Mediterranean pungency of the Knot Garden – lavender, thyme, marjoram and germander – and somewhere away to the left, the sweet molasses smell of the compost heap. I might blunder into one of the Seville orange trees, and get a powerful whiff of citrus from its broken leaves and a bad-tempered jab from its thorns for my trouble. Then a slight drop in temperature, and the dank river smell of the Canal – careful now! – at my feet. And then, wafting on the air, the smell of a thousand roses.

Not one smell, of course, but many – musk, tea, myrrh, apple, fruits of every description – and carried not only by petals, but by leaves and stems and stamens too. Roses betray their origins and allegiances (and sometimes their misalliances) by smell quite as much as by form or habit. Moss roses, for example, arose in the eighteenth century as mutations of centifolia roses. They have thick moss-like encrustations on their leaf- and flower-stalks and on their calyxes (the green outer casing of the flower buds), which exude a sticky highly aromatic resin. When crushed, this gives off a spicy scent like balsam, wholly independent of the sweet 'old rose' perfume of the petals. Deadheading a moss rose like 'William Lobb', especially on a warm day, can be a heady experience. But also try rubbing the flower stems of an ordinary centifolia – 'Tour de Malakoff', for example, or 'Spong' or 'Blanchefleur' – and you will find an echo of the same scent.

Or take 'Manning's Blush', another eighteenth-century rose with pretty blush-white pompom-like flowers and small dark grey-green foliage like a miniature alba. But in fact it's an eglantine: rub its leaves between your fingers and they smell of apples.

But sometimes there is no accounting for the vagaries of scent. Why, for example, should my double white *Rosa pimpinellifolia* smell of lily of the valley, while my pale blush one smells of Turkish delight? And what line of breeding connects the energetic scrambler *Rosa arvensis* 'Splendens' – often known as 'The Myrrh-scented Rose' – with David Austin's much more decorous

English Roses? Many of the English Roses have the same myrrh scent – a very distinctive, slightly aniseed, un-sweet smell – traced back to a rose called 'Belle Amour', via 'Belle Isis' and 'Constance Spry', which was the first of the English Roses, bred in 1960. But there the trail goes cold, for the origin of 'Belle Amour' itself is a mystery.

Perhaps most intriguing of all is the tea scent found in the old tea roses. I had been waiting four years to smell my 'Park's Yellow Tea-scented China' – said to be the original tea rose, introduced into this country from China in 1824. As I rummaged around the garden, sniffing rose scents and making notes for this column, deep in one of the borders, suddenly my heart leaped to see a large, pale, creamy yellow solitary bloom waving up high against the blue sky: 'Park's Yellow Tea-scented China'. Its first bloom, and I might have missed it. And what did it smell of? Not tea at all, but lychees.

21 June 2003

Midsummer's Day

There's a period of suspension between the summer solstice on 21 June and Midsummer's Day on the 24th, when the whole garden seems to be holding its breath. The solstice is the day when the sun stands still (from the Latin '*sol*' and '*sistere*', to stand still). This is the day when the sun reaches the Tropic of Cancer, the most northerly point of the ecliptic, the imaginary line described by the sun in its apparent orbit around the earth. And just as a ball, thrown high up into the air, appears to hesitate for a moment and hang motionless at the limit of its trajectory before falling back to earth, so the golden ball of the sun appears to stand still for a few days over the Tropic of Cancer before 'turning' (hence the word 'tropic', from the Greek '*tropos*', a turn) back towards the equator.

It's a magical time, marked with special ceremony since the dawn of history. And although we may not nowadays light bonfires on Midsummer's Eve or greet the sunrise at Stonehenge (not many of us, anyway), old habits die hard: like the forgotten little rivers of London – 'Effra, Graveney, Falcon, Quaggy,/ Wandle, Walbrook, Tyburn, Fleet' in U. A. Fanthorpe's marvellous poem 'Rising Damp' – they may go underground, but they are still there, running beneath the houses, and they still perturb our sleep with their subterranean rumblings.

The quintessential midsummer text is *A Midsummer Night's Dream* – when, for one night, the rules of the everyday world are suspended, relationships are shuffled like a pack of cards, and the characters emerge blinking into the dawn, seeing the world with new eyes. And a garden is of course the perfect setting. Outdoor performances of *A Midsummer Night's Dream* are now one of the features of an English summer.

What happens to the two pairs of lovers lost in the wood in *A Midsummer Night's Dream* is genuinely frightening, despite the comedy. There was always a strong undertow of anxiety about midsummer celebrations. Midsummer's Day (24 June) is the feast of St John the Baptist – like Christmas, a Christianisation of the old pagan rites held at the solstice on the 21st. And like Christmas Eve and New Year's Eve and Hallowe'en (All Hallows' Eve), the vigil on the evening before was always the most potent time. The sun might be at its highest and strongest, but Midsummer's Day ushered in the hottest and unhealthiest time of the year, the season when crops, herds and humans were all at their most vulnerable to disease, drought or devastating downpours. On Midsummer's

Eve bonfires were lit on the windward side of the fields so that the smoke would drift across the crops and purify them. Cattle were driven through the embers to bring good luck. Special herbs, including St John's wort (so called because it blooms at midsummer), were burnt in the fire.

St John's wort (*Hypericum perforatum*) is a daintier native version of that thuggish incomer, the rose of Sharon (*Hypericum calycinum*), and has similar though smaller shining yellow flowers, and leaves perforated with tiny holes (hence its Latin name). To allay our modern fears and depressions we nowadays take our St John's wort in tablet form. And instead of bonfires we have fireworks: no summer garden party seems complete without an explosion of sound and colour to round off the proceedings. I'm not above a little ritual propitiation myself: the cold dry weather last month has so far kept the black spot at bay on the roses, but my fingers are remaining firmly crossed.

25 June 2005

July

Never trust a July sky

Eryngium giganteum (*'Miss Willmott's ghost'*)

All Change

They are calling it the European monsoon – Glastonbury underwater, a tornado in Coventry, and much of the country hit by flash floods. And like the monsoon, it is becoming eerily predictable. This time last year we had a coach party waiting on the front drive while I rushed around trying to prop up the fallen roses and clear paths through the garden. This year we got off relatively lightly: thunder and lightning crashing all around, the streets running with water in towns no more than a dozen miles away on either side, but here we were spared the battering many other gardens received.

Which is just as well. Mine is a sort of 'live now, pay later' style of gardening. Densely planted, richly fed, everything leaning on everything else, with mounds of long grass and huge rosebushes cascading everywhere. Perilously fragile, in other words. A June thunderstorm can wreak havoc in a garden like this, and if such storms are to become a regular feature of British weather I am going to have start practising the 'Chelsea crop' – shortening the long stems of herbaceous perennials in mid-May to promote more self-supporting, compact growth. And I shall certainly be 'Scarmanising' more of the rose bushes – named after the rose grower John Scarman, who advocated pruning with shears rather than secateurs, leaving all the interlocking twiggy growths in place: it was very noticeable that those given the

Scarman treatment this year stood up to the downpour far better than last year.

The storm hit us just after six in the morning. By half past my youngest cat was on the kitchen window-sill, asking to come in. All through the hottest weather she has slept outside, feeding herself on mice, turning up only occasionally in the evenings to see if anything cooking on the barbecue might be to her liking. Now, after breakfasting on cat biscuits – her equivalent of fast food – she crashed out, muddy and exhausted, in my big white bed while I set off up the garden to survey the damage. At lunchtime I was still deadheading roses, snapping off the sodden heads to lighten the weight, brushing the fallen petals off the leaves before the hot sun could have a chance to bake them hard. It is at times like these that I wonder whether I have too many white roses. But then my old tom-cat came weaving his way through the undergrowth, his raggedy old grey coat in peaks from the rain, a scatter of fallen rose petals across his back. And how delicious the garden smelled! The air washed clean of all the accumulated dust of the recent heatwave. Sounds seemed to carry better: I could hear the steam train at Bridgnorth puffing three miles away, and suddenly all the song thrushes in the world seemed to be singing in my garden.

2 July 2005

Lupins

There aren't enough jokes in gardens. Take *Eryngium giganteum*, for example, the sort of vegetable equivalent of those seventeenth-century water jets which owners used to turn on and off at will, squirting up people's skirts or down their necks. Ellen Willmott, the Edwardian lady gardener, had the right idea. She used to scatter seed of it in other people's gardens. In its first year it passes unnoticed, a meek little rosette of green heart-shaped leaves. Then in its second or third year, behind your back, it thrusts up four-foot flowering stems like big green iguanas with spiky ruffs which turn aluminium-bright overnight like advertisements for Brillo pads and stainless-steel kitchenware. By the time it flowered Miss Willmott was long gone. People call it 'Miss Willmott's ghost'. It seems to like heavy soils, and does best from fresh seed, which it scatters copiously. Every year it never fails to make me laugh.

There's something innately comic too about lupins. Remember John Cleese as Robin Hood, demanding, 'Your lupins or your life!' – and the less than enthusiastic response he received from the poor, showered with lupins instead of loot. Fashionable in the 1950s, they seemed forever associated with the era of the Ford Popular car, Doris Day movies and 'Journey into Space' on the radio. These were the Russell lupins, a strain of brilliantly coloured herbaceous perennials bred by George Russell of York, whose mustachioed picture beamed from every post-war packet of lupin seed. He first exhibited his lupins at Chelsea in 1937, where their four-foot stems and contrasting keels and standards (in shades of blue-and-white and pink-and-white, as well as yellows and all white 'selfs') caused a sensation.

Lupins have the widest colour palette of all early summer flowers, but they are naturally short-lived creatures. After Russell's death his strain of lupins succumbed to cucumber mosaic virus, and the fashion for lupins died with them. But the lupin is now undergoing a rehabilitation, with Pat Edwards (holder of the National Collection of Russell Lupins at Albrighton, near Wolverhampton, where Russell ended his days) patiently rebuilding the Russell strain, and orders flooding in for a new strain of lupins in subtle shades of apricot, salmon, copper and terracotta, bred by Sarah Conibear of West Country Nurseries.

Worldwide there are more than 250 species, most of them originating from North America. The garden lupins are derived from crosses between *L. polyphyllus* (discovered in the western states of America in 1826), which comes in blue, purple and reddish shades, and the yellow tree lupin, *L. arboreus*, brought from California in 1793. We have no native lupin in this country, though the whole centre of the main island of Orkney and the river mouths of the Dee and the Tay used to be blue with *L. nootkatensis* – brought it is said by returning Hudson's Bay traders at the end of the eighteenth century, from Nootka Sound on Vancouver Island. And here and there descendants of the Russell lupins too survive in waste places. There's a swathe of purpley blue ones on a steeply curving bend on the road to Wolverhampton, as if they chose this bank as the perfect place to display their tapering spires. And there are mounds of the fragrant yellow shrubby ones just outside Bridgnorth on the same road, where they self-seed easily in the light sandy soils. Every year I mean to stop and pick seed of them, but the traffic thunders by and I am always racing to catch a train. Perhaps I could start my own seed strain . . .

13 July 2002

Losing Control

'Don't you worry about losing control?' is a common enquiry from visitors to my garden. I admit that my garden is wilder than most supposedly formal gardens, especially this year, when everything has made yards of extra growth. The long grass has fountains of feathery seed-heads weeks earlier than usual. The roses are lolling forward, cascading on to the paths, weaving themselves into one another, insinuating themselves into the lower branches of the trees. The tall blue-and-white spires of *Campanula persicifolia* which seeds itself all round the garden have put on an extra foot in height, and are pitching forward at crazy angles, blocking paths, brushing the grass with their flowers. The half dozen late-flowering clematis I planted at the back of the Rose Border a couple of years ago to furnish the pillars and ropes after the roses had finished have, unnoticed, put out long snaking horizontal shoots, threading themselves through the roses to emerge in the most surprising of places. Not what I had intended, but it's too late now: disarrange a single shoot, attempt to prop things up, try to regain control, and the spell is broken. It's all a beautiful tangle.

My garden has a life of its own, independent of me. I like that. Things come and go, wander in and out of the garden, move themselves around and forge alliances without any regard for what I might have to say about it. They have their own agenda. The salsify (*Tragopogon porrifolius*) I grew one year as a vegetable transformed itself the next into a statuesque, glaucous-leaved, lilac-flowered daisy which energetically seeds itself around the garden, poking its tall fluted snout up through the pink roses to the astonishment of garden visitors. The orange fox-and-cubs (*Hieracium aurantiacum*) which breezed in from nowhere some years ago and took up residence in the dry soil of the hedge-bottoms has this year transferred its allegiance to the top of the little Lammas Meadow, hovering above the surface of the long grass like a cloud of brilliantly coloured hoverflies. And I have a new rose. Suddenly, about a month ago, I became aware that the topmost branches of the crab apples and rowans and whitebeams which divide my garden from my neighbour Bridget's were full of flower buds. At first I thought Bridget must have planted it.

Then I thought it was the 'Rambling Rector', swinging Tarzan-like from his appointed place by the garden gate. But no: one of his offspring, perhaps (the result of a casual fling with nearby 'Adélaïde d'Orléans'?), a stray seedling planted by the birds, now wreathing the trees with garlands of white blossom.

Why do we fear losing control? Is that what gardening boils down to – controlling Nature?

My favourite part of the garden here is the Wild Garden. The whole garden is peopled with the ghosts of those who gardened here before, but I am especially fond of this part of it. I made it for Miss Juliana. 'Fifth and last surviving daughter of Joseph Loxdale Warren', it says on her gravestone, 'fell asleep January 30th 1928, in her 86th year', pre-deceased by Josephine Martha, Wilhelmina Jane, Henrietta Matilda, Lucy Ann, Mary Lisette and Georgiana Mary, seven daughters who lived here together, with their bachelor brother Warenne Fitz Warren, the seventh son. The other boys went out into the world: Joseph was a barrister, Albert went into the church, George into the army. Charles was 'shot through the heart, whilst advancing to the relief of his countrymen besieged in the Residency of Lucknow on September 25th 1857' at the age of twenty-four. His sisters survived him by half a century or more. I think of them growing old here together, the world changing around them, the grass growing longer, the hybrid teas reverting to dog roses, the garden gradually growing wilder and wilder.

I made the Rose Border for their father, Joseph Loxdale Warren, who came to live here in 1875. He would scarcely have approved of it this year. Its formal pillars and swags and standards have been sharing space with hogweed and celandines and self-seeded foxgloves. In April I smothered the celandines with a deep mulch in a futile attempt to discourage them. And I pulled up the hogweed. But that left me feeling rather forlorn. I had admired its big jungly leaves: they added substance to the delicacy of the rose bushes, halfway in height between the soft grey leaves of the cardoons behind and the half-grown, still-green leaves of the eryngiums in front. But I need hardly have worried: hogweed is ferociously deep-rooted, and the plants in the Rose Border shrugged off my feeble attempts at respectability and rose again from the stumps of the roots I had left behind to produce thick curds of white flowers, good strong verticals among the mounds of roses.

No, Joseph Loxdale Warren would not have approved. But I like to think that Miss Juliana might have seen the point.

3 July 2004

In Siberia

Provenance is a word used by book-collectors and librarians to refer to a book's previous history – to its former owners (who may be many, if the book is old), to the various book-dealers through whose hands the book may have passed, and the libraries in which it may have sojourned. Most prized are books which once belonged to their author, or to some other famous person, or which bear some interesting annotation. The sixteenth-century French book-collector Jean Grolier, for example, had all his books sumptuously bound with the generous-spirited motto 'Io. Grolierii et Amicorum', meaning '[This book belongs to] Jean Grolier and Friends'.

But not all book-collectors were rich or famous, and a book does not have to be old for its inscription to tell a story. I have two copies of Leigh Hunt's *The Months* – subtitled 'descriptive of the successive beauties of the year' – originally written in 1821 by the poet Leigh Hunt. He is perhaps better known as the author

of 'Abou Ben Adhem (may his tribe increase!)' and of the enchant-
ing 'Jenny Kissed Me' (which I remember various great-aunts and
uncles inscribing in my autograph book as a child). One of my
copies of *The Months* is a large elegant edition printed in 1936
with line drawings of Swallows-and-Amazons children and smart
ladies in cloche hats walking their labradors under leafless trees.
The other is a little plain green pocket-sized book, printed seven
years before in 1929, which carries two inscriptions – apparently
contemporary with the date of the book's publication:

William H. M. Floyd, Igarka, Siberia.
Lat. 70° 16" N. Long. 86° 12" E.

and, in the same hand,

To Philippa from The Philistine.

I knew immediately where he was: Igarka, on the Yenisei River,
the sixth-longest river in the world, dividing Siberia into two
unequal halves on its journey north to the Arctic Ocean; Igarka,
land of permafrost and tundra, site of a Stalin-era women's gulag;
Igarka, once a boom town, now doomed, dying, half-abandoned
to the encroaching birch forest.

What was he doing there? Who was Philippa? Did the book
ever reach her? Was she sister, lover, friend? And why did she
think of him as The Philistine? I think of her in her English garden,
reading Leigh Hunt's evocation of July, or walking her labradors
under the trees, and of William journeying up that vast and terrible river, my book in his pocket, to where the earth flattens out
towards the Pole and the land seems crushed by the sky. What
became of them both, I wonder?

Whoever she was, Philippa did not annotate her book, unlike Maria Margaretta Jackson, who owned my copy of Mrs Loudon's *The Ladies' Companion to the Flower Garden*. It is the fifth edition, published in 1849, and it was bought for her by her brother Edward from a bookseller in Chester ('George Prichard, late Seacome & Prichard, Bridge-St Row, Chester'). He inscribed it 'from her attached brother, Edward, in remembrance of 26 June 1850. Liverpool'. Did he emigrate to America, I wonder, and was this his parting gift, given to her on the quayside at Liverpool?

It's a pretty little book, with a grass-green cover lettered in gold, and gilt edges. She evidently treasured it: it is still in perfect condition. She marked a passage on sowing annual flowers, and underlined the name *Nemophila*, a low-growing genus which originated from California, still much used for bedding schemes today. ('Penny Black', for example, is a stylish modern cultivar, with little purple-black flowers edged with white.) Like many other plants from the Pacific coast of America it was introduced into this country in the early decades of the nineteenth century. Did Edward send Maria seeds from America?

Partings and reunions, joys and sorrows. Books and plants bring us together, not only with those from whom we are temporarily separated, but with all those gardeners of past times who dreamed the same dreams, grew the same plants.

5 July 2003

Leaving Home

I seem to have reached the age when all my friends' children are getting married. At any rate, it's becoming an annual event to have my straw garden-hat trimmed with fresh flowers for the weddings:

white roses and trails of ivy, white 'love-lies-bleeding' and silver senecio, white lisianthus and swirls of aubergine ribbons, depending on the season.

It's amazing what a hat will do. When I went to collect the hat, the policeman outside the flower shop in Much Wenlock even forgave me for parking on double yellow lines and gave me only a mild ticking-off for not wearing my seat-belt. And at the wedding I fell in love (entirely unexpectedly and, as it turned out, happily) with someone I had known as a friend for thirty-five years.

Restoration fops carried posies of sweet-smelling flowers to ward off the evil smells of the city. Victorian ladies decked the skirts of their dresses with garlands of Bourbon roses, and wore stephanotis and lilies in their hair for evening parties. Nowadays weddings seem to be our only excuse for wearing flowers.

So trim your hat with flowers: it could transform your life.

Picking garden flowers for the house, however, always seems to induce a sort of guilt in me, as if I were being inordinately greedy. I feel I should leave them to bloom in the garden, where they would last longer than if beheaded and stuck in a vase.

Sweet peas are the perfect solution. They must be picked to go on blooming. I grow the old fashioned *grandiflora* type – rather misleadingly named, since they have smaller flowers than the big blooms of the Spencer varieties with their frilly edges, but they have by far the best scent. A small bunch will perfume a whole room. And if you keep on picking them they will last from now until the frosts. What better excuse do you need?

Grandiflora sweet peas come in glorious bicolour combinations like the dark-blue and purple 'Quito', or the maroon and deep-violet 'Matucana', said to have the best scent of all. Then there's the shining lavender of 'Lady Grisel Hamilton' and the pale pearlised pink of 'Prima Donna', the variety from which all the Spencer varieties are descended. My own favourites are the fascinating striped varieties (called 'flakes' by those in the know) like the red-and-white striped 'Queen of the Isles', the pale blue-and-white flake 'Unique' and the warm chocolate-brown-and-white 'Senator'. I sow them in pots in a cold frame (to defeat the mice) in February or even March, because I want them to flower rather late in the season, after the old roses have finished. This means that I would be planting them out in early May, and that they would flower from early July onwards. If you want them to flower earlier, sow them like the experts do in October. Then they will be in flower in June. If you are really greedy, double the amount and sow some in October and some in March. You really can't have too many sweet peas.

To choose some to grow for next year, contact the Henry Eckford Sweet-Pea Society of Wem, in north Shropshire. Named in honour of the nineteenth-century patriarch of sweet-pea breeding who lived in Wem, the society maintains seed of about thirty of Eckford's *grandiflora* varieties. It holds an annual show at the town hall every July. You don't need directions. Just follow your nose.

Talking of scents, the mock orange is in bloom in my garden, and in my father's. It's a scent you could drown in – the scent of my childhood. I have been overwhelmed with memories in the last couple of weeks, clearing the house after his death, disposing of furniture, sorting books and photographs – and all the time the piercingly sweet smell of the mock orange drifting in from the garden he and I made together.

It has never looked lovelier: violet 'Veilchenblau' interweaving with the rosy buds and white flowers of 'Adélaïde d'Orléans', just the way we imagined it; perfect fans of 'Seagull' and 'Francis E.

Lester' clothing those too-new brick walls, just as we planned; Pa's bright hybrid teas spicing up my too-tasteful compositions of old roses, just as he knew they would.

But gardens don't stand still. They are only a temporary truce with nature at the best of times. And they are only ever lent to us. Pa's garden will go on to be someone else's garden now.

So deadhead the roses one last time. Time to say goodbye.

20 July 2002

Cottage Yellows

Harold Spicer was the organist of Manchester College, Oxford. With his ancient rheumy eyes and perpetual shower of dandruff, he seemed as old as Methuselah. I was all of twenty-four, and had come to work in the library. One day Harold invited me to tea. It was a Wednesday afternoon, with Choral Evensong on the Third Programme, and the conversation turned – naturally – to gardening. I was just starting my first garden, and was feeling very much the novice. He remembered feeling equally bemused as a very young husband, charged for the first time with giving instructions to a very elderly gardener. 'I knew nothing, but said I thought I'd like some yellow flowers. "I'll just set you some nice Cottage Yellows then." ' Harold repeated the words, laughing and wheezing so much he could hardly get the words out. 'Cottage Yellows! They flowered all right: lovely big yellow flowers, rambling all over the place. But do you know what?' He yelped with laughter. 'Then they turned into marrows!'

This for me is the essence of cottage gardening: fruit and flowers and vegetables and herbs, all grown together and well manured with plenty of muck. Lilies and lettuces, petunias and potatoes;

food for the table and a store cupboard full of gleaming jars of pickles and preserves. In a word: abundance. There is something deeply unromantic about freezing that surfeit of strawberries, that bumper crop of blackcurrants or raspberries, those plump goose-berries ripening on their spiny branches. I love my larder with its rows of jars, their named and dated labels chronicling the progress of summer – strawberry jam in June, blackcurrants and raspberries in July, damsons in September.

Picking strawberries is back-breaking work, done against the clock – time and tide and strawberries wait for no man – but the blackcurrant harvest is an altogether more leisurely affair. I sit on the grass path alongside the bushes, the dappled sun hot on my back, my head and arms deep in the cool green jungle that surrounds the blackcurrant bushes. The berries are cool and smooth to the touch. I sever the stalks with a thumbnail, gently rolling the berries between forefinger and thumb into a cupped palm before depositing them a handful at a time into a plastic bowl.

It's a child's-eye view down here – or a cat's. I peer through the tall green stems and paddle-shaped leaves of horseradish, like so many miniature banana palms, the blue-green foliage of *Galega* with its lilac pea-shaped flowers like upside-down wisteria (its country name is French lilac). I watch a green shield-shaped beetle delicately negotiating a rose leaf, a flotilla of dark brown bumble-bees collecting pollen, a cloud of metallic black-and-gold hoverflies. Grace, my cat, comes weaving towards me through the jungle shade, her pale fur slashed with sunlight. She rubs against me and then just as suddenly is gone, off about her own business. I'm deeply envious of her subterranean existence in this green world of sunlight and dappled shade.

As I pick, I am aware of the pungent smell of the blackcurrant leaves, the lemon-soap smell of balm (*Melissa officinalis*), the musk of the 'Blush Noisette' rose overhead. I pluck leaves and crush them in my fingers: there's the sweetness of marjoram, the hot peppery smell of feverfew. Layers and layers of different scents. Lilies somewhere, sweet peas. I run my fingers down the bristly flower stems of a white damask rose and put them to my nose: they smell of cloves and cinnamon, the scent of the East.

My favourite blackcurrants are Ben Sarek: early and compact, excellent for small gardens, and with berries as big as marbles. I grow all my soft fruit in cottage garden-style mixed borders. And I don't net the fruit. I find that the blackbirds and thrushes don't raid the bushes, except in exceptionally dry summers. Even then I don't begrudge them: there's plenty for all.

Cottage gardens have always been havens for wildlife. Havens too for old plants. What was thrown out as unfashionable by the big house tended to be preserved in cottage gardens – a matter of economics rather than taste. Many an old *Dianthus* or forgotten primrose, Victorian pelargonium or rose thought lost to cultivation, has been rediscovered blooming in an old cottage garden.

17 July 2004

Gillyflowers

Whatever happened to stocks? Does no one grow them now? Brompton stocks, East Lothian stocks, ten-week stocks – the litany of their names seems as impenetrable now as a Wisden to a non-cricketer. Their gentle sugared-almond colours and sweet smell used to be an essential component of the old-fashioned fragrant garden. Brompton stocks and East Lothian stocks were the biennial ones, following on from the wallflowers and coming before the sweet williams, but they were always a bit more difficult to grow. In the late summer or early autumn, bunches of bare-rooted wallflowers and sweet williams tied up with string would appear for sale on market stalls or outside greengrocers' shops, all ready for planting out. But stocks wouldn't put up with that sort of treatment: you always had to grow them yourself, sowing the seed in a seed-bed in June or July, and planting out in spring. Stocks don't take kindly to the modern garden-centre way of selling them, either: if not in flower, they don't sell, and if already in flower, they won't last once you get them home. Perhaps that's the trouble.

But it's curious how, as flowers like this disappear from our gardens, they reappear as cut flowers in posh florists' shops. English-grown stocks arrive in the flower shops in May and June, with long stems of double flowers like miniature muddled roses in shades of lavender-blue, cream, pink, white, dark purple and burgundy-red. They seem to have more perfume than the Dutch stocks (known as 'Column stocks'), which are taller and narrower and arrive later. The Dutch stocks are grown under glass, and are available for a much longer season. The English stocks are seasonal and much sought-after – and very expensive. They also make wonderful dried flowers.

It's not too late to sow some yourself for next year. All the stocks are derived from *Matthiola incana*, a rather tender southern European native, with grey-green slightly hairy leaves (*'incana'* means hoary), which grows wild on the chalk cliffs of the south coast and the Isle of Wight. There are lots of garden forms – single or double, tall or dwarf, annual or biennial, with branched or unbranched flower stems – but the tall double biennials are best. Double flowers tend not to set seed, so seed is generally collected from mixed patches of singles and doubles, which means that you always get a certain proportion of singles among the seedlings, so it is worth roguing them. You can tell them apart by their leaves:

the doubles tend to have rather paler leaves than the singles, or in some varieties have a notch on the leaf.

If you miss sowing the biennials now, you could sow some of the annual varieties next spring – known collectively as ten-week stocks (*M. incana* var. *annua*). But whatever you do, don't forget to scatter some seed of the night-scented stock (*M. longipetala* ssp. *bicornis*) somewhere where you plan to sit or stroll, or beneath a window: the flowers are totally insignificant by day, but by night they pump out their glorious scent by the gallon. An old trick for fragrance right around the clock is to mix them with the showier annual Virginia stock (*Malcomia maritima*).

Stocks are part of our floral history. The Elizabethans loved them. They called them stock-gillyflowers, meaning gillyflowers with a woody stem. Stocks lost the gillyflower bit of their name around the time of the First World War. The gillyflower itself was the clove carnation – the smaller sort of carnation represented today by cultivars like 'Fenbow's Nutmeg Clove' (which you can still grow from seed), whose sweet clove-like scent both stocks and wallflowers share. Wallflowers were known as yellow stock-gillyflowers or wall stock-gillyflowers. Country people here in Shropshire still call wallflowers 'gillies'. And the taller white or purple dame's violets, also known as sweet rocket (*Hesperis matronalis* – my favourite early summer smellie), were known to the Elizabethans as Queen's gillyflowers or winter gillyflowers. I love them all.

The name 'gillyflower' is said to be derived from the French word for a clove, '*giroflée*', which itself may be derived from the Arabic word for a clove, '*quaranful*', or the Indian '*katakaphalam*', meaning 'tree whose fruit is pungent', by way of Greek '*karyphillon*' and Latin '*caryophyllum*' – which gives us the carnation's current Latin name, *Dianthus caryophyllus*. ('Carnation' itself is a colour word, meaning flesh-coloured.)

I suspect that the demise of the stock is linked with the general demise of bedding-out. Annuals are madly fashionable at the moment. Biennials like foxgloves self-seed and take care of themselves. Perennials will never be out of fashion. But stocks? Quite how out of fashion they are can be gauged by the fact that there is no National Collection devoted to them. No National Collection for wallflowers, either. Unless someone takes them under their wing, they could be lost for ever. And all our gardens would be the poorer.

24 July 2004

July Gap

As the roses fade, I start envying my neighbour Pat's herbaceous border. It is just getting into its stride now, when my garden is fast running out of puff. Once the mainstay of gardens in July and August, the old-fashioned herbaceous border has long been abandoned by many gardeners (including me) as just too much work. But what works for me is to grow some of the more rampant plants from the herbaceous border in long grass in my Wild Garden – New England asters, goldenrod, perennial sunflowers, *Campanula lactiflora*, *Aster macrophyllus*, sea holly, *Cephalaria gigantea* – making an impact late in the summer and into the autumn, their skeletons left to dramatise the empty winter garden. This style is nowadays associated with fashionable European designers, but William Robinson was advocating just this sort of gardening – including the use of grasses like giant oat-grass (*Stipa gigantea*) – a hundred and thirty years ago. There's nothing new under the sun.

Giant hogweed (*Heracleum mantegazzianum*), introduced

from the Caucasus in the early nineteenth century, was another of the plants favoured by William Robinson for the wild garden. It is notorious now for its irritant photodermatitis-causing sap, which can cause severe blistering, and equally unpopular for its almost unstoppable advance (mature plants seem to shrug off most weedkillers). Planting it in the wild is now an offence under the Wildlife and Countryside Act of 1981.

People here have been taking me to task for apparently letting giant hogweed spread unchecked in my own garden. Not so: the undeniably statuesque six-foot-plus stems and huge panicles of white flowers growing in the Wild Garden – and invading the Rose Border – belong to the ordinary native hogweed (*H. sphondylium*). Its usual habitat is rough grassland or wayside verge, in contrast to the streamsides preferred by *H. mantegazzianum*. It is also without the red spotted stem which characterises its bigger cousin. But our native hogweed should still be treated with respect, as it too can cause photodermatitis, especially if reduced to a pulp by a strimmer. So when strimming rough grass it is safest to wear gloves and long sleeves if hogweed is present. But don't stigmatise a lovely native plant on account of a more thuggish foreign interloper.

There are in any case plenty of other irritant or poisonous plants in common use. Are we to banish euphorbias and rue and laburnum and monkshood and all the others from our gardens? Monkshood (*Aconitum napellus*) is one plant I couldn't do without at this time of year, with its tall navy-blue spires of sinister-looking cowled flowers. I'm a sucker for any plant with a sinister reputation – like the mandrake (*Mandragora officinarum*), anciently used as a narcotic, with deeply disturbing prostrate egg-shaped fruits (whence its common name of 'devil's apples') like a clutch of raptor eggs straight out of *Jurassic Park*. Or leopard's bane (*Doronicum pardalianches*), whose big yellow daisy flowers were reputed to keep leopards at bay. Or wolf's bane (*Aconitum lycoctonum* ssp. *vulparia*), with evil-looking snaky yellow-green heads. My favourite is viper's bugloss (*Echium vulgare*), with two-foot-tall hairy spires of tubular flowers in an uncharacteristically cheerful colour for a plant with such a name (it comes in shades of sky blue with lolling pink tongues). The stems at first are curled up and uncoil as they rise, like a snake preparing to strike. It is usually biennial, and dies after flowering, but self-seeds copiously, especially in poor dry soils.

27 July 2002

Other People's Gardens

I'm tired. The garden is tired. The last pink rose is drying to a crisp in the unaccustomed heat. I want to turn back the clock. I want it to be 1 June again, with the days still lengthening and the garden still green and full of possibility. We are both showing our age, the garden and I. Like the aquilegias and the feverfew and the hardy geraniums, I need cutting back and rejuvenating. I need a holiday.

And so I find myself on a train travelling north with my friend Mary, going to visit her mother Winifred, who gardens in the Scottish Borders. And as we travel, the summer miraculously spools back with every mile we go, rewinding itself to a point where the white foxgloves are still in bloom and the roses are in their first flush, to a place where the trees haven't darkened to late-summer heaviness and the burns are still tumbling with water, to a small white house in the hills where the bathwater is peat-brown and soft as old silk on your skin.

Winifred came here thirty years ago. The glen was at that time sheep pasture and high, bare hill. Now a tidemark of green afforestation darkens the valley and clings to the skirts of the hills. Raptors circle above: a peregrine, red kites, sparrowhawks, big black carrion crows. The only sounds are the sounds of the wind and the occasional rattle of a stone dislodged by a Sika deer. Within this, Winifred's garden is an oasis, five acres of colour and scent and grassy walks, sheltered by the soft billowing shapes of deciduous trees – native rowans and willows, birch and elder, ash, field maple and hawthorn.

I wake early, before anyone else is stirring, and I stand at the back door, looking out into the garden. I wonder what it must be like to wake here every morning, to that view, to that silence – to stand on the little bridge over the burn at dawn, sniffing the early morning air; to walk down to the vegetable cage at teatime with a kitchen knife to cut a lettuce or pick raspberries, pausing to smell the sweet peas trained up the wire netting; at night to lie in bed listening to the rising wind which in winter roars down the glen, swooping up over the shelter belts and cuffing the house around the ears. I wonder what it must be like to be snowed in here alone for days on end. And I begin to see how, after the long winter, one would crave colour, as Winifred does – great splashes and swathes of colour against the monstrous indifference of the hills and the sky.

I walk out into the garden in my dressing-gown. I have no slippers – I forgot to pack them – but I go anyway, barefoot. I try each of the seats in turn. Does she sit here beneath the arching branches of St Mark's rose ('Rose D'Amour'), podding peas for supper? Or here, in the sun, looking down the grass path to where the Scottish 'Melancholy Thistle' grows (*Cirsium helenioides*, whose flowerheads droop so pensively), reading or perhaps working on some piece of embroidery? Or here, in the shelter of the willow bower, safe from prying eyes, watching the burn spread itself into the dark pool below? Perhaps she sits in none of them, but instead contentedly works in the garden, looking, weeding, considering, alighting nowhere.

That is too rosy a picture, I know. It's lonely here, and the weather is not always kind. There can be snow in June and frost in August. A short season. And the trees are not a mere backdrop to flatter the flowers. They are arranged in waves, one behind the other, dividing the garden into soft, interlocking compartments to baffle the wind. A single row would not suffice. Without them the garden would not exist.

But I know why she does it. Her soul is here. She made this garden and it continues to nourish her. Ian Hamilton Finlay (whose garden is just over the hills from Winifred's) says some gardens are described as a retreat when really they are an attack. Winifred's garden is neither. It is a statement. It says, 'This is me'.

I make the long journey back south again, and I wake in my own bed to the familiar chatter of small birds in the garden, the flutter of house martins' wings across the window. I can hear the cooing of wood pigeons in the distance, the companionable sound of traffic just beginning on the road. I draw the curtains and look down into the garden. It is green and inviting and mysterious again. I'm home. Thank you, Winifred, for reminding me.

26 July 2003

August

Make hay while the sun shines

Gooseberries

Dog Days

There ought to be a law against August. It's an endurance test, the month most people like least in their gardens. The roses are over, the foxgloves are standing about wanly waiting to drop their seed; even the grass has stopped growing. All the one hundred-and-one shades of green that so excited the eye in spring and early summer have darkened now into a palette of two or three, as inspiring as damp fireworks on the lawn the morning after a party.

These are the dog days, so called because Sirius the Dog Star, the brightest star in the sky, rises and sets with the sun at this time of year. The combination was considered since ancient times to give rise to the hottest period of the year, full of malign influences and unwholesome vapours, synonymous with torpor and inactivity. I'd sleep through the whole month if I could, and wake up in September with the Michaelmas daisies and the first dews, refreshed, like my garden.

Even the great Vita Sackville-West confessed to despairing of her garden at this time of year. Her solution was alstromerias. Mine is agapanthus. I don't want soft-pink and peachy shades at this time of year: I want to turn up the temperature with the sizzling reds of dahlias or cool it down with the silvery blues of agapanthus. Either way, the idea is to have something fresh and exciting in the garden to look forward to.

I love the long, bright green leaves of the agapanthus, welling up when everything else is slowing down. I love their sleek almost-frosted stems as they rise up to flower, and the way the flowerheads expand, each floret gradually separating itself from the others like someone stretching after a long sleep. I keep them in big black plastic pots so that I can move them around and rearrange them, fitting them into the borders wherever they are needed. But this also helps when it is time to divide or repot them (something I do every two or three years): getting a mature agapanthus out of its pot is well-nigh impossible. A plastic pot is expendable – you just make a straight slit down each side of the pot with a Stanley knife, peel the sides back, and lift the whole root-ball out.

Dahlias are also a wonderful tonic for tired gardens and flagging spirits. As a gardening nation we owe Christopher Lloyd a great debt of gratitude for many things: for *The Well-Tempered Garden*, quite the best gardening book I know; for his inspirational garden at Great Dixter, where he famously threw out his roses, replacing them with jungly tropical bedding; and for his championing of dahlias at a time when they were deeply unfashionable. My current favourites are the gargantuan 'Garden Wonder', with huge, bright scarlet, double flowers and bright green leaves; the slightly more decorous 'Bishop of Llandaff', with shining red-cardinal semi-double flowers above gorgeous plum-dark foliage; and dusky 'Arabian Night', the colour of slightly unripe blackcurrants. I team them with scarlet cannas and big clumps of *Lobelia cardinalis* – a hardy relative of the little bedding lobelias, with three-foot-tall spikes of pouting snapdragon-like scarlet flowers. I start them all in pots under cover in March or April, and use them to fill the gap when I lift the last of the tulips in late June. By this time the dahlias will often have made as much as two feet of growth, and could easily be damaged if tipped out of their pots in the normal way.

This is where the split pots left over from the agapanthus come in. If the dahlias are planted in the split pots (each split pot placed inside a whole pot to hold the cut edges together), you can just peel the pot away at transplanting time without danger of damaging the brittle flower-stems.

This year I am trying three new dahlias. It is too early yet to say how they will perform, but 'Dark Desire' is catching everyone's eye in the garden here just now, with single flowers as dark as bitter chocolate and a central knot of stamens like gold wire. 'Ragged Robin' is a charmer, with deeply incised foliage and small semi-double dark red ragged flowers intriguingly split and twisted at the ends of the petals. 'Royal Blood' is a little like 'Bishop of Llandaff', with dark matt foliage but darker ruby-red single flowers. All three are protected by Plant Breeders' Rights, but I wonder whether 'Royal Blood' is one of the Bishop's offspring. A seed mixture known as 'The Bishop's Children' has been around for some years, producing dahlias in a mix of fiery colours, all with the Bishop's distinctive dark foliage. Perhaps the Bishop wasn't so decorous after all.

31 July 2004

Rain

I woke the other morning to find the bonfire yard in flames. In a neat piece of wish fulfilment the intermittent crackling noise had woven itself into my dreams as dripping water – the longed-for rain we had been missing all month. But when it was joined by the smell of smoke I found myself suddenly awake and leaping to the window. The yard is shared by all the neighbouring gardens, and with ten people enthusiastically gardening it's easy to amass a heap the size of a small bungalow in no time at all. And the whole lot had now apparently spontaneously ignited.

That's how hot and dry it has been. I was away for the inside of a week at the Benedictine abbey of Belmont near Hereford, where we alternately baked in the sun or dodged showers of tropical ferocity. But here the grass stopped growing, dark moss roses turned bright cerise with stress, strawberries and raspberries shrivelled in the heat, and the Seville oranges in the Canal Garden grew pale, drooped, and dropped their leaves.

So the rain when it finally came a day or two later was a blessed relief. I heard it in the night and got up at dawn and walked out into the still-wet garden in my dressing-gown and slippers, pottering about until hair and slippers were sodden with the wet. There were puddles on the hoggin like torn pieces of sky, pond-skaters and water beetles diving in the Canal at the vibration of a footfall – in their element in this new watery world – blackbirds and thrushes running about like small chickens hunting worms in the grass. There was a raindrop on the point of every needle of yew, great viscid globules of water dangling from every ripening apple. And scent – wave upon wave of jasmine, lavender, sweet peas, lilies – all wafted on billows of liquid air. Paradise.

At Belmont I had been leading a retreat which had gardens and gardening as its theme, and one of the things that came up was the origin of the word 'paradise' and how it relates to the concept of the Garden of Eden in various religious traditions. 'Paradise' apparently derives from an old Persian word meaning an enclosure or walled area. The connotations of earthly delights came later when the word was adopted by the Greeks to refer to the beautiful walled gardens they found in Persia. These were princely gardens of perfumed flowers, rippling water courses, fruit trees and dappled shade, and were divided into four quarters by four streams symbolising the four rivers that flowed out of Eden.

Whatever work was done was certainly not done by the gardens' owners. In the Jewish tradition, on the other hand, Adam and Eve worked in the Garden and reaped the fruits thereof. The Garden of Eden was a place where work and reward were equally balanced, where man and Nature were in perfect harmony.

That's the thing about gardens: work and reward. Digging new potatoes is a case in point. It is one of the great pleasures of life, worth any amount of hard labour. Every year it's like digging for buried treasure. They come out of the ground white and smooth and faintly warm like new-laid eggs, smelling sweet and grassy like summer itself. Their skins are thin and slightly damp, and you can rub them off at the touch of a thumb.

Potatoes don't keep when they are like this (which is why supermarkets don't stock real new potatoes – they stock so-called 'baby potatoes' instead, which are just disappointing little old ones).

I grow waxy creamy-white 'Belle de Fontenay' as a first early, followed by floury 'Sharpe's Express' and purple-skinned 'Edzell Blue' as second earlies, with 'Kerr's Pink' and 'Pink Fir Apple' as main crops. Anything less and I feel deprived. For the other great pleasure of course is eating them.

3 August 2002

Black & White

Black and white: the ultimate in chic. Zuleika Dobson's pearl earrings, the marble floor in a painting by Vermeer, black type on a white page. Black linen and white cotton for summer, white silk and black wool crêpe for winter. 'White Triumphator' tulips with

'Queen of Night'; 'White Cloud' poppies with *Papaver somni-ferum* 'Black Peony'; *Nicotiana sylvestris* with black hollyhocks; sultry *Veratrum nigrum* with white lilies.

White lilies are my salvation at this time of year. After the crimsons and magentas and purples of the old roses, I'm glutted with colour. I long for the satiny gleam of a white throat: in late June, *Lilium regale* and *L. regale* 'Album', blooming as the roses start to fade, filling the garden with their heady, intoxicating scent. In early July, *L. candidum*, the chaste white madonna lily of medi-eval paintings. In late July, *L. longiflorum* with its long, long, narrow trumpets washed with a hint of green. In August, the hybrid oriental 'Casa Blanca' – totally O.T.T. with its huge flowers and chocolate-coloured stamens, but I can't help but love it. And finally, in September, if the weather is kind, *L. speciosum* var. *album*, with its crumpled swept-back flowers like a cloud of hover-ing white moths.

I don't remove the stamens. Lilies produce copious amounts of pollen which is shed into the flower, especially after heavy rain, and some people find this unsightly. Lily pollen can also leave indelible stains on clothing and soft furnishings, and eat into the surface of wooden furniture, which is why many florists do remove the stamens. Removing the stamens is also said to make the flowers last longer. But how sad and shorn the lilies look, without their wonderful saffron- or cinnamon- or snuff-coloured protruber-ances! And I suspect that much of the lilies' scent comes from the stamens. Indoors it may be an advantage to defuse what can be an overpowering scent, but out of doors I want all the scent I can get.

No flower is really, truly, black. Black is the colour of ripe fruit: black grapes, sloes, damsons, blackcurrants. My favourite summer dessert is not summer pudding (though it comes close, with its white sides stained by the brilliant red-and-black juices of the fruit) but black fruit salad, steeped in Earl Grey tea, or – even better – black fruit jelly made with black fruits and a bottle of claret.

The blackest black in the garden, without a hint of colour, is the blackcurrant. And what better way to while away a summer's day than sitting on an upturned bucket picking blackcurrants for cassis? Pick them shiny and firm and black for the best jam in the world: sweet, but with a kick of acidity which is perfect with clotted cream and scones. But leave them slightly longer, until they acquire a soft sheen like Zuleika's pearls and are bursting with sweet juice, and then they are perfect for making cassis.

Making cassis is a five-yearly ritual in our house. For four years out of every five the blackcurrants are bottled, frozen or made into jam, as the occasion and the harvest dictate. But in the fifth year we make cassis. Cassis is a liqueur based on blackcurrants, red wine and brandy, which can be drunk neat but is usually added to chilled white wine or sparkling water to make a long summer drink. (I also pour it over the top of summer pudding if I'm feeling especially greedy.) It's a slow process: at no time must the mixture rise to simmering point, let alone boil. Something above blood heat is what you are aiming at. As the mixture slowly thickens, I test the temperature by dipping my finger into the glistening purple-black liquid – and who could then resist putting that finger in their mouth, and savouring the thick warm alcoholic fruitiness as the evening gently slips away?

The dried fruit we all know as currants are of course nothing of the sort. They are dried grapes, as are sultanas and raisins. Sultanas (made from pale yellow grape varieties) traditionally came from the Smyrna area of Turkey. Raisins are dried muscat varieties, traditionally from Malaga in Spain. Currants, on the other hand, are made from black grape varieties, and originally came from Corinth in Greece – hence their name. They were known in this country as early as the fourteenth century, whereas *Ribes nigrum*, the blackcurrant, did not arrive until the sixteenth century. The blackcurrant got its name from the fact that it was at first imagined to be the source of the 'raisins de Corinthe' or 'currants' which it so much resembled. Prunes of course are dried plums.

1 August 2003

Summer Pruning

Julia and I have just been summer-pruning the cordon apples and pears. Or, I should say, Julia has: I trapped a nerve in my spine last week, and have been spending much of my time prone on the floor. Or, as Julia insists I should correctly call it, supine. She is a doctor, and on the days when she is not summer-pruning my apples and pears for me, she works in the NHS, so she should know. Prone (or prostrate) is, she says, to lie face down. Supine is to lie on one's back – which was what I was doing.

How did I do it? Heaving out the remains of an old tree stump? Carting barrowloads of soil about all day? Digging potatoes? No: searching for a lost cat – Blackberry, my neighbour Bridget's sleek black tom, who had been missing for a week. I jumped down from a fence and landed badly on the other side. And the cat? He came home as soon as it rained. As I knew he would. So here I am, limping about, relegated to deadheading the sweet peas while Julia gets on with the summer pruning.

The point about summer pruning is that it encourages the production of fruit spurs – those short knobbly shoots with fat buds which carry the flowers and fruit. Fruit spurs only grow a few centimetres a year, in contrast with extension growth, which has long narrow buds and can put on as much as eighteen inches or more every year.

To encourage extension growth – for example, to make the frame-work of a young tree – you prune the leaders (the main branches) in winter. To encourage fruit spurs, you prune the laterals (the side shoots) in summer, cutting them to a couple of buds (not counting the cluster of buds at the base). This system is used for apples and pears grown in any sort of trained shape – fans, espaliers, cordons, and so on – but it can also help to improve fruiting in bush and even young standard trees which are slow to come into bearing. The shoots should be nicely firm and woody for at least a third of their length before you prune, indicating that the trees have finished growing for the season. Don't summer-prune until they reach this stage, or you end up with secondary growths shooting out at all angles like a very untidy hedgehog. And don't summer-prune the leaders.

There are a few varieties of apples and pears which don't tend to produce fruit spurs, bearing most of their crop instead on the tips of their shoots. These are known as tip-bearers, and are better grown as bush or standard trees rather than trained forms. They include 'Irish Peach', which is the earliest dessert apple to ripen in my garden, and 'Cornish Gillyflower', one of the last, both with a superb flavour. But somehow I have never quite got the hang of pruning them: pruning of any sort, summer or winter, would seem to entail cutting off the tips and therefore losing next year's crop, but doing nothing has meant that the apples have got steadily smaller and fewer each year.

So how should I prune my tip-bearers? According to the experts of the RHS, I should remove some stems entirely each year to maintain the trees' vigour, and cut back the stronger laterals to about six buds to create more branches and therefore more fruit-ing tips. The weaker, unpruned laterals will then still give me a crop of fruit. Simple, when you know how.

21 August 2004

Sour Grapes

It's been a wonderful year for gooseberries (mercifully mildew-free for once). Gooseberries have rather slipped out of fashion in the past few decades, and many good old varieties have been lost, but 'Whinham's Industry' (a dual-purpose variety – a cooker when green, good enough for dessert when ripe) is one of the best of the handful which survive, a reminder of the glory days of the nineteenth century when more than two thousand gooseberry varieties competed for the attention of gardeners the length and breadth of the land.

This year the fruit on my four bushes of 'Whinham's Industry' has swelled to prodigious size, and for the last couple of weeks I have been patiently waiting for the moment when the berries turn from green to deep wine-red, their succulent insides oozing with golden juice and translucent seeds, promising a whole shelf-ful of gleaming jars of bottled fruit for the winter. But when I finally went up the garden to pick them, I found that the whole crop had vanished overnight.

Putting two and two together, I suspected that a badger might have been the culprit. I had been finding mysterious large seedy droppings all around the garden in the day or two leading up to the disappearance – but there was none of the digging and scraping that one associates with badgers, and no damage to the bushes themselves. Then I remembered Aesop and the story of the Fox and Grapes, famous from a thousand pub signs. I had read that foxes eat rowan berries and other fallen fruits in autumn, and my vine-growing neighbour Ian confirmed that they will also eat grapes. And if grapes, why not gooseberries too?

I couldn't remember how Aesop's story ended, so I rang my

husband at his bookshop in Ludlow and he produced an edition dated 1665 with parallel English, French and Latin texts, complete with a fetching engraving of the fox lusting after the grapes.

The point of the story is that the fox, for all his wiles, can't reach the grapes because they are grown Italian-style, up a tree, but he consoles himself with the thought that the grapes were in any case 'green and tart, not worth his stay'. Which of course is the origin of the expression 'sour grapes'.

I might well apply the same moral to my penstemons. This winter they all succumbed to the Shropshire climate – though whether to January's low of 5°F (minus 15°C), or February's double ration of rain I don't much care. I never liked them anyway.

No, that isn't strictly true. I did like the variety called 'Sour Grapes' – a lovely deep violet with a hint of blue at the base. Even better, I liked the variety frequently sold as 'Sour Grapes' but correctly called 'Stapleford Gem'. 'Stapleford Gem' is the colour of the prince's castle in the Cinderella book I won at the age of seven – a pale shimmering confection of blue-grey and lilac-pink with a haze of pearly white at the throat, shot through with veins of purple. Truly an aristocrat among penstemons.

The muddle about its identity has a suitably aristocratic pedigree, too, traceable to Margery Fish and Vita Sackville-West, both of whom apparently sent out 'Stapleford Gem' plants mistakenly labelled 'Sour Grapes'. The two varieties remain thoroughly confused to this day – certainly my 'Stapleford Gem' came to me only a year or two ago still labelled 'Sour Grapes'.

But as Margery Fish says, the penstemon provides continuous colour throughout the summer, and heaven knows I could do with that. The trouble is, few penstemons are truly hardy and in this garden things have to sink or swim: I haven't time to mollycoddle them. A good rule of thumb is that the larger the flowers and the broader the leaves, the less likely the variety is to be hardy. So 'Stapleford Gem', with its narrow leaves and smallish flowers, should be among the hardiest. It's also less tall than many varieties, and so less likely to suffer from wind-rock in winter. But everything depends upon local soil conditions and aspect, as well as the weather.

Luckily penstemons root easily. The solution is to take cuttings in late summer and overwinter them in a greenhouse or cold frame. You could even give some to friends. Just make sure you don't mix up the labels.

10 August 2002

Rapunzel, Rapunzel

The average person spends a third of their life in bed. I probably spend more: it's my favourite place to read, to write, to daydream, gazing out of the window at the garden, planning. I even don't mind being mildly ill so that I have an excuse to spend more time there, curled up with the cats. And one of the delights of having a rather rambling house is that I can migrate from room to room according to season, choosing a bed and a bedroom according to whim or the weather.

My winter bedroom faces east, to get the best of the early morning sun. I can chart the shortening of the days by the progress of the sun's rays across the room. From here I look out towards the church and the churchyard. I can hear the church clock striking the quarter hours. If the weather gets really cold, I might migrate into the smaller room next door, with a tall old-fashioned single bed – the snuggest room of all, lined with books from floor to ceiling.

My favourite bedroom for summer (where I am writing this now) is in the north corner of the house, cool and shady, with the casement window thrown open on to the garden. I can hear the blackbirds below the window-sill squabbling over the ripe morello cherries trained on the wall. I can hear the fluttering of house martins' wings as they swoop down and up to reach their nests under the eaves. And I can smell jasmine, wafting in through the open window in great sweet billows.

This is *Jasminum officinale*, the common white summer-flowering jasmine, which thrives here on the north wall of the house despite being slightly tender (it is reputedly hardy only down to 23°F (minus 5°C)). This seems to be because it is growing through a thicket of winter-flowering jasmine (*Jasminum nudiflorum*) which protects and supports it. If only the winter jasmine had the scent of a winter-flowering witch-hazel (any of the *Hamamelis* would do – they are all intensely fragrant), I might be tempted to sleep here all year round.

The thought prompted me to consider what other sweetly scented climbers – one for each season of my peripatetic existence – I could plant beneath my other bedroom windows. I decided to consult my friend Louisa Arbuthnott, who specialises in climbers and wall shrubs. The garden attached to her nursery at Stone House Cottage, near Kidderminster in Worcestershire, has enough flower-draped walls and romantic creeper-clad towers to prevent Rapunzel pining for her prince altogether. What would Louisa choose for spring?

'*Stauntonia hexaphylla* without a doubt,' she said. 'The scent is very exotic, very carrying. You can smell it right across the garden. Like the sort of summer holiday you can't afford. You need a big wall to accommodate it, and the flowers themselves are only modest' – like little bunches of drooping snowdrops, white tinged with violet – 'but the fragrance is unforgettable.'

What next? Wisteria. I have always envied my next-door

neighbours the ancient wisteria which in early summer wreathes their bedroom windows. Theirs is Chinese wisteria (*W. sinensis*), which flowers in May with fragrant, violet-blue trailing blossoms, before the leaves appear. Japanese wisteria (*W. floribunda*) flowers in June, when the young leaves are emerging. Its blossoms are longer than *W. sinensis* – up to two feet or more – but *W. sinensis* has the advantage of flowering again later in the summer. For sheer fragrance, however, Louisa recommends another, less well-known wisteria, *W. venusta* (now more correctly known as *W. brachybotrys* 'Shiro-kapitan'). The racemes are shorter than either *sinensis* or *floribunda*, but the individual florets are larger – shining waxy white. The leaves are lovely too, covered with silky silver hairs.

What about a rose for midsummer? It would have to have healthy foliage and the sort of wafting musky perfume which is carried on the air. 'Rambling Rector', perhaps, or the late-flowering musk rose, *Rosa moschata*, which flowers on well into autumn, with big trusses of single white flowers. Or perhaps one of its descendants, such as the sweetly scented double 'Princesse de Nassau', which has white flowers, barely flushed with pink.

And then a honeysuckle. What would Louisa recommend here? The vigorous evergreen climber *Lonicera similis* var. *delavayi* for late summer and autumn, followed by the smaller shrubby semi-evergreen *L.* x *purpusii* for winter and early spring, both with deliciously fragrant creamy white flowers.

That brings me nicely round to my *Stauntonia* again, which flowers in April. 'But what about wintersweet (*Chimonanthus praecox*)? You can grow it as a shrub but it's even better on a wall. And it has the best winter scent of all.'

I'm clearly going to run out of wall space.

7 August 2004

Bees on the Lavender

Bombus – now there's a wonderful onomatopoeic word – Latin for bumble-bee. I've just been watching two young *Bombus lapidarius* queens feeding on my Old English lavender, and the word perfectly conveys the sound – a deep resonant hum – as well as their bumbling progress from flower to flower.

It's one of the delights of lavender, especially the late-blooming kinds like Old English (*Lavandula* x *intermedia* Old English Group), that it attracts so many different kinds of bee. There are at least six different sorts of bumble-bee feeding on my lavender at the moment – little lion-maned Carder bees (*Bombus pascuorum*); the occasional small black *B. pratorum* with a yellow stripe up around her neck; a whole flotilla of big black and yellow striped ones (*B. terrestris*, *B. lucorum* and *B. hortorum*), all with buff or white tails – but it's the two female *Bombus lapidarius*, the large red-tailed bumble-bee, which caught my eye. With their plump velvety-black bodies, red tails like fox furs, and huge shiny black transparent wings like glossy fifteen-denier stockings, they look like what they are: princesses – sleek, well-fed and with the world at their feet.

Like honey-bees, bumble-bees are social insects, and operate within a similar caste system of queen, workers and drones, but unlike honey bees they do not store honey, and each colony dies out at the end of the year. Only young mated queens like the two *Bombus lapidarius* will survive the winter. The big jazzy males are still bombing about, eating and drinking themselves silly, unaware that the end is nigh. But then one morning you will find them still clinging to the spikes of lavender, sleeping it off as usual, except that today it's that little bit colder, and the sun takes that little bit longer to reach the garden, and stays more fleetingly. And like solar-powered cells, their batteries start to run flat. As the sun's rays reach them, they'll slowly heave up one leg, then another, then stop in mid-movement. Left out in the cold, they'll be dead soon. Meanwhile, the new young queens snooze the winter away, snug in hibernation, until they emerge in spring to found a new colony.

Bumble-bees are very important pollinators of early crops. They emerge before the honey-bees and fly in lower temperatures – even in light rain. They also have longer tongues which enable them to pollinate flowers the honey-bees can't. And increasingly they are being used in greenhouse culture as pollinators of crops like strawberries, courgettes and tomatoes. They are especially important now with the decline of wild honey-bees due to the parasitic mite Varroa. But unless we mend our ways and plan our gardens with at least some thought for them, they will become a lot more scarce than they are now. Insecticides are a major problem. Bumble-bees are particularly vulnerable because many of them sleep on the flowers at night, so there is no safe time to spray. Another problem is the modern regime of silage-making in June (instead of haymaking in August), which destroys the nests of ground-breeding species.

I went to ask my ninety-year-old friend Natalie Hodgson what one can do to help. She runs a pick-your-own lavender field on a sloping site overlooking her home at Astley Abbots, just over the hills from me. It's impossibly picturesque: the black-and-white half-timbered house with its jumble of roofs, the blue haze of the lavender stretching across the hillside, a long line of beehives. She has been keeping honey-bees for years (they famously live in a village 'street' of beehives disguised as village shop, school and pub), but in response to the current worries about bumble-bees she has started raising them too.

Natalie's advice for helping bumble-bees is to plant early flowers like pulmonarias, hellebores, heathers and crocuses, as well as catkin-bearing trees like pussy willow. Bees also prefer single flowers to double forms. And they love lavender. You can ensure a succession of lavender from May to the first frosts by planting *L. stoechas*, followed by *L. angustifolia* (cultivars include the navy blue 'Hidcote' and the pale-blue 'Munstead'), followed by *L. vera* (now *L.* x *intermedia* Dutch Group), with *L.* x *intermedia* Old English Group bringing up the rear. And then (especially if you trimmed them back after their first flowering) in a good year the *L. stoechas* varieties will repeat.

It's also a help not to be too tidy in the garden: the different species all have different nesting and hibernation requirements, and piles of stones or twigs and patches of long grass may all provide sites – as will the pocket of your garden coat left hanging up in the toolshed all winter, or the grass bucket of your old lawnmower. But don't worry: bumble-bee nests are usually quite small, and although bumble-bees can sting, they rarely bother to do so. And if you do use insecticides, use them early in the morning or late in the evening, and make sure there are no sleepy bees in the way.

17 August 2002

Autumn Raspberries

It's amazing what the placing of a seat will do. My garden is notably short on seats. Good seats are so expensive for one thing. And for another, I never have time to sit down. Not, you understand, that I am always working away, hell-bent on pulling up every weed. No, it's rather that my way of relaxing in the garden is to wander about, looking at things – picking a flower here, nibbling a plum there, just cogitating.

Then the other day, while rummaging in the garage for something else entirely, I came across an old folding wooden bench with several slats in the seat missing, rescued from a bonfire years ago. I had meant to have it mended, but then forgot it.

I took it up to the garden, and set it down at the end of a path against the high yew hedge. And I sat on it. (Carefully.) Suddenly an anonymous part of the garden became a place in its own right – square and enclosed and really rather nice. The path now had a point. The plantings on that side of the tunnel came into focus, instead of just being the other side of somewhere else. More than that, it completely altered my perception of the rest of the garden, seen from that vantage point.

And it was gloriously placed to catch the early evening sun. The next evening I went back and sat on it again, experimentally, nibbling a handful of autumn raspberries. I think it might become a habit . . .

Talking of autumn raspberries, many things are worth waiting for, but autumn raspberries come pretty near the top of my list. Larger and better flavoured than their summer relatives, they arrive just when soft fruit is disappearing from the shops. I grow 'Autumn Bliss', which starts bearing in mid-August and goes on almost into the first frosts. It fruits on the current year's canes, unlike summer raspberries, so you cut all the old canes right back to the ground in February.

Making jam from autumn raspberries is a terrible indulgence. They produce fruit at a more leisurely pace than the summer varieties, so there is rarely the same need to deal with a guilt-inducing mountain of fruit, but it's difficult to resist making a few delicious pots. But what is it about jam-making which seems to require that it be finished after midnight? However early I start, I always end up working into the small hours of the morning. The other night I staggered once more from a hot kitchen out into the cool night – and saw a shooting star. And then another. And another. These were the Perseids, the annual August meteor shower radiating from the constellation Perseus, only visible after midnight. Quite worth making jam for.

31 August 2002

Dewpoint

Something has changed. A different smell, a different cast to the light. I open the door and there it is: not midsummer, not high summer, but almost-autumn. Overnight the seasons have moved on a notch.

It's the dew: the first heavy dewfall of autumn, drenching the grass, silvering the feathery tops of the uncut yew hedges. I can smell its cool self-contained stillness from the door. After days of heat, I want to lap it like a cat.

My footprints trail behind me in the grass. I peer at the secret snares of spiders' webs, made visible overnight. Rose-hips ghosted with chilly dew-breath. Crimson honeysuckles bowed down with the weight, cold and pale like party girls at dawn. And as if on cue, the water-boatmen have all vanished – packed up, stashed their oars and flown away, leaving the Canal vacant, untenanted, like an end-of-season beach.

It was cold last night, after a warm and humid day, and there was a clear sky. It was the first time I had seen the Milky Way in weeks. Perfect conditions for a heavy dewfall, though not usually

so heavy or so early. But the pink and cream of the ripening viburnum berries and the rectangles of bleached stubble where the long
grass has been cut tell the same tale. Already I have that old familiar back-to-school September feeling, a compound of anxiety and
suppressed excitement, reluctance to leave the summer behind and
anticipation of what is to come.

We have nearly finished cutting the long grass. I have the same
mixture of contradictory emotions. I delay and delay, loathe to
lose the swaying sea of seed-heads. But once we start I find the
process oddly elating – a rediscovery of spaces half-forgotten, in
area somehow bigger than I remember, straining at the perimeters
of the garden. I like the bleached-out colour of the cut stubble
too, against the dark green of the yew hedges. I have six areas of
long grass (seven if you count the drive), each managed for different flowers. They are not vast: the largest no more than an average
lawn in size, and two of them little more than strips up each side
of the garden.

Bulbs in long grass are easy: one simply waits until the foliage
has died down before cutting. But in managing meadow areas it is
crucial to decide which season one is aiming for, and to let the wild
flowers drop their seed before the grass is cut. Here the Snowdrop
Walk is cut first, in early summer, followed by the long grass with
daffodils and lady's lace on either side of the drive. Then in June
the Plum Walk, to clear the way for the autumn crocuses. The
Nuttery, underplanted with April- and early May-flowering things
– primroses, bluebells and leucojums – used to be cut in June, but
now that the tree canopy has grown sufficiently heavy to smother
the long grass, it needs little more than hand-pulling to discourage
any nettles or docks before the cyclamen start to emerge. The patch
of the Wild Garden given over to May-flowering things (various

forms of white *Narcissus poeticus*, camassias and *Iris sibirica*) used to be cut in early July, but is gradually being colonised by wild blue cranesbill (*Geranium pratense*), so we now cut it a few weeks later to allow the cranesbills to set seed.

The last area of long grass to be cut is usually the Lammas Meadow, with purple and white fritillaries, wild yellow tulips and self-seeded orange hawkweed, cut in time for Lammas (1 August). But this year cutting has been delayed. I have been waiting for the yellow rattle to set seed. I sowed it into the coarsest grass last September as an experiment. It is a British native wild flower, a semi-parasitic annual which reduces the vigour of the grass into which it is sown. It has certainly worked here. The results were immediately apparent as soon as the grass began to grow in spring. And the yellow rattle is itself an attractive addition to the meadow in its own right, with neat dimpled green leaves and the bright colour of a cowslip.

By ten o'clock the dew has vanished, and as I wander around the Wild Garden, peering to see if the tiny scrolled candelabra of the cranesbills have whirled their seeds into the air or whether the pale bladders of the yellow rattle are empty yet of seed, I disturb a cloud of orange butterflies, feeding on the shaggy yellow heads of the *Inula hookeri*: gatekeepers, the heralds of autumn.

9 August 2003

AUTUMN

September

*Summer comes with a bound;
winter comes yawning*

Michaelmas daisy (& peacock butterfly)

Seen from a Train

I have just returned from my long-hoped-for, long-planned – long-postponed – seven-hour journey along the margins of England and Wales, on the stopping train from Ludlow to Penzance, en route for the Isles of Scilly, watching the hydrangeas turn from pink to blue, the soil from red to black; conifers giving way to camellias, sumachs to echiums, apples to palm trees; peering down from bridges and diving into tunnels, teetering across viaducts and clinging to cliffs – twenty-eight stations from the broad water-meadows of Herefordshire to the stone walls and steep little fields of Cornwall. And all the way I was mesmerised by people's back gardens.

Front gardens are where you keep up appearances; the back garden is where you keep the hamster. Back gardens are where people let it all hang out – and not only the washing. It's like the difference between superego and id. In the front garden you do what is expected of you. In the back garden you are yourself. Here you indulge your innermost passions: grow those prizewinning fuchsias, that giant sunflower, those magnificent tomatoes; lounge on those white plastic chairs, tinker with that beloved old bike, scuff the lawn into brown patches playing footie with the kids. All safe from prying eyes – except from the train.

From the train we see you as you really are, back to front, inside out – from the bottom up: compost heap before conservatory, straggly boundary hedge before perfect flower-beds, muddy patch of nettles before immaculate lawn. But you don't give a fig. Why should you? We are gone in a flash. We are dumb. Back gardens turn us all into exhibitionists.

I lived for several years as a child in a house sandwiched between the Great North Road and the main LNER line from London to Edinburgh. There was just enough space for the house, the garden, and an allotment at right angles to it, reached by climbing through some loose planks in the wooden fence at the bottom of the garden. The allotment was where my father grew our vegetables – rows of cabbages and Brussels sprouts, turnips and beans, all neatly set out at regulation distances. Back gardens are more private and less purposeful than allotments: on allotments there's always someone looking over your shoulder. The back garden was where he indulged his passion for trees. But the allotment was where he had his garden shed, and where he liked to strip off his shirt and sit smoking a pipe as the trains rumbled by to Scotland.

I like to think of him in his prime sitting in his allotment, his dark skin turning copper-coloured in the sun, as the people on the train stared out of the window or turned the pages of their newspapers. Glimpses of other lives seen from a train have a particular poignancy. One of my father's favourite poems was 'To a Fat Lady Seen from a Train', by Frances Cornford. It seems a pretty rum thing now to have written in a child's autograph book:

> O fat white woman whom nobody loves,
> Why do you walk through the fields in gloves,
> . . . Missing so much and so much?

But I have never forgotten the alliteration of the first line, or the strangeness of the central image: the isolation of both viewer and

I like 2 p.m., too. Show time! A last-minute scramble to tidy the hose away, put out the chairs for tea, shove the mower out of sight. A quick peek over the garden wall to see how many cars are in the car park. Then the visitors arrive: couples on holiday from Norfolk and Somerset, Derbyshire and Scotland; the family who found us on the internet, and the people who just happened to be passing; people seeing the garden for the first time, and people making their second or even third visit of the year – all bearing tales of their own gardens, asking questions, sharing observations, wanting advice. What nice people gardeners are.

At 6 p.m. the lengthening shadows bring back the depth and perspective lost in the glare of mid-afternoon. Scents, cowed under the sledgehammer of the sun, start to revive. Colours become deeper, and more rich: the green of grass and hedge is never more lustrous than now. Blues and purples glow as the light fades, the flowers seeming even larger than they really are: a late-blooming clematis which looked coarse at 3 p.m. now looks huge and velvety, like something from a tropical isle. Early evening is perhaps the best time of all to visit a garden, and tonight there's a party of ladies from the W.I. The ladies are on time, jolly, well-informed, and great fun. They make me look at the garden again with fresh eyes.

By 9 p.m. the last of the visitors has gone, the plates scraped clean of crumbled scones and clotted cream, the dishwasher loaded, the borrowed chairs returned. The bumble-bees are already asleep on the lavender, the honey-bees long ago headed for home. I can feel the dew between my toes as I bring the last of the tables in from the lawn. Quick shapes flit at the corners of my vision: pipis-trelle bats, with their zigzag flight. Or perhaps Grace the cat, stalking me. My fingers brush the sticky green leaves of *Nicotiana sylvestris*, and I catch a whiff of its perfume – the sour pungency of the leaves augmented now by the piercing sweetness of the flowers. The white trumpets float, disembodied, in the gathering dusk. There are small, silvery moths in the lavender now, fluttering among the dark furry shapes of the sleeping bees.

I can't bear to go inside. I don't know what time it is. Sounds are magnified. I can hear the trickle of water as it falls into the Canal – a small sound almost lost in the cheerful babble of daylight hours. The shapes of hedges and trees are blurred with darkness now, only their outlines showing dark against the stars. I go back to fetch a torch to finish clearing up. The light catches the red eyes of moths feeding on the electric-blue thistle-heads of the cardoons, the shiny brown bodies of earwigs twisting out of sight behind the petals of the scarlet dahlias. I find more moths, wings folded, gorging on the ripe plums; snails champing unconcerned on the tender leaves of the hydrangeas. I feel like a voyeur.

I see to my surprise that it's nearly eleven when I return to the house. The door is still standing open, as it has all day, the house full of the scent of the garden like the scent of the sea. Reluctantly I close the door. Only seven hours to go before I can open it again.

4 September 2004

Two Elegant Ladies

I look at petunias with new respect. No longer will I see them simply as brightly coloured garden wallpaper. Evidently they have minds of their own. Plant breeders in search of a more intensely purple petunia have found – to their astonishment – that their experiments produced not a purple petunia, but a white one. This peculiar behaviour led scientists to the discovery of a powerful immune system working at the genetic level – a discovery which has been called the most important medical breakthrough of the last decade, promising to revolutionise the treatment of a range of diseases, including AIDS and cancer.

The lynchpin of this newly discovered system is a form of double-stranded RNA called RNAi (or RNA interference). Single-stranded RNA has been known for many years as the messenger between DNA (which carries the coded information defining each unique organism) and the proteins which carry out or 'express' that information. Thus, in theory, when the plant breeders added more of the messenger RNA to make more of the protein which makes petunias purple, the result should have been a more exaggerated expression of the relevant gene: a more intensely purple petunia. The actual result – a white one – is a phenomenon known as PTGS or Post Transcriptional Gene Silencing.

PTGS had been thought to be a peculiarity of petunias and a few fungi (where the phenomenon is known as 'quelling'). But it is now understood that PTGS is caused by the presence of RNAi, which is taken as a signal to destroy anything similar to itself – the original messenger RNA – in the same way that the immune system responds to a virus. This means that the relevant gene is 'switched off', which means that the gene stops doing its job.

In any living organism, including human beings, there are thousands upon thousands of genes. Their position on the genome may be known, but the function of the vast majority is still unknown. By injecting targeted RNAi, each gene can be silenced in turn, allowing researchers to identify its function. Thus, eventually, it is hoped to be able to identify and switch off the genes responsible for diseases such as cancer – all thanks to the humble petunia.

There are two very elegant ladies in my garden at the moment: the soft apricot-coloured tea rose 'Climbing Lady Hillingdon' and the rich purple clematis 'Lady Betty Balfour', growing together through the same wall-trained plum. The blue-purple stems of the rose echo the colour of the clematis, and the extravagant boss of creamy stamens in the centre of each clematis in turn echoes the colour of the rose. The plum is Coe's Golden Drop, whose deep amber flesh and purple-spotted golden skin perfectly complements them both. It's a marriage made in heaven. All I could wish for is a little more scent from the rose, though the fragrance of ripening plums more than compensates, as the red admiral butterflies agree, ignoring the flowers and feasting on any fallen plums in a *memento mori* straight out of a Dutch seventeenth-century flower painting.

Earlier this year the rose was dug up and moved to accommodate a new May-flowering *R. banksiae* on the same sheltered south-facing wall. I asked a friend (who is not a gardener) to help me by cutting 'Lady Hillingdon' right down to the ground. He took me at my word and cut it very hard indeed. I was rather taken aback, but the hard pruning seems to have done nothing but good. It used to be said that you should get your worst enemy to prune your roses (the idea being that the harder you prune your teas and hybrid teas the better), to which I would now add that your best friend could also do it – anyone, so long as they are a not a gardener.

Emboldened by this, I asked the same friend a few weeks ago to prune my evergreen myrtles (*Myrtus communis*). They, like the two roses, are slightly tender, and I grow them in big tubs with handles so that they can be dragged into shelter in winter if need be. I had never dared prune them and they had grown into large untidy non-flowering pyramids full of bare stems. I averted my eyes. He chopped. The result? Masses of fresh green aromatic leaves and now, in September, an explosion of fragrant white blossom. Give the man a medal.

13 September 2003

How Does Your Garden Go?

Mary, Mary, quite contrary, how does your garden go? This way or that? Clockwise or anti-clockwise? The other day I found myself at Studley Royal in North Yorkshire, and was halfway round the circuit of the garden before I realised that I was walking the 'wrong' way. All the great landscape gardens of the eighteenth century were composed of a series of set pieces, designed to be viewed in a certain sequence from predetermined vantage points. At Studley the climax of the garden is the distant view of Fountains Abbey, suddenly revealed at the end of the river valley as you look down from the Gothic 'alcove' known as Anne Boleyn's Seat. It is a magnificent *coup de théâtre*, and it is totally lost if you follow the current signposts and start at the abbey itself.

I sympathise with the National Trust and English Heritage. They understandably want to divert traffic away from the village of Studley Roger. But to appreciate the garden as its maker intended you need to start from the deer park, which can only be accessed through the village. This quite rightly costs you an extra £2 for parking (unless you are a National Trust member), and you will also need a copy of the guidebook (£3.50), which gives you directions for seeing the garden the 'right' way round. But it's worth it, for following the original route also gives you the best views of Studley's sublime formal water garden with its lake, canals and reflecting half-moon and crescent-shaped ponds, set in turf like green velvet.

On the other hand, parking is free at the visitor centre, near the abbey end of the circuit, and you could, as my long-suffering companion suggested, simply walk backwards. As I walk round my own garden these days I am often accompanied by my parents' little brown tabby cat, Beattie, who has now come to live with me. Despite her advanced years, she has proved to be the most adaptable of creatures: after a life spent almost entirely indoors (three years in a cat rescue centre followed by five principally sitting on my mother's lap), she has rapidly turned into a country cat – climbing trees and catching mice as if to the manor born.

She and I always walk round the garden the same way. Today our mission is to see whether the walnuts are ready for pickling. We go across the Plat with its late summer bedding of scarlet *Lobelia cardinalis*, maroon-black *Cosmos atrosanguineus* and dark red dahlias, then up through the Canal Garden, where we both pause to peer into the brown depths of the water to watch the water-boatmen diving – and are divebombed in our turn by a large jade-green dragonfly which buzzes around our heads like a mechanical toy. Then out between the yew hedges to the Plum Walk, where Beattie chases the red admiral butterflies feasting on the fallen plums, and I gorge on the last of the delicious 'Reine Claude'. Then up into the Wild Garden, where the long grass has been mown down to stubble height like a bleached cornfield, and the rose-hips blaze – *Rosa setipoda* with glossy Chinese lacqueur-red hips and long trailing sepals like a school of small scarlet jelly-fish swimming through the air; *R. moyesii* with huge twisted orange flask-shaped hips, hanging in bunches like red hot chilli peppers; *R. villosa* with cherry-red hips, round as a crab-apple, bristly as a burr – and finally into the cool dimness of the Nuttery.

I planted the walnut trees in 1991 – 'Buccaneer' and 'Broadview', two varieties specially adapted to the English climate (walnuts can be susceptible to late frost) – and I planted two so they might pollinate one another, as walnuts are not always reliably self-fertile. This is their first decent crop, and I had been dreaming of making my own pickled walnuts – spicy and black and with an almost indescribably crunchy, papery texture. I ransacked my husband's old cookery books and came up with several recipes, all of which stipulated the knitting-needle test: that is, if any resistance to the point of a knitting needle is met, the nuts are too old to be pickled (though maddeningly none said when in the ripening process that stage might be reached).

So I plunge a skewer (the nearest thing I can find to a knitting needle) into the succulent green rind of the nearest nut. It proves as obdurate as me at Studley Royal. I wonder if they sell pickled walnuts in the supermarket?

14 September 2002

[*According to the many people who wrote or emailed in response, St Swithun's Day (15 July) is the last day for pickling walnuts. In France (and perhaps in the south of England), late June is a better time, around St Gervais' Day (19 June). In France, St Gervais interestingly seems to have the same properties as St Swithun here: 'Pluie de St Gervais, Pluie quarante jours après.' The same was also said in England of rain on St Mary Magdalen's Day (22 July), and in France she too is associated with the walnut harvest: 'A la Ste Madeleine, Les noix sont pleines.' At any rate, the consensus seems to be to pickle your walnuts in late June to mid-July, depending on where you live. So I was at least two months out with my knitting-needle test – no wonder the nuts were hard.*]

All Passion Spent

There's a peacefulness about September: all the strivings of July and August forgotten, all that 'trying to keep things going', that nightly watering of dry soil, that conscientious deadheading, that picking-off of every yellowed leaf. 'Sorry there's so little colour' (with the implied reproach, 'Why didn't you come last week/last month/ *anytime* but now?'). Who are we kidding? Let's stop pretending. Time passes: gardens show their age. We shouldn't apologise.

But thank God it's September. The earth is damp again, and the air is full of liquid sounds – the swoosh of thrushes' wings, the burble of house-martins. I can smell the dampness in that rich September aroma of leaf mould and late blue lavender, bonfire and white summer jasmine, see it in the pale yellow roses which are gently starting to repeat, the Michaelmas daisies which are unfurling their cool blue heads, the new young seedlings – long despaired of – starting to emerge from the damp, still-warm soil. I can breathe a sigh of relief: summer is over at last. Am I just being perverse?

There's time now to look, to stand and stare. To see the whole world upside down in a dewdrop. To watch, as if oneself taking root, a chestnut leaf slowly flushing from amber to russet, the veins of crimson colour slowly spreading around the hard green circumference of an apple.

Time too to rediscover the stars. Earlier nights and lower temperatures mean clearer skies. As I put away the garden tools I can see Cepheus and Cassiopeia overhead – the unlucky parents of Andromeda who lies for ever chained to her rock just out of their reach – and the angry red eye of Mars, still there like the all-seeing eye of Sauron in *Lord of the Rings*, but joined now by Aldebaran, the red eye of Taurus the bull, harbinger of autumn.

This week sees the equinox, and already we are well into the season of equinoctial gales, with its characteristically turbulent skies. Winds back and veer as the fronts race across the hillside, scattering sunshine and shadows. Weather systems stack up above the garden like aeroplanes in a holding pattern. I stand transfixed, watching: great hammerheads of cumulo-nimbus, growing still larger as I watch; icy skeins of cirrus, way above, torn into tatters by stratospheric winds; warning puffs of little fracto-cumulus, queuing up along the squall line.

Our present system of classifying clouds and the words we use to describe them were devised in 1802 by Luke Howard, a London pharmacist, amateur meteorologist and keen botanist. Howard took as his inspiration the revolutionary binomial system of plant nomenclature devised half a century earlier by the Swedish botanist Carl Linnaeus. Linnaeus divided plants by family (genus) and, within genera, by species. Following the same method, Howard identified four genera of clouds, and gave them internationally understandable Latin names: cirrus (meaning a whisp or curl of hair), cumulus (a heap), stratus (a blanket or covering) and nimbus (a storm). Each genus was then subdivided into various species according to size, shape and formation (cirro-cumulus, cirro-stratus, cumulo-stratus and nimbo-stratus). Later the species were in turn subdivided by the addition of epithets such as castellanus ('with turrets') or calvus (meaning 'smooth' or 'bald'), in the same way as plant species are divided into various forms, giving rise to compound names such as cumulo-nimbus incus (from 'incus', an anvil, the final stage of a big storm cloud). Howard's descriptions of cloud formations inspired a generation of poets and artists, including Shelley, Turner and John Constable in England, and Caspar David Friedrich and Goethe in Germany.

As I stand and stare, or quietly potter about the garden not doing very much, I find that my September mood is summed up by the title of one of Vita Sackville-West's novels, *All Passion Spent*. It is the story of a widow who at the end of her life stops pretending and defies the wishes of her family to do at last what she herself really wants to do. Vita wrote a dozen hugely success-ful novels as well as numerous books of poetry, travel and biography. It was largely through her books that she was able to finance the garden at Sissinghurst. Five of her novels are still in print in the Virago Modern Classics series, including *All Passion Spent*, *The Edwardians* and, my own favourite, the wry and whim-sical little *Seducers in Ecuador*. Do try them.

20 September 2003

'What is that wonderful tree?'

'What is that wonderful tree?' That is the question most often asked by visitors to my garden. It is tall and narrow – perhaps fifty or sixty feet high – with a massive spiralling trunk and deeply fissured bark fretted into squares. In summer its leaves are as dark as a thun-dercloud, in autumn butter-yellow, the ground beneath alive with blackbirds and thrushes and fieldfares feeding on the red-and-gold fallen fruit. In winter its gaunt crown stands head and shoulders above the surrounding trees, craggy, venerable, enduring. In spring its tall crown billows out into foaming promontories and plateaux of creamy white blossom mid-way between the chalk-white of plums and the rosy pink-and-white of apple blossom.

It's an ancient pear, probably planted here in the middle of the eighteenth century when the house underwent a radical transfor-mation from its old Elizabethan self to its smart new Georgian one. Three hundred years is a not uncommon age for a pear.

Old pear trees have a presence in the landscape akin to English elms: high and narrow and seeming immemorially old. But neither is truly English: both are ancient introductions, probably brought here in Roman times or before. And both have now largely vanished from the countryside.

Pear orchards used to be a common feature of the English landscape. Each county had its own regional varieties, like 'Knapper', 'Late Treacle' and 'Lumber', three surviving varieties of perry pear from Gloucestershire. 'Tettenhall Dick' (reputed to be 'hard as a brick') comes from the Black Country, while 'Hessle' is a hardy variety from Yorkshire which is still widely available. Using locally raised varieties meant that pears could be grown successfully as far north as Jedburgh in south-east Scotland, in areas which might be considered unsuitable for growing pears on a commercial scale today.

The pears would be planted as much as sixty feet apart, with sheep and cattle grazing underneath, following the traditional pattern of medieval wood pasture. Elsewhere they might be inter-cropped with corn, or interplanted with smaller fruit trees like apples and damsons in mixed orchards, with the pears providing valuable shelter. The smaller, shorter-living trees would be cut down after a hundred years or so. My pear is a 'Forelle', a German variety introduced into this country at the end of the seventeenth century (translated into English as the 'Trout Pear', from the brown stipples on its skin). It is the last remaining tree of a mixed orchard planted on top of what appears to be builder's rubble generated during the eighteenth-century renovations.

But since the end of the Second World War nearly three-quarters of all our old orchards – not only pears, but apples, plums, damsons and cherries, too – have been grubbed up. In some counties like Wiltshire and Devon the figure may be as high as 90 per cent, a tragedy almost comparable to the loss of the elm trees in the 1970s.

As a part of the farmed landscape pears are now almost extinct. Fragments of old perry-pear orchards can still be seen at Weir Green and Waterend on the banks of the River Severn in Gloucestershire, and elsewhere they survive here and there as hedgerow specimens. But in many places gardens have been their only refuge.

But now under the auspices of Common Ground, the charity dedicated to saving Britain's orchards, and other organisations like the Woodland Trust, new orchards are being planted all over the country. Many of these are 'community orchards', providing not only fruit but a communal open space and a haven for wildlife. The cities are getting in on the act, too. The city of Worcester, which has three black pears on its coat of arms, has given a 'Worcester Black' pear to each school in the city. (The 'Worcester Black' also figures in the coats of arms of Worcestershire itself and Worcestershire County Cricket Club.) And at Malvern, fifty-nine local varieties of pear have been planted around the Three Counties Showground. Orchards need not take the conventional form, either: at Ebley, near Stroud, a 'linear orchard' of seventy standard old pear and apple varieties has been planted along an ex-railway line, now a cycle track.

'Worcester Black' is what is known as a 'warden' pear – a type of very long-keeping culinary pear, named after a famous cooking pear which grew at Warden Abbey, near Biggleswade in Bedfordshire, in the fourteenth century. Such pears will keep in a shed or barn until April or May, though they never soften enough to be eaten raw like dessert pears. Other warden pears still available include the two old French varieties 'Catillac' and 'Bellisime d'Hiver' (as plump and speckled as a mistle thrush), both of which turn pink on cooking.

Most big old pear trees like my 'Forelle' are general purpose varieties which can be used for cooking, eating or to make perry. True perry pears are much too tart ever to eat, and were never widely planted outside the three counties of Gloucestershire, Herefordshire and Worcester. Perry has been made in this country since at least the sixteenth century, and probably from as early as Norman times. It is considered by many to surpass cider in terms of delicacy and flavour, and is even claimed to rival good wine.

Those luscious melting dessert pears which we now take for granted are relative newcomers, dating from the eighteenth and nineteenth centuries. Many of the best come from France, and they are happier grown in restricted forms like espaliers and cordons, so that they can benefit from the shelter of walls. 'Glou Morceau' is still one of the finest late pears, raised in about 1750 by Abbé Nicolas Hardenpont of Mons in Belgium, one of the earliest hybridisers.

But for those of us without walled gardens, the old English standard trees will always have a place – both in our gardens and in our hearts.

7 September 2002

Old Potts Way Traffic Island

I nearly crashed the car when I caught sight of it. A blaze of yellows, oranges and reds rippling over a traffic island on the outskirts of Shrewsbury. Not your usual municipal bedding – more like a Van Gogh cornfield or a mad technicolor Liberty print, with corn marigolds and Shirley poppies and black-eyed susans sparkling in the September sun.

I was desperate for a closer look. But where on earth to park?

I went on to the next island and circled back, went round the island
again – twice, more slowly, to the fury of homeward-bound
commuters – went off at a tangent to another traffic island, came
back and circled again, almost gave up, then in desperation
mounted the curb and parked on the grass verge. All very foolish,
I know, and not to be recommended, dear reader – I still don't
know if pedestrians are even allowed on traffic islands – but it was
worth it. The island, when I reached it, was alive with bees and
colour and movement.

I called the Parks and Gardens Department, who passed me on
to the designer of the roundabout, David Wassell, who told me
that the planting was based on one of the 'Pictorial Meadows' seed
mixtures devised by Dr Nigel Dunnett at the University of Shef-
field. These are very clever mixtures of native and non-native hardy
annuals which flower over an extremely long period from mid-
June to early November. Properly speaking, they are not meadows
at all, because they do not include grass seed, but there is something
of the meadow in their waving, naturalistic appearance, and the
way dozens of different wild-flower species are interwoven to
produce a swathe of more or less uniform height – the whole thing
then turbo-charged with a succession of brilliantly coloured
garden annuals.

These mixtures are not suitable for conservation plantings in
rural areas outside garden boundaries (because of the addition of
non-native flowers), but they are perfect for urban parks, private
gardens, school grounds, play areas, urban highways, verges and
roundabouts. There's no need to strip off the topsoil, either, as
you would with a real wild-flower meadow. Just sow thinly into
a good seed-bed, having first removed any perennial weeds. Maintenance is minimal, and the seed-heads can be left to overwinter.
Some of the species will self-seed, but in most instances it will be

necessary to re-sow the meadow each year. David is hoping to underplant the traffic island with a mixture of cottage garden tulips, planted deep, which can be left in the ground from year to year. These will then provide colour in early spring, before the meadow gets into its stride.

It is the succession of flowers in the meadow which is the really clever bit. The mixtures are made up of five elements: long-season species, which form the backbone of the planting, such as blue cornflower (*Centaurea cyanus*), yellow corn marigold (*Chrysanthemum segetum*) and the delicate white umbellifer, false bishop's weed (*Ammi majus*, a native of the Mediterranean); rapid flowerers, such as the annual *Linaria maroccana* (a more compact, quicker-maturing version of our own native perennial purple toadflax), to shorten the period between sowing and the beginning of an effective display; late-flowerers, including many North American prairie plants such as tickseed (*Coreopsis tinctoria*); a few 'emergents' such as tall purple orache (*Atriplex hortensis* var. *rubra*), to add drama; and lastly what Dr Dunnett calls 'star performers', including *Phacelia tanacetifolia*.

I agree with him about *Phacelia*. It is a highly decorative native of western North America, where it is used as a cover crop on fallow land, and as bee forage. When I saw a patch in flower recently in the walled garden at Hampton Court, Herefordshire, every plant was alive with honey-bees. At Hampton Court they use it as a green manure, digging it in before flowering (otherwise it can be a prolific self-seeder), but this year they have left it to flower, with stunning effect. Its American names are fiddleneck and scorpion weed – both alluding to the shape of the soft blue-mauve flower spikes, which coil over like emergent ferns – and wild heliotrope, alluding to its lovely colour. The leaves are softly grey-green and densely hairy, and the flowers have long protruding stamens, giving the whole plant a soft, dotted effect. Absolutely lovely.

27 September 2003

Yew Clipping

It's a record: my yew hedge has just yielded 805 kilos of yew clippings. They fill the shadowy interior of the trap-shed in springy green resinous piles almost as tall as me. The weather this year, so trying in so many other ways, has been kind to the yews at least.

The hedge is seven feet tall by just under one thousand feet, and it has been bristling with twelve-inch-long new shoots ever since July. We cut the hedge once a year, usually in late August or early September. The timing depends on which of my kind friends incautiously come for a lazy weekend at that time of year and find themselves instead at the sharp end of a wheelbarrow.

It takes four of us: one to cut, two to fill the barrows, and one to trundle backwards and forwards between the garden and the trap-shed. We always cut the yew on to long sheets of plastic, gathering the full sheets up, ends to middle like newly washed bed sheets, to tip the clippings into the barrow. While this may seem like a great palaver, it is certainly the neatest and quickest way to clip any hedge. No raking up or stray bits lingering afterwards. The whole job takes us seven hours, with three breaks.

And then early the next morning the clippings go off to be deep-frozen and freeze-dried before being shipped to the end-user, the French agrochemical giant Aventis, which makes the cancer drug Taxotere.

The discovery of taxane, the active property in yew, is a fascinating story. In 1967, as part of a routine scanning of some 35,000 plants for possible medicinal use, scientists working in the US came up with the Pacific yew (*Taxus brevifolia*), the dried bark of which was found to have astonishing anti-cancer properties. Human trials began in 1983, and from the early nineties onwards Taxol, a taxane-based drug, became widely used in the US in the fight against cancer. However, taxane proved to be a very difficult molecule to synthesise, and concerns were soon voiced by conservationists who feared for the future of the great strands of Pacific yew on the west coast of the US, and for the future of the spotted owl which nested there.

Enter the European yew (*Taxus baccata*). It was found that the potency of taxane extracted from the needles of young growth such as that annually clipped from miles of yew hedges growing in English gardens was up to ten times greater than that extracted from bark. Moreover it came from a totally renewable source. This was patented by Rhône-Poulenc (now part of Aventis) under the name Taxotere.

I planted my hedge in November/December 1989 – whiskery little nine-inch-tall plants, two feet apart. The planting distance depends on the finished height you want (the lower the hedge, the closer together you space the plants). Small bare-rooted trees are much the best and certainly the cheapest option, as young trees establish better than bigger ones. And autumn is much the best time to plant.

Now, thirteen years later, you can see the pattern of the hedges from the hill above the garden – a dark chequerboard of yew with a central circle around the Turf Maze. Nearer to the house you can see the billowy profiles of older yews, planted in the eighteenth century, though these are mere juveniles compared with the ancient yew in the churchyard on the opposite hill. As big around as a group of dancing children, its hollow trunk split and twisted by a thousand winters, it seems inconceivably ancient and yet perennially young.

The church was built in 1840 (uncharitably described by Pevsner as 'of only too well-preserved yellow brick'), but there was a wooden church here before that, dating back to the Normans, and the tiny hilltop churchyard has the round shape that suggests a Saxon burial ground or some even older religious enclosure. Yews are the oldest living things in Britain, said to have been venerated by the Druids, and churchyard yews are the oldest of all.

Perhaps the Druids were right: the yews did turn out to contain the secret of life after all.

28 September 2002

October

Clear autumn, windy weather;
Warm autumn, long winter

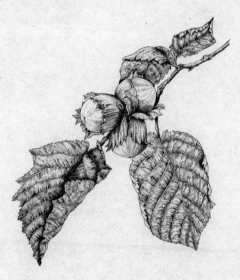

Hazelnuts

Eat Your Greens

The agronomy of my garden has slipped four or five thousand years into reverse. I've reverted to hunter-gatherer mode. I no longer seem to grow my food: I discover it. Instead of cultivating the soil and dutifully making my last sowings of salad leaves and winter spinach, I scuffle about in the fallen leaves like a truffling pig, looking for nuts: pale-shelled walnuts still damp from their fleshy green pods, smelling of vanilla; sweet chestnuts nestling in the long grass like small green sea urchins, their pursed mouths opening a little to reveal the shining brown of the nuts inside. I fill my pockets with fallen cobnuts and filberts until they bulge like squirrels' cheeks. I raid the feral blackberries that have lassooed the clipped box in their uncouth, prickly embrace; compete with the blackbirds for the sloes in the hedge. At dawn I trail wet footprints through the dew, looking for giant puffballs; scour the ground under the pine trees for parasol mushrooms; dip my fingers in dripping combs of stolen honey.

Who needs green stuff when you have riches like these? The first walnuts are alabaster white inside their shells, with translucent skins like the lining of a bird's egg. The taste is delicate, the texture cool and smooth on the tongue. They lack the harsh bite of dried walnuts. I think I'll make baklava with them, interleaving layers of filo pastry with chopped walnuts and dollops of honey – with more honey poured over the top of the pastry when it comes, puffed up and golden, hot from the oven.

I used to be a very fussy eater as a child. At infant school the dreadful prospect of school dinner would hang over me all morning, blighting my life. Frogspawn I could cope with, ants' eggs too, at a pinch. But Brussels sprouts? Never. Eventually, kept in long after the other children had been let out to play, my retching or the bell for afternoon school would trigger my release. But now, tossing them with chopped walnuts in a mixture of hot olive oil and butter just before serving, I can face Brussels sprouts with equanimity.

Nuts like walnuts and hazelnuts are high in protein and fats. In dietary terms they are treated as an alternative to meat: they don't, for example, count towards your five recommended portions of fruit and vegetables a day. Chestnuts are higher in starch than other nuts – higher even than potatoes – and are more like pulses in texture. In parts of France and Italy (and especially in Corsica) they are milled into flour. It will be a long time before I have enough chestnuts for that. But after an autumn of evenings spent roasting them in the fire I should still have a few left to cook with some prunes and Armagnac as stuffing for a goose at Christmas.

I suppose I could buy salad stuff. But who, after reading Felicity Lawrence's *Not on the Label: What Really Goes into the Food on Your Plate* (Penguin, 2004) could eat another bag of pre-packed supermarket salad leaves, when you learn that it has been washed in a chlorine solution twenty times stronger than that used to disinfect a swimming pool? We British have never been especially keen on vegetables in any case, whether eaten raw or cooked. In medieval England vegetables were believed to cause wind and melancholy. Fruit was thought to be even worse for your health, bringing on 'putrefying fevers'. Virtually the only vegetables grown in the medieval kitchen garden were herbs, garlic, onions and masses of leeks. What people chiefly ate was bread and meat:

beef and mutton if you could afford it, pork (preserved for the winter as bacon), poultry, eggs and 'white meat' – the name then given to dairy produce such as cheese. Visitors from abroad thought us conspicuously well-fed, at every level of society. Even the poorest peasant, such as Chaucer's 'poure widewe' in *The Nun's Priest's Tale*, had a pig or two, a sheep, and a cock and hens, and most villagers had a cow as well. And the wealthier you were, the more meat you ate – up to two or three pounds of it *a day*.

The combination of bacon and eggs – still a staple in twenty-first-century households – is quite possibly one of our oldest British dishes. It was not until the late seventeenth century that fruit and vegetables began to be consumed in any quantity. Fruit-growing became fashionable first, followed by a taste for green vegetables and salads. By the time John Evelyn, that other famous diarist of the seventeenth century, came to publish his book *Acetaria: A Discourse of Sallets* in 1699, he could list seventy-three different 'sallets' – from alexanders and artichokes to turnips and viper's grass (forms of salsify and scorzonera) – with dozens of different ways of preparing, combining and dressing them. Five portions a day? Easy-peasy.

23 October 2004

The Poetics of Space

A footbridge is a mysterious and wonderful place. A place of temptation, not without a frisson of danger. Footbridges are engrained deep in our folklore and our language. We speak of 'building bridges' and 'bridging the gap', but bridges can separate as well as link. They are defensible spaces, places of trial – think of Little John, Horatius on the bridge, those silent and visored knights-in-arms who challenge all-comers in Malory's *Morte d'Arthur*. A footbridge creates a third place between the two spaces it links, becomes a place in itself. It isn't really anywhere: like A. A. Milne's halfway down the stairs, neither up nor down. Or like the mirrors in Cocteau's *Orphée*, we feel it could transport us somewhere else instead.

Jim Partridge is a maker of footbridges. He has been fascinated by bridges since he was a child. A photograph taken as an adolescent of a single old timber used over a fast-flowing stream still adorns his studio walls. He says, 'Footbridges are emotionally charged places. They work as physical metaphors of the other journeys and crossings in our lives. A footbridge will only be successful if it tries to lead us towards those feelings, not just to the other side of the road.' Both his prose and his footbridges are as spare and as beautiful as Japanese haiku.

The first Jim Partridge bridge I encountered was as an exhibit in an art gallery, but you are just as likely to see one in rough terrain on Forestry Commission land or spanning a mountain stream on a remote Scottish island. That is, if you notice it at all. Jim's bridges are not the brilliantly coloured and laquered bridges of Japanese gardens, admiring the perfect 'O' of their reflections in the water beneath, nor the perfectly placed eye-catchers of an English landscape garden, going somewhere or nowhere, spanning a dribble of water dammed to make an artificial lake. Nor do they have the folksy self-importance of American carpenter-built bridges, all roofs and windows and criss-cross side beams. Jim Partridge's bridges spring out of their site as naturally as trees, as perfectly formed as a wren's wing, beautiful, functional, invisible.

The exhibition was called 'Making Buildings', at the New Art Gallery in Walsall. I walked right past the bridge the first time around. A plank raised on two low wooden supports. Left over from the building works, perhaps. Somewhere to sit while contemplating the other exhibits? But then I saw that it was not one plank, but two, one on top of the other, clamped together at each end and sprung apart in the centre by wooden wedges, its strength based upon that empty air – that hole in the middle – the principle of the lenticular truss.

Jim takes this story as a great compliment. His father was a printer, and Jim's childhood was spent surrounded by books and the appreciation of fine printing. The first rule of good typography is to be invisible, to let the words shine through. And the second rule is that the spaces around the letters are as important as the letters themselves.

He trained as a craftsman furniture maker, producing beautiful chairs and other pieces, and becoming known initially for his exquisite wooden bowls which, like the footbridges, play with ideas of space – exploring the limits of inside/outside, the point of contact where this side meets that side. But as a furniture maker, he always had difficulties with the idea of exclusivity, of producing one-offs, feeling that logically there was no reason why his chairs should be made in editions of one. Each of his footbridges, on the other hand, is unique because made for a specific site, and because he prefers to use found materials gathered on site, sometimes using fallen timber or thinnings, sometimes choosing a single tree to fell.

In his outdoor work Jim collaborates with his partner Liz Walmsley, and together they were commissioned by the previous Lord Bute to make a footbridge for his estate on the island of Bute. Here the shape of the bridge was suggested by a tree growing nearby with a particularly beautiful curve, a single polished plank of which, like a sheet of peat-brown water, now forms the bridge, its momentum echoed by the curve of a single handrail cut from the same tree. Some of their more complex structures use wedges again, in combination with steel cable, to make high arched pre-stressed bridges which need none of the abutments of traditional bridges. The cable pulls the wooden blocks together, the wedges spring them apart. Hedgehog-like, these bridges bristle at you in mock alarm. Other bridges double as steps, springing like moun-tain goats up a hillside, daring you to follow.

But even bridges designed to meet the rigorous health and safety standards demanded by public bodies, like the one at Barnard Castle in Northumbria, are approached with the same thoughtfulness and delicacy of touch. The bridge curves easily as you approach it, drawing you in, then narrows abruptly once you're hooked, the sudden bounce of the wood and changed sound signalling a setting-out, something embarked upon – peril-ous possibly, exciting certainly – then encourages you to relax and pause in a smaller curve in the middle, before sending you off with a final flick of its wrist in the opposite direction, to a path hidden from view.

In their most recent project, harking back to the simplicity of that first single plank, Jim and Liz have used seven tall young trees side by side to span the outer ditch of a former sea fort guarding the harbour of Rozel in Jersey. An eighth tree, split in half, forms the two handrails. Following the natural taper of the trees, the bridge narrows by eighteen inches as it approaches the stone doorway of the old fort, emphasing the narrowness and the length of the bridge and reminding those who cross it of its ancient defen-sible purpose. Green English oak is Jim's preferred material, but here he uses straight French oaks blown down in the storm which devastated so much of northern France. As Jim's father might have said, when internal logic and function coincide, it must be good.

22 September 2001

The Colour Red

As Alice famously said, 'What is the use of a book without pictures or conversations?' I'm inclined to agree with her, but there is something wonderfully seductive about completely blank books. I have a little collection of them, mainly publishers' dummies. And even they can tell a tale. I remember the Professor of Bibliography at Oxford demonstrating how he could tell which dummy was for a novel, which was for a piece of scientific writing, and which was for a scholarly work, just by the weight and feel of the blank paper. (The novel had soft thick paper to make it appear longer than it really was; the paper destined for the scientific text was smooth and glossy to accommodate all the diagrams and photographs.)

But a new notebook is something completely different: like fresh snow, it is very tempting but terribly daunting at the same time. I got over this myself a long time ago by writing my garden diary in pencil on scraps of paper, thereby liberating myself to scribble down my unconnected thoughts without constraint. But last week my husband gave me a new garden notebook, promptly resulting in instant writer's block.

Begin by making a list, I thought, that's always a good way to break the ice. So, several people having written in to ask for a list of old roses which will reliably repeat flower, off I went into the garden to make a list of the roses in flower last week. And here it is, in no particular order, and bearing in mind that these are just some of my personal favourites: the yellow climbers 'Céline Forestier', 'Alister Stella Gray', 'Desprez à fleurs jaunes' and of course 'Gloire de Dijon'; white climbers 'Sombreuil', 'Souvenir de la Malmaison' and the indispensible 'Mme Alfred Carrière'; pink climbers 'Blush Noisette', 'Narrow Water' and the redoutable 'Mme Isaac Pereire' (who is happy either as a big shrub or a climber); plus a mass of shrub roses from blush pink to deepest crimson, including 'Old Blush China', 'Stanwell Perpetual', 'Rose du Roi', 'Rose de Rescht', 'Jacques Cartier', 'Comte de Chambord' and 'Mousseline'. And the star of them all, as people have asked to me repeat, is the Portland rose, 'Jacques Cartier', blooming his head off with never a black spot in sight.

As gardeners we all love our reference books, crammed full of information, but oddly one of my most jealously guarded reference books contains hardly any words at all. It's the *Horticultural Colour Chart*, published by the British Colour Council in collaboration with the Royal Horticultural Society (though 'chart' is a bit of a misnomer, as my edition consists of two hundred separate loose leaves). I was consulting it the other day to remind myself of the precise signification of the various words for the colour red. At this time of year I adore the brilliant hue of pure primary red – by which I mean the colour of the red cactus-flowered dahlia 'Garden Wonder', of some rose-hips, and of the berries of honeysuckle and guelder rose (*Viburnum opulus*), which are all blazing in the same corner of my garden against the deep bottle-green of a mixed holly and yew hedge. According to the colour chart, this is properly called scarlet (think red geraniums), with vermilion on the orange side of it (think poppy red) and crimson on the blue (think ripe cherries and old roses).

Curious to know why I only like scarlet flowers in autumn and spring, I telephoned the garden photographer Andrew Lawson, who wrote the best book about colour I know (*The Gardener's Book of Colour*, Frances Lincoln, 2003). He said that in spring and autumn the angle of the light is lower and redder, enhancing pure reds, but that all colours look brighter at this time of year because the light is less intense, and often more diffuse – in contrast to the bright white light of high summer which tends to drain the colours of their vitality. But the real secret, he said, was that I had planted my reds against their complementary colour green – a recipe guaranteed to make them fizz with brilliance.

12 October 2002

Choosing Tulips

Within its high yew hedges, the garden here feels like an oasis of green at the moment. I garden on a belt of sticky clay on top of the Old Red Sandstone, and it's in weather like this that I am grateful for my heavy moisture-retentive soil. For while I have been basking in this Indian summer, the gardens of friends as close as twenty miles away (and as far afield as Somerset and Suffolk) have been suffering from serious drought. It seems ironic that half the nation's gardeners are putting up their flood defences, while the rest are desperate for water. And even here I have young trees prematurely shedding their leaves and herbaceous flowers shrivelling on the stem.

A good way to take one's mind off it all is to think ahead to the delights of next spring. So I've been ordering more tulips. I plant them in eleven-inch black plastic pots which I then sink into the ground. Growing tulips like this is the perfect way to try out new colour schemes without committing oneself. So if my imagined colour combinations don't quite come off, or the timing doesn't work, I can rearrange the pots, or even tactfully remove them altogether if the whole thing is a disaster. (I remember one year planting some which turned out to be a particularly horrid shade of salmon pink.)

And then, after flowering, I'll whisk the tulip pots away and replace them with something else like lilies, tender lavenders or agapanthus. This is also a good way of growing tulips if, like me, you garden on heavy soil, which tulips tend to dislike. Once the stems of the tulips can be bent without breaking (meaning that the bulbs have stopped growing), I let their pots completely dry out. This way they get a good baking. Then the following autumn I'll pot up the best of them in new compost.

This year I'm trying a new orange and flame-coloured scheme which includes the golden-apricot and rose-flushed parrot 'Professor Röentgen', the bright tangerine lily-flowered 'Ballerina' (which is also – apparently almost unique among tulips – scented), the strange but lovely 'Princess Irene', in pale orange-terracotta with plum-purple shadings, and the more delicately coloured 'Libretto', another parrot tulip, in rich cream shaded with old rose. Or is that over-egging the pudding, do you think?

Tulips come in every colour from almost-blue and just-about-black (the silvery lilac-coloured 'Blue Parrot' and the sumptuous 'Black Parrot', for example) to sunshine yellow and sizzling red, with every shade and combination in between, as well as in half a dozen shapes, from tall elegant lily-flowered varieties to short fat double peony-flowered ones. Go on, indulge yourself.

I find that one of the hardest things to do in my garden is to be really ruthless with herbaceous plants once they have flowered. I'm just too soft-hearted. As long as they have a single tattered flower left I'll leave them alone. But looking at other gardens now I can see that had I cut the flowered stems back early enough lots of things would now be in bloom again. This is true of delphiniums, all the herbaceous geraniums, lots of easy space-fillers like *Galega* and *Linaria* and double white feverfew, and that mainstay of the spring garden, the bright silver-leaved *Anthemis punctata* ssp. *cupaniana* with its fresh white daisy flowers. The Irish gardener Helen Dillon is famously severe – like the Red Queen, at the first sign of a yellowed leaf, it's 'off with their heads'. Everything then gets a good feed and plenty of water to stimulate them into new growth. Gertrude Jekyll even used to cut down half of each clump in early summer *before* flowering, to lengthen the first flush, and then cut down the other half of the clump as usual *after* flowering, to provide a second flush. Such dedication! But it certainly pays dividends at this time of year.

19 October 2002

Bread & Roses

We don't usually associate flowers with social reform. They make powerful symbols, of course – of national identity, peaceful protest or the trials of love. But revolution?

I was wondering recently about the origin of the political slogan 'Bread and roses'. It would seem to be a reworking of the Latin poet Juvenal's dismissive characterisation of the Roman populace, *Duas tantum res anxius optat, / Panem et circenses* – 'They want only two things: bread and circuses', i.e. food and entertainment (and the nastier the better).

There are also biblical echoes: 'Man doth not live by bread alone' (Deuteronomy ch. 8, v. 3, and Matthew ch. 4, v. 4). But in fact the answer lies nearer to our own times. The phrase 'Bread and roses' was coined in the context of a strike in 1912 by the textile workers of the US town of Lawrence, Massachusetts. A new law had just been passed by the state legislature limiting the maximum number of hours worked by children to fifty-four hours a week. In response, the factory owners cut the working hours of all employees to fifty-four hours, with a commensurate cut in wages. In an unprecedented display of solidarity, all 35,000 workers walked out. For the first time, members of the skilled English-speaking craft unions campaigned side by side with lower-paid women workers and the disenfranchised non-English-speaking unskilled majority. The strike lasted for nine weeks and made headline news throughout the US.

During one of the demonstrations a group of women workers carried a placard saying, 'We want bread and roses too.' The poet James Oppenheim picked up the phrase and made it into a poem which included the lines 'Hearts starve as well as bodies; give us bread, but give us roses!' The poem was later set to music, and became one of the great songs of the American labour movement. Even today the phrase is still identified with the rights of women and ethnic minorities to a living wage and equal pay for equal work. In the 1990s it was adopted by the Los Angeles 'Justice for Janitors' campaign, on which Ken Loach based his film of the same title, *Bread and Roses*.

Neither do we associate the flower-arranger Constance Spry with social reform. But as a new exhibition at the Design Museum makes clear, the famous Constance Spry Flower School had its origins not in an attempt to provide amusement for idle middle-class ladies but in order to train young working-class women in floristry – one of the few crafts then open to them, and a rare opportunity for them to run their own businesses. Spry began her career working in social welfare in England and Ireland, and in 1921 was appointed headmistress of the Homerton and South Hackney Day Continuation School, teaching teenage factory girls on day release the practical skills of cookery and dressmaking. She also started to teach them flower-arranging, so that they could beautify their own homes, using simple garden flowers and every-day containers.

Spry was of working-class origin herself, the daughter of a Derby railway clerk turned civil servant. She was also for a time a single parent: in 1916 she escaped an unhappy marriage in Ireland by fleeing to England with her four-year-old son, supporting herself by working in Barrow-in-Furness as a welfare supervisor.

Her transformation into society flower-arranger came about almost by chance. She was invited to arrange the flowers for the perfumiers Atkinsons of London, whose windows looked out over Bond Street and Burlington Gardens. At the time, floral decoration was characterised by Edwardian opulence, extravagance and downright snobbery. Upper-class homes were filled with expensive hothouse flowers – raised on their owners' country estates, naturally – with never more than one kind in each vase. (It was said to be 'very vulgar' to mix flowers, because it might look as if you could not afford enough of them.) Spry filled the windows of Atkinsons with huge vases full of lichened branches, wild arum lilies, moss-studded primroses. She plundered the hedgerows for wild flowers, berries, hips, used anything and everything. The arrangements created a sensation.

By 1936 she was doing the flowers for every royal occasion, and there was not a society wedding for the next twenty years for which she did not provide the flowers. But at the outbreak of war she was still capable of lecturing on austerity cooking and turning out a book exhorting people to grow their own vegetables. She believed in hard work and self-improvement. But even more passionately she believed that everyone, even the poorest of people, had a right to things of beauty around them: to bread and roses, in fact.

2 October 2004

The Eponymous Lord Derby

What a wonderful thing it is to have good neighbours. All last winter the rats and mice were getting in under the eaves of the fruit store. They gnawed the potatoes and gorged on the apples and carried the nuts off to their nests. The cats did their best, but to no avail. Eventually the rat-catcher from the local council office had to be sent for. And now here we are, apple-picking time again, and still no nearer a solution to the problem. Or so it seemed. But then I discovered that, while Julia and I had still been pondering whether we could manage to board up the eaves, and whether that would do the trick, my neighbour John had quietly done the job for us.

The apple store in winter is one of my favourite places. It's like finding your way into a treasure chamber: the dim interior lit only by the light of a torch; the indistinct shapes of the apples in their trays receding into the darkness, their gleaming colours caught by the flickering beam. The fruit feels smooth and cold and hard in your hand as you browse the racks. Do I feel like a 'D'Arcy Spice' today? A 'Cornish Gillyflower'? The pungent smell of the ripening apples triggers the flow of saliva at the back of your mouth. Perhaps an 'Ashmead's Kernel'?

These are all late-season apples, not quite ready to be picked yet. 'D'Arcy Spice' is traditionally picked on Guy Fawkes' Day or the day of the Lord Mayor's procession, and will then keep until Easter or even May in a good year. Outside we are still picking the mid-season apples. Their colours are even more intense this year than usual: 'Pitmaston Pine Apple', with tiny deep-gold conical fruit like golden apples in a fairy tale; 'Margil' – a very old apple indeed, reputed by some people to have been brought over by the Romans – slightly bigger, round, brilliantly coloured, with gleaming crimson streaks over a bright orange ground; 'Rosemary Russet', bigger again, with a soft pillowy shape, as if someone had just laid their head on a big feather pillow – hardly russeted at all, with pale greeny yellow skin ripening to an apricot tan; and the curiously named 'Winter Banana', its smooth bright skin and vivid pink-and-gold colouring lighting up the garden like a series of Chinese lanterns. Who needs flowers when you can have colours like these?

We have all been having a glorious time tasting each variety as it ripens. 'Pitmaston Pine Apple' came out on top of Julia and her partner Pete's tasting this week, with 'Margil' a close second. 'Pitmaston Pine Apple' has a dense, rich, honey taste which reminds me of the smell of the beehives, sweet and complicated, and full of the scent of flowers. It is perfect cut up into muesli at breakfast time. 'Margil' has creamy coloured flesh, crisper, tangier, a little like old-fashioned pear-drops. This to me is the perfect dessert apple. My own current favourite is 'Rosemary Russet', sharp, crisp, mouth-watering – not usually ready to be eaten until November, and then keeping until February or March – quite different from the drier texture and nutty flavour of 'Egremont Russet', which we picked earlier in the month.

Almost all the older apples are dual-purpose varieties – cookers and eaters – which keep their shape well when cooked. With a few exceptions, the big acid-flavoured green cooking apples are all nineteenth-century in date, like 'Lord Derby', a huge green dumpling of a cooker which falls to a perfect snow. 'Lord Derby' is a very heavy cropper, and one of the earliest to ripen. This year we used it to make pies for the Harvest Supper at the beginning of October.

Quite by accident, I find I may have discovered the identity of the eponymous Lord Derby. I was going to a session of the

Cheltenham Literary Festival last week devoted to Homer's *Iliad*, and thought I would do a bit of homework beforehand. I was rereading Christopher Logue's *War Music*, a modern English version of *The Iliad*, and found in the introduction mention of a nineteenth-century Lord Derby who translated *The Iliad*. A quick search on the internet revealed that he was also three times prime minister. Those were the days, when prime ministers translated Homer and had apples named after them.

25 October 2003

Taking Stock

As the days get shorter there's a paradoxical feeling of expansiveness about the garden. It's something to do with the light – those full, round, golden days of September and October, when you seem to have all the time in the world. Now is a good time to wander round the garden and take stock of the year, to decide what pleased you and what didn't, what surprised you and what bored you, what worked better than expected and what went unexpectedly wrong. And write it down, before you forget. (As the philosopher George Santayana once rather gloomily observed, 'Those who do not learn from history are doomed to repeat it.')

One of the things which pleased me most was my new allium border. I like their crisp shape as a contrast to the blowsiness of midsummer. Even the ordinary leek (*Allium porrum*), if left to go to seed, will produce dramatic football heads of pale violet flowers on four or even five-foot stems. I chose mainly late-flowering species of alliums to fill the gap that yawns between mid-July and the end of August, and planted them among some bushes of tall, late-flowering Old English lavender, with an edging of pinks. (One disadvantage of many ornamental alliums is that when they are coming into flower their foliage is at its worst, so they look best planted with something else around their shins.) The star was *A. sphaerocephalon*, with small dark crimson-maroon egg-shaped heads on long, wiry stems. Its English name is 'roundheaded leek', and it is a rare British native, growing wild around the Avon Gorge, near Bristol. It is one of the cheapest and easiest alliums to grow, and increases well. All the alliums are very long-lasting in flower and keep their shape afterwards, so they continue to enhance the border even after flowering. And they are wonderful in flower arrangements or as dried flowers. So resolution number one for next year: extend the allium border.

Sometimes of course one does get it spectacularly wrong. A few years ago I planted three young *Wisteria sinensis* 'Alba' as standards, and started to train them into mopheads, each on a stout six-foot post. (This is a handy way of growing wisteria if you don't have enough wall space. You can even try them in a container: nail a cross-shaped piece of wood horizontally on top of the post, to help you make the mophead.) But I knew almost immediately that they were in the wrong place. I moved one straight away. This is now flowering again for the second time this season, and I sniff it appreciatively every time I pass. But I can now see that the other two must also be moved: there simply isn't enough room or light where they are, and they have never produced a flower between them. So resolution number two for this winter: move the wisterias.

What went better than expected? In the Wild Garden, the purple-leaved filbert (*Corylus maxima* 'Purpurea') is laden with nuts, each encased in a long intriguing dusky-red husk. The young sweet chestnuts (*Castanea sativa*) too are bearing for the first time. Even the walnuts (*Juglans regia*) are doing well. Whether the squirrels beat me to the nuts remains to be seen. But I don't really mind: I love them all for their colours and textures and shapes – especially the walnut, with its leathery, feathery, aromatic leaves. There has also been a wonderful crop of hips on all the species roses, lighting up the Wild Garden like little lighthouses with their vivid colours and extraordinary shapes. On the downside, the wasps have had a field day in the plums. But what has gone rather better than expected was the nicotianas. I sowed masses of the very tall white-flowered *Nicotiana sylvestris* in gentle heat in spring, and then planted them out, three to a twelve-inch black plastic pot, and dropped them (still in their pots) into the Rose Border in July as quite big plants, to act as fillers. They have been a great success. In the ground, these wouldn't have stood a chance: they would have been crowded out by other things and eaten alive by slugs and snails. And there is the added bonus that if I can overwinter them in their pots in the polytunnel, they should then sprout again from the rootstock next spring.

The nicotianas are a continuation of a theme which begins in the garden in June with the *Lilium longiflorum* – the same shining white trumpets and heavenly smell – but what surprised me about the lilies this year was the almost total absence of lily beetles. Have the birds finally got the message that these brilliantly coloured strangers are in fact good to eat? Or was it the fact that the lilies were kept in the polytunnel in their pots until the very last moment before being set out around the garden, so that the lily beetles failed to notice them? Or was it simply the weather?

What bored me? It has been a year of ups and downs in which the garden has alternately delighted and infuriated me, depressed and consoled me, exhausted and refreshed me in that roller-coaster of emotions which gardeners know so well. But bored? Never.

16 October 2004

'Do you remember an inn, Miranda?'

For several nights the mercury in the maximum-and-minimum thermometer has been hovering only a degree or two above freezing. I stand at the open door and sniff the early morning air. Colours seem intensified: the spiky red of the dahlias, the violet-blues of the Michaelmas daisies, the pulsating crimson and plum of the leaves on the cockspur thorn (*Crataegus crus-galli*). I'm suddenly acutely aware of smells: the last of the sweet peas in a vase on my desk, the penetrating musky odour of white *Rosa moschata* flowering now as never before.

I'm a bit of a late bloomer myself. I sometimes think that, like the peacock butterflies, I undergo a period of diapause in late summer – defined by my *Collins Field Guide to Butterflies* as 'a period of suspension of activity or development'. The more familiar form of diapause is hibernation (from the Latin word for winter). Midsummer diapause is called aestivation (from the Latin '*aestas*', meaning summer), and is defined as 'a state of torpor in summer heat or drought'. That's me, all right. People who suffer from SAD syndrome (Seasonal Affective Disorder) have the opposite problem: they experience a waning of vitality and lowered mood at the onset of winter, a condition linked by some doctors to an atavistic need to hibernate. Whereas at the first nip of frost my spirits start to soar.

The nights may be getting cold, but in the meantime the days are hot, and the air above the lavender in the Knot Garden is full of the shimmer of wings: the polished topaz of bees' wings; the devoré velvet of peacocks and tortoiseshells and painted ladies; the white silk chiffon of cabbage white butterflies spotlit against the grey stone of the house; even a pair of hummingbird hawk moths. I pull an old green deckchair on to the gravel in the sun and sit and watch. The hummingbird hawk moth (*Macroglossum stellatarum*), unlike most moths, flies by day, and with its furry mouse-grey face, blur of rapidly beating orange hind-wings, and distinctive tufts of black and white hair, it could indeed be mistaken for a tiny hummingbird. Its movements are restless and erratic, zooming up and suddenly down, hovering in front of the lavender with its body drooping and its long proboscis reaching into the flower, for all the world like a miniature Concorde.

Like the painted lady and the red admiral butterflies, the hummingbird hawk moth is a migrant, and will migrate south again before the cold weather starts, but the peacocks and the small tortoiseshell butterflies will soon be looking for somewhere to hibernate, perhaps in one of the outhouses or in the log pile, or often in the house itself, whose windows and doors still stand open all day long. The search for hibernation sites is also on for the newly mated queen bumble-bees and the big brown-and-yellow hornets (surprisingly pacific, despite their fearsome appearance) – the Harley-Davidsons of the insect world, with a deep resonant buzz quite unlike the Suzuki whine of the black-and-yellow wasps which have terrorised us all summer.

In the house the Rayburn has been re-lit. The 'Garden Open' signs are stashed in the garage, the teacups put away in the dresser, the visitors all departed. Upstairs the study is cleared for action, and the eight chapters of my book are laid out in neat piles waiting for me: first drafts, redrafts, new material, afterthoughts, the all-important preface. Ah yes, where was I? . . .

But somehow my attention wanders to the scene outside the window. I can see the blackbirds down on the lawn making little rushes and sallies at one another, fighting over fallen apples, backing and advancing like the Spanish dancers in Hilaire Belloc's poem. The pull of the garden is too strong. I switch off the computer and go back outside again. Not quite time to hibernate just yet.

11 October 2003

November

Winter finds out what summer lays up

Iris foetidissima

Little Sparta

It seemed the right thing to be doing – to be approaching Little Sparta on foot, alone, in the wind and the rain, climbing the long stony path up the bare hillside to the grove of trees at the top. It's that sort of place: wild, remote, lonely, embattled; a place of intellectual rigour and Spartan simplicity; a place of beauty and poetry, pity and terror, like the ancient Greek city-state invoked by its name. The farmstead was originally called Stonypath, and was rechristened Little Sparta by its owner, the poet-artist Ian Hamilton Finlay, in pointed contrast to what he saw as its effete urban neighbour over the hill, Edinburgh, the 'Athens of the North'.

Little Sparta has been called the most important garden of the last half-century, the only truly original garden made in Britain since 1945. Its owner's battles with orthodoxy and the establishment (both of the left and the right) are only too well known, and the images chosen to represent the garden by magazines and newspapers are inevitably those with the greatest power to shock: the machine-gun juxtaposed with the opening lines of Virgil's Eclogue VIII ('Flute, Begin with me Arcadian notes'); the gigantic hand-grenades which take the place of stone pineapples on the gate piers of the 'Hypothetical Gateway to an Academy of Mars'; the great brazen head of 'Apollon Terroriste' cast in the likeness of the French Revolutionary Louis Antoine de Saint-Just, architect of the Terror – beautiful, terrifying, deadly.

But the casing of the machine-gun barrel is pierced like the finger-holes of a flute, the flute in turn recalling the idealised pastoral landscape of Virgil – a presence whose shade pervades the garden, every bit as potent as Saint-Just. You are ambushed by inscriptions, by hidden meanings, challenged to think. The whole garden seems to say, 'Watch your step.' It's a sacred grove with Apollo/Saint-Just as the presiding deity, but there is also tenderness, lyricism and playfulness. Paths cross and re-cross the garden – among trees, over streams, across little pools – on sequences of stepping-stones, each inscribed with a single word, a phrase, a fragment, connecting one to another, you to the completed phrase, bank to bank. Gaps become links and links become gaps, inviting rearrangement, alternative meanings, fluidity. A quotation from Saint-Just, 'The present order is the disorder of the future', is broken into single words scattered on gigantic stones across the hillside. The place where water gushes from one pool out into another has the tiny inscription W AVE – the fractional gap between the W and A suggesting the watery salutation '*Ave*', the Roman greeting.

This is not a sculpture garden. The trees, plants and water are part of the sculpture, indivisible. On the edge of the Front Garden, looking out through the trees to the windswept hillside, is one of many inscriptions linking interior and exterior soundscapes: SONG WIND WOOD/WIND SONG WOOD/WOOD-WIND SONG. Elsewhere the wind in the trees recalls the sound of waves and the sea: a wooden seat looking out over the fields is inscribed THE SEA'S WAVES/THE WAVES' SHEAVES/THE SEA'S NAVES, invoking the image of a sea of corn waving in the wind, playing with the Latin word '*navis*', meaning boat. Names of boats are everywhere, repeated like litanies: CORVETTE and CARAVEL, BARQUE and BRIGANTINE. Finlay's father was a sea captain, running bootleg rum out of the Bahamas to Prohibition America.

After two hours I had hardly got beyond the Front Garden. 'But there's fourteen acres!' Finlay gently chided. After two more hours I had barely got further. 'Will you have a cup of tea?' So we sat and talked about William Shenstone, the eighteenth-century poet-gardener who filled his garden with inscriptions; and about Henry Vaughan, the seventeenth-century poet who dreamed of eternity like a ring of light; of Rousseau's heroine Julie, who spurned court life in favour of a life of quiet contemplation in her garden; of Virgil and Epicurus and all the other shades memorialised here. 'Can you not come back?' he said. 'Will you come back?'

It is a garden to visit again and again and again. Jessie Sheeler's new book, *Little Sparta: The Garden of Ian Hamilton Finlay* (Frances Lincoln, 2003), is the indispensable guide. Sheeler gives transcriptions and translations, explains sources and allusions, offers interpretations. The photographs by Andrew Lawson are simply superb.

1 November 2003

After the Storm

I like rough weather. I like the sound of the wind roaring in the chimney. I like being able to light the fire at three o'clock with a clear conscience. I like being shut in the house while the weather prowls up and down outside. The growing distinction between inside and out is one of the pleasures of autumn. All summer long the doors here stand open on to the garden, and the house is scented with lavender and jasmine and the smell of newly mown grass. But now the big door in the hall is closed. Inside, the house smells of wood smoke and quinces slowly stewing on the Rayburn. Outside, the garden smells of wet leaves and fallen apples. In here it's silent, apart from the crackle of the fire and the hum of the computer. Out there a storm is brewing: I can hear the wind growling.

I can't resist it. I switch off the computer, making the excuse of a last-minute check of the garden before the storm arrives. When I open the kitchen door, the wind slams it back against the cats' dishes with a clatter. The orange trees in their tubs already lie scattered like ninepins across the front of the house. I battle my way around the garden to the polytunnel, to check that the bolts are secure. Then up into the Nuttery to check on the beehives. Back down through the apple and pear tunnels, where most of the apples have already been picked, as a precautionary measure, but the rambling roses at each end are still in full leaf, catching the wind like great sails. If they had been pruned already it would have reduced the danger of the whole structure collapsing. But there's nothing to be done now except wait.

It is still raining when I re-emerge from the house the next morning. The grass is thickly pasted with wet yellow leaves, whirled down before they had a chance to colour. The dahlias are dulled and sodden, the *Crocus speciosus* flattened, the Michaelmas daisies leaning at crazy angles, their blues and purples quenched by the downpour. No structural damage, thank goodness. But suddenly I feel dispirited. The whole garden seems to have moved a notch closer to winter – not the sort of winter you see in aspirational gardening magazines, all crisp edges and elegant seed-heads outlined with December frost, but a murky wet winter of ragged edges and mud.

Then something bright catches my eye: the orange seeds of a clump of *Iris foetidissima*, their colour undimmed by the storm.

The big straw-coloured pods are split open into three, like over-sized violets, and each segment is crammed with a double row of seeds like brilliantly coloured sweetcorn. A spark of cheerfulness on a dark and dismal day.

It's a disobliging name, *foetidissima*. *Foetida* (meaning stinking) would be bad enough. But *foetidissima* is the superlative form, meaning 'stinking very badly indeed', or even 'most stinky of all' – apparently from the superlatively dreadful smell of the foliage when crushed. But not in my experience. Even when vigorously rubbed, the leaves only give off the mildest of pongs. The source of its English nickname, 'roast beef plant', is similarly mysterious.

The leaves in themselves are handsome, evergreen, dark and sword-like – a welcome sight in winter. They are the source of the plant's Old English name, '*gladwyn*' or '*gladdon*', from the Latin '*gladiolus*', meaning a little sword (a diminutive of '*gladus*', a sword). All our native irises used to be known as gladdons: *Iris pseudacorus* was the water gladdon; *Iris foetidissima* was the stinking gladdon; and the very rare wild gladiolus itself (*Gladiolus illyricus*, found growing wild only in the New Forest) was the corn gladdon.

The flowers of *Iris foetidissima* are a sort of pale violet-white in colour, tinged with yellow. They are small and inconspicuous compared with garden irises, but that hardly matters. The seeds are why one grows it. The wild plant has bright orange-scarlet seeds, the colour of rose-hips, but there are yellow-seeded and white-seeded forms too. There is also a yellow-flowered form (*I. foetidissima* var. *citrina*), and one with variegated silver foliage ('Variegata'), though that has a reputation for being less free-flowering. The seeds have the virtue of clinging to the pods and not dropping to the ground even when the pods are fully open, so *I. foetidissima* will continue to light up a corner of the garden all the way until next spring. The seed pods also make very handsome cut flowers.

In classical mythology, Iris was the goddess of the rainbow. Just as the rainbow reaches down from the heavens to the earth, so Iris was the messenger of the gods, passing back and forth between gods and men. The genus *Iris* seems to have got its name from the rainbow hues of its flowers. But it is an approriate name for a flower which can give so much pleasure after a storm.

6 November 2004

An American President

Almost exactly two hundred years ago, in 1804, another American president had just been elected for a second term: a president who thought that the greatest service a man could render his country was to add a useful plant to its culture; a president whose detailed observations of the weather helped to lay the foundations of the modern science of meteorology; who engaged in passionate debate with European intellectuals about climate and the effect of environment upon a country's inhabitants; whose curiosity and intellectual scope knew no bounds; whose personal collection of books formed the nucleus of the nation's great storehouse of knowledge, the Library of Congress. Thomas Jefferson, philosopher-statesman, scientist and gardener, the man who in 1776 drafted the Declaration of Independence, the founding document of the United States of America.

Jefferson inherited the hilltop estate he later named Monticello from his father in 1757 at the tender age of fourteen. He began to plant there in 1767, and for the next fifty-seven years he kept a Garden Book in which he recorded trees planted, seed sown, fruit and vegetables harvested, the times when flowers bloomed, the successes and failures of the year. He used his garden as a trial ground for testing new crops and new varieties to see if they were suitable for the Virginian climate. If his crops succeeded, he distributed seeds and cuttings to other people in order to promote their wider cultivation. If they failed, he continued to experiment with other methods and to search for other varieties which might prove more suitable.

One of his failures was the olive: in March 1774 he sowed fifteen hundred olive stones, but apparently without success; of the five hundred olive trees he imported from Italy in 1773, only one survived the vicious winter of 1776. One of his successes was upland rice: he imported seed from Piedmont, Egypt and even Timor in the East Indies, in an attempt to find a variety which would thrive without the need for flooding the fields. 'I have the success of this species of rice at heart,' he wrote, 'because it will not only enable other states to cultivate rice which have not lands susceptible to inundation but because also . . . it may take the place of the wet rice in the Southern states, and superseding the necessity of overflowing their lands, save them from the pestilential and mortal fevers brought on by that operation.'

His aim was to improve the diet and health of the American people, but he also grew all the fruit and vegetables for his own household. Like every other eighteenth-century gentleman, he was inordinately fond of peas and competed with his neighbours each year to be the first to have peas ready for the table. In the course of his long gardening career he experimented with fifty different varieties of peas, forty-four varieties of beans, and more than thirty different sorts of cabbage, almost all imported from Italy – including the now so fashionable 'Cavolo Nero' – each with its Italian name carefully noted down in his Garden Book.

He also loved flowers. While in Europe, as American Minister to the French Court between 1785 and 1789, he was an indefatigable garden visitor as well as an avid enquirer after the best agricultural practices. He conceived of Monticello as a botanical garden at the service of the nation, and filled his garden with all the latest discoveries and most beautiful flowers, both from home and abroad.

Jefferson retired from public life in 1809 at the end of his second term as president, though he continued to be acknowledged as the intellectual leader of his party. With more time to devote to the purely ornamental aspects of gardening, he redesigned his flower garden with oval flower-beds and informal shrubberies on either side of fashionably winding walks. For Jefferson, gardening was a continual process of discovery. Towards the end of his life he wrote, 'No occupation is so delightful to me as the culture of the earth, no culture comparable to that of the garden. Such a variety of subjects, some one always coming to perfection, the failure of one thing repaired by the success of another . . . though an old man, I am but a young gardener.'

There is no use in repining for an age when presidents grew their own vegetables. The past is a foreign country: they do things differently there. But when did we last have a president (or a prime minister, for that matter) who knows – or can imagine – what it is like to be dependent for your food and for survival itself upon the whims of weather and the growing uncertainties of climate. Ferried from one air-conditioned room to another by motor car and jet, do they even know when it rains? Millions of dollars are spent on presidential election campaigns, billions more on foreign wars. Meanwhile, 800 million people worldwide still do not have enough to eat. It's a mad world, my masters.

13 November 2004

Autumn Colour

From the window of my writing room I look out over the garden. I shouldn't: my mind should be on the writing. But it's hard not to – especially this year, especially now, when the annual pageant of autumn colour has been playing out with even greater theatricality than usual. Sitting at my window, mug of tea cooling in my hand, I'm an audience of one, a packed house, all attention.

It's the last act. First there was the bonfire of the big American trees up above the Canal Garden, beginning to smoulder as early as late August or the first week in September – the sugar maples (*Acer saccharum*) sending up incendiary rockets of scarlet and gold; the red maples (*A. rubrum*) flushing from forest green to bright red, then darkening to the deep crimson of mulled wine; the cockspur thorn (*Crataegus crus-gallii*), all fizzing sparks of orange and flame and vermilion, then collapsing into a plummy heap beneath the glowing embers of its shining red berries – all extinguished now by October's wind and rain.

Then, as the colder nights began to bite, there was the red-gold of the horse chestnuts, the deep rose and plum and gold of the medlars, and the buttery yellow of the big old pear tree, flushing brighter flame on the side nearest the sun. And, at the far end of the garden, the chrome yellow of the hazels in the Nuttery, poking their heads up over the dark green of the hedge. All too now gone, only a stray leaf clinging here and there like tattered standards after a battle.

Only the little native trees in the copse I planted to the east of the house seemed to go on and on: silver birches, still covered with tiny golden leaves like a shower of gold coins; field maples, declining now into yellow ochre and tan; the wild service tree (*Sorbus torminalis*), with its maple-like yellow leaves veined with rosy chestnut and malachite blue-green. I wonder why these all last so long – the field maple in particular (our native acer, *A. campestre*), which goes unnoticed in the hedges all year long and suddenly emerges into the limelight in early September, lighting up the roadsides with its bright mustard leaves, and blazing on into October and November. Is it the smaller size of the leaf? The fact that they are native?

But now, finally, their leaves are beginning to fall. From my window I can start to see through the little copse again, to see the bones of it, the lines of trunk and stem and branch. I begin to imagine snowdrops, and carpets of winter aconites, and cold frosty air. Backlit by the low sun, the hips and berries seem suspended now in mid-air – the great shining bunches of scarlet fruit dangling from the branches of the guelder roses (*Viburnum opulus*), the smooth vermilion hips of the eglantines (*Rosa rubiginosa*) packed full of flat papery seeds like red hot chilli peppers, the satiny shocking-pink cushions of the spindle berries (*Euonymus europaeus*), spilling out their stuffing of vivid orange seeds.

While I sit glued to the window, watching, the book languishes unwritten, the bulbs unplanted, the apples unpicked, the garden untidied. But there are two messages that should be engraved on every gardener's heart at this time of year: don't panic . . . and don't feel guilty. Allow yourself time to enjoy the garden, time to look. After all, the trees won't mind if the fruit isn't picked, and the birds will bless you for it – and for the straggle of dead and dying herbaceous stalks which will provide them with seeds and shelter all winter long.

And there is still time to plant those bulbs. I have often been reduced to planting tulips at Christmas or even on New Year's Day, and they seem to come to no harm. There is even an argument for deliberately delaying planting now that our autumns and early winters are so mild and wet. According to tulip-grower Steve Thompson, tulips will not start to make roots until the soil temperature drops below 52°F (11°C), so if planted too early (the argument goes) they will sit dormant in wet soil, at the mercy of slugs and susceptible to disease. The bulbs then need twelve to sixteen weeks below 52°F to produce a complete root system. Apparently in really warm places like Australia, which do not have a prolonged cold period, gardeners have to chill their tulip bulbs in the fridge before planting. If global warming continues, we may have to do the same. So, for the moment, just chill out.

16 November 2002

Queen Olga's Snowdrop

Did you ever wonder who Queen Olga was? This is just the time of year when you might catch a glimpse of her in a garden near you: *Galanthus reginae-olgae*, the autumn-flowering snowdrop. For committed galanthophiles, the season starts now, and Queen Olga opens the ball. But you would have to look in grander gardens than mine: snowdrops like Queen Olga are going to set you back £5 or £6 for a single bulb.

But who was Queen Olga, and why does she have a snowdrop named after her?

Almost the only thing I know about her is that she was apparently very short-sighted. It seems a curious qualification for someone involved (even tangentially) with snowdrops, for the defining characteristics of most named snowdrops are so miniscule that, as my mother would say, a blind man would be glad to see them. Wife of George I, King of the Hellenes, she was a Romanov, a granddaughter of Tsar Nicholas I of Russia (and grandmother of our own Prince Philip). They were married in the Winter Palace in St Petersburg. George himself was a member of the Danish royal family, and had been invited to become King of Greece in 1863. He was assassinated for his pains in 1913.

I confess that I'm no galanthophile. I think there are few lovelier things than a carpet of our own wild native *G. nivalis*, left to their own devices in woodland, or scattered around the stones of an old churchyard. Quantity not quality is what I want. However, *reginae-olgae* is different. For one thing, she makes it possible for us, if we wish, to have a whole succession of snowdrops from September through to March. And for another, coming from Greece, the adopted country of her namesake, she reminds us that not all snowdrops need shade. *Reginae-olgae* likes nothing better than a sunny position, so plant her (if you can afford her) at the front of a border to brighten up your gloomy autumn days.

It's worth remembering also that many snowdrops from that part of the world – Greece, Turkey and the Balkan states – have similarly useful characteristics. *G. elwesii*, for example, is a springflowering species which also enjoys a sunny position. *G. ikariae*, a green-leaved species, is one of the last to flower, in March. And neither will break the bank.

23 November 2002

The Patient Mulberry

I can feel my spirits rise with every degree the temperature drops. A week ago the view through the Canal Garden was closed by the butter-yellow foliage of the mulberry. Now, as the leaves drift down, the Temple is revealed for the first time. It's not a real temple, hardly five feet deep. Just a covered stone seat, really, ornamented with a pediment and columns. But delicious in summer, hidden behind the mulberry: a secret place to sit, all dappled shade and the scent of roses. You would hardly know it was there. But now, as the mulberry drops its leaves and the white columns and the gilded motto beneath the pediment glint in the low sun, the Temple is revealed as a grand gesture, a formal eye-catcher closing the long vista all the way from the house to the top of the garden: a transformation of a Romantic garden into a classical one.

The mulberry is one of the last trees to come into leaf in spring, so I will be able to enjoy my new view for six or seven months. Visitors to the garden are amazed that I haven't cut the tree down. But I couldn't, I simply couldn't. Ten years ago it was rescued from a small town garden where it had outgrown its welcome. It took six of us to heave it on to a lorry. The prognosis was not good: it had no root ball at all, just three fat white shallow roots as thick as my arm. Worse, there was nowhere here to put it. Mulberries are not fussy about soil, but to fruit well in the Midlands and the North they need some form of shelter, and my recently planted hedges scarcely came up to the mulberry's shins. But it was do or die: in its current home the mulberry was otherwise destined for the bonfire. So I erected a square enclosure of shelter netting, planted the tree, tied it to two stout tree-stakes, and hoped for the best.

The first year its leaves were scarcely bigger than a thumbnail – barely a couple of inches across, compared with the generous five or six of a healthy tree. But it survived. Despite its improvised shelter, the topmost shoots were annually pruned by the wind where they projected above the netting. But still it survived. Gradually the yew hedges grew up around it, until finally they were high enough to protect it. And this year it fruited for the first time.

Once you've tasted a mulberry (*Morus nigra*) you'll never want anything else. The berries are long, black and knobbly, bursting with dark delicious juice. They are too fragile to be transported, so they are rarely if ever seen for sale: all the more reason for growing your own. If you have space, a venerable mulberry in the middle of a lawn or against a south-facing wall would be a fine specimen: multi-stemmed, leaning on its elbows, no tree speaks so strongly of Olde England. But you can also prune a mulberry to keep it within bounds. This also has the advantage of making the fruit more accessible. According to the Victorian fruit growers' bible, Hogg's *Fruit Manual*, they can even be grown in tubs as small bushes or pyramids: 'The Mulberry is a tree endowed with great powers of endurance, and does not require a pampered treatment; and it is, therefore, one that is very patient under any experiment it may be subjected to.' I can vouch for that.

27 November 2004

Ghost Story

There's something magical about arriving at an old garden late and out of season. As the garden handyman waits patiently for you to finish reading the display boards in the converted orangery so that he can close up for the night, and you venture out into the garden, conscious of being the last visitor of the day, alone now, there's a feeling of transitions and transgressions – the garden ready to lapse back into its own private self – as if you shouldn't really be there at all, as if anything might happen . . .

I was tired. I had been giving a garden history workshop all day in west Gloucestershire, and I was trying to map-read my way across country, following my nose. I was heading for Bradford-upon-Avon, where I was to stay the night with my friend Fritz, but I was lost already. It was then that I saw the brown sign.

I knew about the garden, of course. Painswick Rococo Garden. A sleeping beauty of a garden, designed in the 1740s and rediscovered in the 1980s beneath an impenetrable thicket of overgrown trees, brambles and old man's beard. A unique survival from a time when gardens combined the formal and the informal – intimate, personal, quirky gardens, reflecting the personalities of their owners. A garden, moreover, that had been immortalised by its creator in a painting that had haunted me for years by its pale, strange beauty. I looked at my watch. There was still time: Fritz wouldn't be home yet, and I needed to unwind.

The car park was empty, the staff preparing to lock up. No, they said, that's fine, just close the gate in the wall as you leave. I stepped through, and found myself high up on the edge of a secret valley. The garden was quite small, surrounded by dense shrubberies and big trees, with serpentine paths winding around the outside of a grassy dell in the middle. Through the trees I caught glimpses of little fences, flowers, a pointed stone window here, what seemed to be a row of Gothic pinnacles there, the columns of a tiny Doric temple away to the left. The garden was peppered with strange, charming, diminutive buildings – one painted dark red with an odd, asymmetrical facade, half curving up, half swooping down; the white-painted Exedra with a spiky profile like something crafted out of spun sugar; the faintly alarming presence of the Eagle House on the skyline, its squashed hexagonal bulk straddling the exit; and in the distance, the grey dome of the Pigeon House.

I almost gave the Pigeon House a miss. It was in the furthest-flung corner of the garden, away from everything else, but it was given an oddly prominent position on the painting, and I was curious to see it. Close to, it seemed bigger than I had imagined, with a door and a narrow stone staircase in the octagonal outer wall, leading to a circular upper room. The mismatch was in itself disconcerting, but so too was the gradual realisation as I climbed the steps that I was not alone. As I rounded the last corner in the staircase, a solitary white dove was watching me from the top step. The building was unused, the louvres long ago wired up. How long had he been there? How had he survived?

He consented to be carried into the open air, perched on my hand like a small white falcon, and together, as dusk fell and the mist began to rise, we completed the circuit of the garden – along the beech walk, past the big pool with the tunnel arbour reflected in its inky surface, up the hill beside the formal vegetable garden with its ponds and espaliered fruit trees and long grassy walk crowned by the white Exedra, now glimmering in the dusk – finally rounding the corner towards the lawn below the Eagle House, where the trance-like stillness was broken by a quicksilver flash of movement from a dozen does and hinds startled into flight by our approach. They were gone almost before I saw them, only the turned sods of their hoof prints in the damp grass testifying to their ever having been there.

And as I stood, breathing in the air stirred by their flight, with the claws of the white bird holding fast to my fist, watching the moon rise over the garden, I could almost have sworn that down there, standing in the deepening shadows, was a white unicorn, poised to step into the moonlight.

30 November 2002

Frost Warning

It seemed as if the frost would never come. Late November, and there are still lush mounds of bright green nasturtium leaves around the feet of the yew cones in the *plates-bandes* – the trailing sorts, spilling out in their exuberance over the little box hedges which are themselves sprouting soft new growth after the August clip which should have seen them safely into winter.

Pots of violet-blue streptocarpus which should by now be over-wintering on the bathroom window-sill are still lining the steps up to the back door. There are white geraniums and raspberries still. Roses too, of course – Portlands and Chinas, moschatas and noisettes – even a solitary pink bloom on the blue-steel foliage of 'Queen of Denmark'. And all the tender evergeens are still outside: a single precious ball of phillyrea, three tall pyramids of myrtle, and fifteen big standards of Seville oranges which will take two of us to shift when the time comes. In a normal year they would already be tucked up in the house.

And tonight there's a rising wind from the north. As darkness falls I can smell the cold. On the six o'clock news there are pictures of snow in Scotland and on the east coast. It's too late to move things now. I go back out again to swathe the orange trees in fleece, drag the myrtles and phillyrea into shelter, move the geraniums and streptocarpus closer to the walls of the house. The wind whips the fleece out of my hands, unravelling. I go back in to fetch string and scissors and a flashlight. By the time I finish, the cold is pinching my nostrils and striking up through the soles of my canvas shoes.

In our house we call this the 'homework on the bus' sydrome. It's always the same: however much time I have, I always seem to be behind it. It's partly of course because the garden is too big, too complex: an acre and a half of formal gardens. But this was what I wanted when we came here in 1988 – to make a garden that would possess me, body and soul. No use complaining now.

But it's also because I seem to spend a lot of time just gazing about. Take the bulbs I should be planting. Huge fat purple-flushed lily bulbs like fleshy upturned claws, white golf balls of *Allium stipitatum* splitting their papery skins to reveal waxy yellow insides like hand-rolled balls of marzipan, plump silvery skinned hyacinth bulbs and tulips as bright as conkers for the *plates-bandes* on either side of the Canal Garden, camassias for the long grass beneath the yellow species roses in the Wild Garden. And instead of getting on with it I'm turning them over in my hands, feeling the weight of them, sniffing them (the *Allium stipitatum* bulbs turn out to have a foxy stink like crown imperials), just looking.

One year I was still planting hyacinths and daffodils and tulips in mid-December. I broke off to go to a lunchtime pre-Christmas drinks party at a neighbour's house, and emerged in mid-afternoon to a weather forecast of 21°F (minus 6°C) that night. I had just spent days laying the bulbs out on the grass on either side of the Canal – two thousand of them in an intricately composed pattern of mingled colours and heights and times of flowering. And now they were going to freeze solid unless I finally got them planted. With the aid of three torches – one pointing in front, one pointing back, and one held in my hand as I shuffled along on my hands and knees – I worked until after nine o'clock, the grass freezing around me, glueing the bulbs in place, growing crisp and white in the light of the torch. But I did it. And leaning back on my heels to ease my aching back I saw, springing right across the sky from Gemini to Orion in a single flashing arc, the most wonderful shooting star I have ever seen.

1 December 2001

WINTER

December

If the ice will bear a goose before Christmas,
it will not bear a duck after

Helleborus niger *(Christmas rose)*

Inside Out, Outside In

It's going to be an interesting winter. For the next few months I shall be sharing the house with fifteen fully grown orange trees, a dozen small ylang ylangs and fifty pink bananas. And that's just the drawing-room, the hall and the upstairs corridor. In addition, two big myrtles and a phillyrea are sheltering in the porch, an adolescent ginger lily and a pair of burly argyranthemums are sharing the kitchen, rows of agapanthus and lilies are dossing down in the cellar, and a fascicularia and a yucca are glaring at one another in the scullery – not to mention the swarm of blue streptocarpus which has settled in the bathroom.

Then there are the cats vying for prime position beside the Rayburn, the black newts foraging for woodlice in the cellar, the hibernating tortoiseshell butterflies asleep in the bedrooms, the jackdaws roosting in the roof space, and what I hope are mice rather than rats in the cavities between the walls. As soon as the temperature begins to drop, in they all troop.

Admittedly, the temperature in here is warmer than outside, but it's all relative, of course. (Visiting humans inexplicably demand extra sweaters.) The point is, I haven't got a heated greenhouse, but then I haven't got anything which passes as proper central heating in the house either. Heat and dryness are the enemies of citrus and other big outdoor plants which need to be overwintered in shelter, so the house itself serves pretty well as a greenhouse instead. It's cool and a bit damp, with some big east-facing windows. When overwintering plants indoors, light levels can be a problem, but if the temperature is low enough things stop growing, and you can in any case periodically rearrange things so that everything gets some light some of the time. With a bit of ingenuity, it's surprising how many different types of habitat you can contrive indoors.

The myrtles (*Myrtus communis*) will stand a degree or two of frost, but in Shropshire I find it safer to bring them into the shelter of an open porch for the winter, and wrap them up in fleece when a hard frost threatens. The oranges need a temperature of between 45 and 60°F (8–15°C) – any warmer and the lack of humidity causes them to drop their leaves – so they have the coolest spots indoors.

The ginger lily and the bananas are new. They occupy the warmest and lightest parts of the house, and I must take care never to allow them to dry out. I grew the bananas from seed earlier this year. They are *Musa velutina*, which has incredible lolling dusky pink inflorescences and short stubby pink fruits (full, unlike most banana species, of shiny black seeds). *M. velutina* is shorter than most other bananas – only five to seven feet – but keeping fifty full-grown bananas indoors every winter would be a very tall order. So I'm aiming to keep a few plants going as mature container specimens, and try overwintering the others in the cellar, with the pots of deciduous agapanthus and tender lilies, in a state of induced dormancy. This means cutting the tops off and keeping them cool and dry and dark.

Meanwhile, the kitchen is starting to look even more like a rainforest, as the Rayburn belches heat and the condensation trickles down the windows. Two large preserving pans of fragrant deep-red pulp splutter and pop on top of the Rayburn. I'm making quince paste (soft, amber-coloured French *cotignac* to eat with cream cheese, and dense dark Spanish *membrillo* to cut into slabs and eat like Turkish delight). It's one of the small disappointments of life that quinces won't keep for ever – their voluptuous shape, that intense yellow colour, the fragrance of them. But then I put my finger in the paste and lick it. Heaven.

7 December 2002

The Art of Looking

I admit I was tired. And my feet hurt. So it seemed natural to sink down on to one of the benches and continue to look, albeit from a distance. But I was unprepared to find myself still sitting there twenty minutes later, gazing at the same small painting.

The painting was *The Dandelion Field* (1892) by William Nicholson, a tiny slice – barely eight inches by five, dwarfed by its ornate gilt frame – of sloping sunlit meadow blazing with dandelions. It is often said that if dandelions were not so common we should see them for the magnificent plants they are. Here it is their prodigality that is precisely the point.

The painting is one of a series of tiny minimalist landscapes, strange rather melancholy portraits and sublime still lives, on show in the Nicholson retrospective at the Royal Academy. This is the first major London exhibition of Nicholson's work since 1942. He seems to have stood aloof from the cataclysmic upheavals of twentieth-century art – one of the reasons for the neglect his paintings endured after his death in 1949. Today he is perhaps best known for his early work as a printmaker, represented here by the striking theatre posters, the *Almanac of Twelve Sports*, the woodcut *Alphabet* (including E for Executioner) and the boldly simplified black-and-tan images of icons of the age – Kipling, Sarah Bernhardt,

Queen Victoria – all as fresh and exciting now as the day they were made. But graphic art didn't pay and, with a young family to support, he chose instead to make his living as a portrait painter.

Among the portraits in the exhibition is the famous image of the gardener Gertrude Jekyll, painted in 1920 when she was seventy-seven. She was a reluctant sitter, believing that 'ugly people had better not be painted'. But when it was finished, she thought it 'quite a good picture – very strong and direct'. She is shown in half-profile, peering through the lenses of her wire-framed eyeglasses, her plump fingers arranged into a restless little steeple. It was painted during the long winter evenings, as she refused to spend time away from the garden during daylight hours. To while away the time as he waited for her, Nicholson painted the equally famous companion piece, *Miss Jekyll's Boots*, shown here side by side with the portrait. The battered old boots not only share the sitter's obstinate, obdurate persona – making the point too that gardening is tough work – but also have a life of their own: affectionate, long-suffering, enduring. It is as if painter and boots share a fellow feeling: equally subject to their mistress's whims, they keep one another company, like a suitor playing with his mistress's dog while she keeps him waiting.

It has been said that Nicholson painted still lives as if they were portraits of objects, and portraits as if they were still lives of people. Many of his sitters appear wrapped in their own thoughts, like Miss Jekyll, turning away from the painter. They seem impenetrable, preoccupied. The objects in the still lives, on the other hand, gaze back at us with a wholly self-conscious and rather disconcerting gaze. Nicholson collected jugs and other containers all his life, and painted them repeatedly. Often they are filled with flowers, and there are some lovely examples here: white lilies of the valley in a clear glass tumbler, grey stocks in a silver jug, fragile pale-coloured Shirley poppies against a polished pewter salver, orange and pink zinnias in a blue glass vase. But it seems to be the containers themselves which hold the painter's – and our – attention, as in the sumptuous *Lustre Bowl with Green Peas* (1911), reproduced on the cover of the exhibition catalogue. Here the container is placed centre stage: a silver-lustre bowl and a scattering of pea pods on a white tablecloth, spotlit against a densely black background. The reflections in the sides of the bowl shift and waver, drawing us in. The effect is mesmeric.

Reflections and reflective materials like silver, pewter, porcelain and glass – no less than bunches of flowers – are staples of the still life, but in Nicholson's hands these jugs and vases and bowls look back at the painter, returning his gaze, watchfully regarding the domestic setting in which he sits, and rearranging it: the room, the windows, even the painter himself, are all reflected and subtly changed in their gaze: the see-er seen.

Nicholson was, reportedly, shy of talking about his art. In an interview he gave shortly before his death, he said that all he could do was to invite people to look at the pictures. 'Words, well, words are' [. . . he gestures a little helplessly and once more falls to scrubbing and smearing out on the back of a stray piece of cardboard . . .] 'words.' All we can do is sit and look. And look.

11 December 2004

Metamorphoses

The garden is wet, green and dishevelled. Raindrops hang like single pearl earrings from each down-drooping branch of the tree in the middle of the Turf Maze. The Canal is pock-marked with rain, the little round pond overflowing, its outlets blocked with fallen leaves. In the Orchard, a single Cornish Aromatic still clings to its branch, vivid scarlet against the black of the tree. The ground is carpeted with fallen fruit, slowly melting into the still-growing grass. As I walk up the garden the blackbirds scatter, squawking in protest at being disturbed during their feast.

Perhaps because of the unseasonably mild weather, we are not, apparently, spending enough in the run-up to Christmas. High-street spending is down nearly 5 per cent according to one report. It certainly doesn't feel as if Christmas is only a couple of weeks away. Or perhaps it is the economic climate which is to blame, rather than the meteorological one. Perhaps people have got fed up at last with the endless exhortations to consume. Perhaps they are simply bored by what is on offer in the shops. Three cheers! One of the nicest presents I ever received was a little posy of winter evergreens, pretty enough to sit on the table for a festive dinner, but each green sprig capable of being rooted to form a new plant. That little posy, years later, still furnishes my garden, and keeps the memory of the friend who brought it as fresh and evergreen as the plants themselves.

I suspect I'm not a frightfully good friend – I'm the sort that sends Christmas cards once a year with a scribbled message about keeping in touch. And this year I shan't even manage to do that. I've lost my address book. Left it in a taxi somewhere in London. Or perhaps on the train? Twenty years, more, of addresses. Friends scattered to Australia and America. So the only Christmas cards I'll be sending will be those I can deliver in person. But there's some comfort in that, and honesty too – trudging around the lanes on Christmas Eve, having time to chat to anyone who's in, standing on the lighted doorsteps, exchanging news.

As I walk down to the church, the cattle-grids are brimming with muddy water. 'A green Christmas makes a full churchyard', so the saying goes. The newer graves are still gay with flowers – bunches of autumn chrysanthemums and florists' lilies, sprays of carnations, pink hyacinths in pots – but also with brilliant plastic marigolds, livid purple and green roses, silk sunflowers. I don't seem to mind them being artificial: the rain gives them a sort of living sheen, and their immutability seems to match the stoicism of the dead – the young man killed in a road traffic accident two Christmases ago, the old soldier who survived two world wars to die at last in his bed. In their grass-covered graves they sleep soundly, snuggled comfortably down under their green duvets of grass.

The leaves of the churchyard trees have all dropped now, revealing the mistletoe in the bare branches of the young maple tree – arguing, it seems to me now, not just for continued life, but for a different sort of life, a transformation. The ordinary life of the tree transformed, as it were, into the white berries of the mistletoe – like the sleepers beneath, undergoing a sea change into something rich and fair:

> Full fathom five thy father lies;
> Of his bones are coral made;
> Those are pearls that were his eyes . . .

In our local hospital the flowers are all fresh, as pale and delicate as the patients in their white turned-down beds. I put the flowers I have brought by my mother's bedside where she can see them, and I sit, holding her hand. The monitors bleep their own sort of song. In another part of the hospital, Graham, who cuts the grass in the garden, is welcoming his new grandchild. Julia, our garden trainee, has just got married. I wonder if the sprigs of evergreens in her bridal bouquet will root? Flowers for the newborn, flowers for the dying. Life in all its wonderful variety goes on.

13 December 2003

'And what will the robin do then, poor thing?'

This year was wonderful for us humans, with blazing autumn leaf colour and long warm days right into October, but it is going to spell disaster for many of the other inhabitants of our gardens unless we help them. Creatures like hedgehogs and other small mammals store their winter food reserves in the form of body fat built up during the autumn. Other creatures like birds rely on a continued supply of food throughout the winter in order to survive. This summer the drought prevented many trees and shrubs from setting a decent crop of nuts or berries, and killed many insects. This means that wild birds and mammals are going into the winter already dangerously emaciated.

This was the poorest year I can remember for hazelnuts, and although there is no love lost between me and the squirrels, hazelnuts are also a prime winter food source for voles and mice. And as the smaller mammals decline in numbers, the larger predators like the birds of prey and the foxes start to suffer too. The whole food chain is in danger of coming apart. Badgers are digging in the churchyard here, searching for the few remaining earthworms, their principal food. Hedgehogs are wandering about looking for something to eat when they should have been asleep weeks ago. The holly trees in the garden are devoid of berries, threatening the thrushes and blackbirds with starvation. The berries of the spindle, honeysuckle and elder – a major food source for robins and other smaller birds – are already depleted. Pheasants are surviving on mistletoe: I found the remains of one that had been taken by a fox, its craw stuffed with white berries.

Badgers digging in gardens have been a particular problem ever since the summer. This was not because of an explosion in

Autumn in the New Flower Garden: *Acer rubrum* and *Acanthus mollis*

The Apple Tunnel in September

Autumn harvest: clockwise from top left, Apple 'Egremont Russet', the flagon-shaped hips of *Rosa moyesii*, Quince 'Meech's Prolific', Apple 'Catshead'

The Knot Garden with seedheads of purple orache spotlit by the sun (*overleaf*)

Nasturtiums and clipped evergreens in the Canal Garden

Michaelmas daisies in a corner of the Fruit and Vegetable Garden (*above*)
The yew cloister with leek seedheads and clipped shapes of myrobalan (cherry plum) (*below*)

The leathery leaves and bristly seed-cases of sweet chestnuts carpet the Wild Garden in late autumn.

badger numbers – far from it. According to the National Feder-
ation of Badger Groups (NFBG), the number of badger cubs
raised over the last two years has been lower than at any point
in the last thirty years – another consequence of the drought.
But this year the badgers seemed to be especially drawn to lawns.
The reason seems to have been that as the ground baked hard,
and the earthworms retreated deep into the soil, gardeners
(unhampered by the hosepipe bans of the past) tried to keep their
lawns green by watering them – thus luring the earthworms
closer to the surface, and inadvertently attracting the badgers. If
this happens again next year, the advice given by the NFBG is
to water your lawn last thing at night so that the earthworms
will rise just when the badgers are looking for them. Better for
the lawn and better for the badgers. And you will have the delight
of watching the badgers feeding, rather than the irritation of
having your lawn dug up.

So when you are tucking into your Christmas dinner, spare
a thought for the wild creatures outside. Peanuts, wild birdseed
and fat (for example in the form of dripping from the joint) will
all be gratefully received by the smaller birds. Apples or other
fruit which has begun to go soft will help to keep the blackbirds
and thrushes going. (I never feel guilty about leaving windfall
apples and pears: I let them lie where they fall, knowing that
the birds will find them when they need them.) Tinned pet food
is a good emergency ration for badgers and hedgehogs. And
don't forget that both birds and mammals need clean fresh water
every day. Then it can really be a Happy Christmas, for one
and all.

20 December 2003

Mistletoe

You can tell you are nearing Tenbury Wells by the forest of gaunt black hop-poles receding into the distance on either side of the road, and by the great swaying globes of mistletoe hanging from the trees. A fully grown mistletoe can measure as much as three feet across, and these are ancient. They glow greeny yellow in the wet early morning light, almost dwarfing the little apple trees in the orchards.

Tenbury Wells stands at the meeting place of three counties: Hereford, Worcester and south Shropshire – the heartland of mistletoe country. And the first two weeks of December are the time when Tenbury holds its annual holly and mistletoe auctions. The mistletoe is harvested annually, much of it picked by the travellers who work in autumn in the cider orchards and in spring and summer in the hop gardens. They stand around the auction yard now, waiting to see what prices the crop will bring. It is laid out in lines in the yard, in huge bundles, each tagged with its lot number. According to Stanley Yapp, a local farmer who has been bringing mistletoe to the sale all his life, it's a good year for mistletoe: well over a thousand lots, with even more expected at next week's sale. 'Holly's going to be expensive,' he says. 'The dry summer has meant far fewer berries.'

All the holly and mistletoe on sale here will have been cut from local apple orchards and woods within a few miles of Tenbury. Elsewhere in the country mistletoe may be imported from France, but here the buyers will have none of it. 'It's poor stuff compared with ours,' says Stanley. And far from declining, mistletoe seems to be on the increase everywhere in this country. In a survey conducted for the conservation charity Plantlife, Dr Jonathan

Briggs discovered that mistletoe is actually extending both its geographical range and its choice of hosts, spreading in recent years into many towns and cities, where it thrives in parks and gardens. Mistletoe's traditional host was the cultivated apple, which still accounts for nearly 40 per cent of the sightings, despite the nationwide decline in apple orchards, but mistletoe is now very common on hybrid limes (especially *Tilia* x *europaea*), hawthorn, hybrid poplars, maples, willows and false acacia (*Robinia pseudoacacia*), as well as occuring on plums, pears and rowans. It has even been found on many ornamental tree species, including amelanchier, laburnum, almond, japonica and even walnut. It remains rare on oak, though according to Stanley there are half a dozen examples in Herefordshire alone.

The tradition of decorating houses with evergreens at midwinter as a symbol of the continuity of life through the darkest part of the year predates Christianity and is widespread throughout Europe and Asia. But the current British fascination with mistletoe probably dates back no further than the writings of the Rev. William Stukeley, an eighteenth-century Lincolnshire antiquary with a bee in his bonnet about the Druids. As for the tradition of kissing under the mistletoe, this seems to be a Victorian invention – though Stanley remembers old crop fertility rites involving mistletoe still being carried out around Tenbury only forty years ago.

The future for mistletoe, according to Stanley, lies in medicine and cosmetics. A well-known brand of shampoo now contains mistletoe extract. The dried young twigs were a traditional remedy for epilepsy, and they are still used in herbal medicine to lower the heart rate in cases of high blood pressure. The berries themselves are poisonous, but an extract derived from them is being used to treat patients with cancer. In a second survey carried out by Dr Briggs on the London mistletoe populations, he found mistletoe growing in nineteen London boroughs, some of which he suspects may be attributable to the plant's past use in herbal medicine. Mistletoe was reported to be growing on limes in Hampton Park, for example, in 1720.

Worldwide, there are some fifteen hundred members of the mistletoe family – most of them in the tropics, and some with vividly coloured berries, unlike the pale moon-glow of our own mistletoe. Our mistletoe (shared with the rest of northern Europe) is *Viscum album* ssp. *album*, which prefers soft-barked deciduous trees as hosts. *V. album* ssp. *austriacum* and *V. album* ssp. *abietis* grow in central and southern Europe and prefer pine trees and fir trees respectively.

If you want to grow your own mistletoe, use ripe berries. The ones you kiss under at Christmas will have been harvested unripe, so persuade a friend to net a clump of theirs to prevent them from being eaten by birds, and harvest the berries in March. Select a good-sized branch on your would-be host tree, and squash the sticky berries into flaps cut in the bark. Germination is rarely better than one in ten, so for the best chance of success choose berries from a plant growing on the same species of tree as the one you intend to use as a host, and use lots of berries, as mistletoe is dioecious (with separate male and female forms), so both sexes need to be present to produce the berries. And be patient: it may take three years for the first true mistletoe leaves to appear.

29 November 2003

Christmas Tales

Oh! The shiver of it when the Punch and Judy man tells Kay 'The wolves are running' in *The Box of Delights*. And the delicious lurch in the pit of your stomach when Mr Dawson tells Will 'The Walker is abroad, and this night will be bad, and tomorrow will be beyond imagining' in *The Dark Is Rising* – the very title is guaranteed to send a chill down your spine. I think all the best children's books are set at Christmas – or, more precisely, in that period between Christmas Eve and New Year's Eve, when there seems to be a suspension of time, a magical time out of time. Perhaps it's the darkness. Or the sense of urgency – the importance of getting things done in time, of getting things right, putting them right. It's a time when Herne the Hunter is abroad, a time when everything is in the balance. The hinge of the year. Think of the Frank Capra film *It's a Wonderful Life* – that Christmas perennial – quite dark in tone and not nearly so soppy as the idea of Clarence getting his wings might suggest. Or Scrooge in *A Christmas Carol*, come to that. It's a time for reflection, for re-evaluation. No wonder everyone gets anxious about who is having Christmas dinner with whom and where.

But I've decided to be alone this Christmas, and try to get on with the book. I've already retreated into one room with the cats and my papers and the computer. I keep the fire burning day and night – my one great indulgence: big logs of yew and tulip wood (windblown timber from a neglected old garden near by), smouldering for six or seven hours overnight; dry bits of apple wood from the orchard to throw on the hot ashes in the morning and fill the room with sweet woody fragrance; smooth grey-skinned birch logs smelling of *cuir de Russie*, leaping into mid-morning flame and gone by midday; green holly, flaring and spluttering like hot wax; red-fleshed alder (known as wallow or waller round here – perhaps on account of its watery habitat?), good to slow the fire down before I go to bed; the occasional bit of sulky chestnut, hardly worth burning at all; one or two left-over logs of larch or pine or spruce, from the trees felled years ago down the back drive, resinous and sticky and smelling best of all – but banging and crackling and spitting out sparks on to the carpet until I have to leave off writing and go and fetch the fire-guard.

The smells of Christmas are very evocative: wood fires and beeswax candles, hot cloves and cinnamon, goose fat and pine needles. I had thought I wouldn't decorate the house this Christmas as I will be on my own, but now some deep atavistic longing is possessing me, making me want to fill the house with the pungent boughs of evergreens from the garden: sharp citrus-smelling juniper, holly, quills of pine, flat branches of spruce, yew, tree ivy with its curious black geometrically precise seed-heads, mistletoe. If I don't watch out, I shall be steaming Christmas puddings before I know it and asking Nick and Les down at Morville Heath to cut me a Christmas tree. (The nicest Christmas trees are always the ones freshly cut at the last minute – like Scrooge's goose, an afterthought, just when you thought you had missed Christmas altogether. Green and wet and rustling, smelling of the forest. Or at any rate the plantation: don't let's get too romantic here.)

But one thing I will do is make a holly wreath for the door. And take the bees their annual Christmas treat of bee candy. I like the idea of the bees inside their hives under the hazel trees, glowing with heat like little hearths. I can almost imagine warming my hands at them. They don't hibernate: they keep moving in a perpetual humming vibrating ball clustered around the queen, eternally changing places – the ones inside moving to the outside and those outside moving to the inside – beating their wings to keep warm, all winter long. They manage to maintain a temperature of 65°F (17°C) even in midwinter, raising it to an amazing 92°F (33°C) in January, when the queen starts to lay again. So I won't let the cold air in. I'll just lift the roof of each hive enough to check that the colony is OK and to slip my gift of white bee candy quietly on top of the crown board without disturbing them.

It has just occured to me: I wonder whether the bees, like us, have a myth about a strange muffled figure appearing in the dead of winter, out of the sky, bearing presents . . .

21 December 2002

Paper-clips & Diaries

I have a thing about paper-clips. Or perhaps it would be truer to say, I have a thing about single paper-clips – solitary paper-clips encountered on their own, in odd or out-of-the-way places, left-over paper-clips. If I see a stray one, dropped on the pavement or left behind at a Post Office counter, I cannot resist surreptiously picking it up and pocketing it. It's a sort of talisman.

Of what, I wonder? Of connecting disparate facts and trying to make sense of things, I think, reminding me of writing my thesis, years ago, when a paper-clip connecting two pages of notes – two odd scraps of information put together – meant some exciting new insight. Of 'getting my act together' too, as perhaps the young don't say any more, of things coming together. Possibly too, especially at this time of year, of the bonds which unite us with family and friends. 'Only connect,' as E. M. Forster said.

But if the truth were known, I have a bit of a thing not only about paper-clips but about the entire contents of stationers' shops: pens, pencils, blocks of paper, notebooks, diaries – especially diaries. I suspect that I'm not alone in this. There must be more diary writers among gardeners than among any other section of the population. There are certainly lots of posh gardening diaries: week-to-view desk diaries illustrated with Monet's paintings of Giverny; smart white Royal Horticultural Society ones illustrated with botanical drawings; spiral-bound ones with dreamy close-up photographs of peonies and roses; ones with details of seventeenth-century flower paintings or twentieth-century flower fairies; diaries devoted to tulips or to pictures of dewy grapes and plums; even diaries by celebrity gardeners, pre-filled with encouraging advice and dates to remember.

These are what used to be called engagement diaries. A real gardening diary needs space to expand where necessary, to be flexible enough to have things attached to it or enclosed in it; big enough for you to draw plans and sketch ideas for planting, but cheap and plain enough not to be intimidating (so exquisite leather-bound volumes of handmade paper, however lovely, are out) – and without printed dates so that you don't feel guilty on the days when you don't write it. I used to write mine in school exercise books. Now I write on the backs of draft copies of whatever else it is I am supposed to be writing – a sort of parallel narrative.

You don't have to start on New Year's Day. Begin whenever the mood takes you. Write in it how the delphiniums were the best ever this year. How you walked up the garden that morning in June before anyone else was awake and saw that the first rose was out. How in February you stood and stared until your feet were frozen, watching the sun glinting through the frosted seed-heads of the fennel. Come next New Year's Eve, you'll be glad you did.

But I do also need a printed diary. Not only to keep from forgetting the dentist's appointments and the interesting lectures on 'Year-round Iris' or 'The Woodland Garden' (which despite my New Year resolutions I will never manage to get to), and the litany of saints' days – Aelred of Hexham on 12 January, Thomas Aquinas on the 28th – and the pattern of Sundays running like a thread through the year – the second Sunday after Epiphany, the fifth after Easter, the fourteenth after Trinity – but also (and especially) for the phases of the moon. I love that printed disc of black ink which gradually fills with light as the new moon ripens into the round white 'O' of the full moon. I know all I have to do is look out of the window to see it, but I love to see this printed moon too, wandering through the pages, interweaving with Bank Holidays and royal birthdays, medieval saints and garden openings.

For people living by the sea and by the great tidal estuaries, the phases of the moon of course mean much more than that, as they also do for the gardeners who follow the biodynamic system. They use a special calendar which indicates the best days on which to sow or harvest, prune or plant, according to the position of the moon. I struggle to get things done in the right month, let alone at the correct hour of the correct day of the correct month. But there is an undeniable appeal in this gentle way of gardening, responding to every aspect of nature. 'Only connect.' It's a good maxim.

27 December 2003

Christmas Eve

By nine o'clock on Friday morning Elizabeth Bacon will be crossing the muddy field down to the Mor brook in search of Christmas tree branches. Cut fresh like this, the spicy fragrance of the spruce is almost overpowering, and the resin oozing from the branches makes her hands sticky as she works. It's Christmas Eve, and she is gathering foliage to decorate the village church at Morville. She looks for contrasting shapes, textures and colours: big glossy leaves of bergenia; sprays of tree ivy with their bunches of angular green-and-black fruits; the shining leaves of holly – both green and variegated; a bit of golden *Cupressocyparis leylandii*; the grey leaves of Jerusalem sage (*Phlomis fruticosa*). She's hoping someone else will bring her some blue cedar. 'But not yew,' she says, 'and certainly not mistletoe! Not in the church.'

Flowers are a bonus. There are usually a few blooms of the Christmas rose (*Helleborus niger*) for the altar, but this year the weather has been so mild that there are some white Lenten roses too (*Helleborus orientalis*), not usually in flower until February. Even the spring-flowering *Skimmia japonica* is in fat pink bud. Once she has got all the flowers and foliage gathered together she starts to condition them – giving them what she calls 'a good long drink'. She puts the greenery in cold water, and the flowers in tepid water to encourage the buds to open. 'It's a plain old country church,' she says, 'originally a Norman monastery, so the arrangements are always quite simple.' But sometimes she adds red carnations from the local florist, because they last so well. 'One arrangement of ivy and red carnations last year was still in place on Ash Wednesday,' she says. 'I think the ivy had taken root in the Oasis!'

Meanwhile, Charlotte Petherick is walking up the headland to the tiny church of St Levan, at Porthpean in Cornwall. She is carrying white camellias picked from her own garden. 'We are right beside the sea here, and we rarely get frost, but we get frightful winter gales. Only the other week we had a gale which destroyed the boat slip next door.' But there's always a sheltered corner somewhere in the garden where she can find enough camellias for the altar and the font. The little double white *C. japonica* 'Campsii Alba' and the bigger white 'Conrad Hilton' are always out in time for Christmas, but this year she may also have the rich red of *C. sasanqua* 'Belinda' – 'The colour of beetroot soup!' she says. It's one of the Paradise strain of *sasanqua* camellias, given her by a friend in Australia. 'The *sasanqua* camellias are wonderful. They flower in autumn and winter,' she says, 'and they don't get the petal blight which sadly so many other camellias now do.'

At 3.30 p.m. Elizabeth is in the church and ready to start arranging the flowers, her portable radio already tuned to the Nine Lessons and Carols. She uses the evergreens with their leathery leaves inside the church, because they can withstand abrupt changes of temperature – 'The church goes from icy cold to suddenly hot – we've got a new heating system!' – but she saves the garden flowers for little arrangements outside in the porch where it is cooler and where people can see them up close: tiny scented things like *Viburnum* x *bodnantense* and *Sarcococca humilis* (known as 'Christmas box' from its box-like leaves and habit), and fragile trails of yellow winter jasmine (*Jasminum nudiflorum*).

By this time it's almost dark in Orkney, off the north coast of Scotland. Jean Wallace and her friends on the island of Shapinsay have been hard at work all day, collecting greenery from their gardens – escallonias, hedge hebes, *Olearia* x *haastii* (or 'Hasty O'Leary' as the islanders call it), and the grey-leaved *Senecio cineraria* which overwinters here. Orkney is virtually frost-free, but the wind and the wet mean that there are few flowers in the gardens in winter, and not a lot of colour. All the flowers to decorate the church at Christmas have to be brought in from the mainland. 'I can remember a time when there wouldn't have been flowers in the church at Christmas – not like this at all. It was just an ordinary working day,' she says. 'Even the postman still came!' But now there is a Christmas tree in the church, and candles and flowers and evergreen foliage.

Jean lives at Girnigoe, on the west side of the island. Her garden looks out over a sweep of silver sea, populated by the dark humps of other islands – Rousay, Egilsay and Wyre, Eday, even far Westray. As the last of the light dips behind the western horizon they look like a school of whales settling down for the night. Jean sniffs the air. It's a magical time. Later in the evening the lights will be switched on in the church, and the flowers will blaze with colour. But maybe tonight the greatest show of all will be outside, filling the enormous northern sky with rippling, cascading colour: the Aurora Borealis. Maybe tonight, on this special night of nights . . .

18 December 2004

January

If January calends be summerly gay
It will be wintery weather till the calends of May

Sead-heads of Clematis vitalba *(old man's beard)*

Midwinter Bonfires

I'm a bit of a pagan at heart. Equinox and solstice, New Year's Eve and Midsummer Night, there's nothing like a bonfire to mark the turning wheel of the year. That first whoosh of flame, the intoxicating crackle, the sparks spiralling high into the air. The roaring glowing red-hot hollow heart of it. I love it. And that sense of being not quite in control: feeding the beast, diverting its attention, directing its energies – keeping one step ahead. I like the aftermath of the bonfire, too: methodically raking up the half-burnt debris, returning it to the fire, clearing the decks, tidying up – all of that – only to poke the smouldering heap back into life the following morning with a fresh load.

Despite a vigorous programme of composting and shredding, our bonfire always used to grow to gargantuan proportions, curling round the bonfire yard like a sleeping dragon with its tail over its nose, while we waited for weather and inclination to coincide. Too wet, and the bonfire wouldn't burn; too still, and we choked in smoke; too ferociously windy, and we were in danger of losing control altogether. And never on a Monday: someone might have washing out on the line. But eventually the perfect day would dawn. One year we had a bonfire which burnt for a week and had finally to be extinguished in response to pleas from the neighbours. Now we try to moderate our atavistic urges.

The best bonfires are at night. Not Guy Fawkes' Night: a

Roman Catholic upbringing has left me queasy about celebrating the evisceration and incineration of that poor Catholic gentleman (though I suspect that the continued popularity of Guy Fawkes' Night may have considerably more to do with the proximity of the pagan feast of Samhain – the precursor of Hallowe'en – than with some hazy recollection of a seventeenth-century treason trial.) And not in summer, though there are ancient traditions of bonfires both at Beltane, the pagan feast on 1 May which celebrated the beginning of summer, and on Midsummer Night, the eve of the feast of St John (24 June), close to the summer solstice. But on a winter's night, when you can see the stars and feel the cold at your back – one of these nights I might even be tempted to leap over it, in true pagan style.

Midwinter fire customs used to be much more widespread than they are today. Those that survive are a hodge-podge of ancient and modern, like Up-Helly-Aa, the most splendid midwinter festival of all. It is celebrated in Shetland on the last Tuesday in January, and involves a Viking longship, dragged through the streets of Lerwick by hordes of Viking-costumed men bearing flaming torches. At a pre-ordained spot the men throw their torches into the boat, and the longship is ritually burnt. The name derives from 'Upholiday', Lowland Scots for the Twelfth Day of Christmas (6 January), the date when Up-Helly-Aa was originally celebrated. All splendidly barbaric.

In fact Up-Helly-Aa dates from about 1870. It was an attempt by the local Total Abstinence Society to divert the islands' young men from the drunken revelry customary at New Year. But although the ritual is modern, Up-Helly-Aa taps into a much older tradition of midwinter 'saining' – purification by fire – which is still found not only in Shetland but here and there around the rest of the country. Saining dates from a time when it was vital to keep demons and evil spirits at bay if herds and crops – and therefore the people who depended upon them – were to survive the winter. In the Highlands of Scotland, branches of juniper were burnt on New Year's Day in houses and byres to protect the cattle. In Herefordshire and south Shropshire, groups of twelve small bonfires, all in a row, plus one bigger than the rest, would be burnt in the fields on Twelfth Eve, and hoops of mistletoe were carried flaming across the fields within living memory. (I have my own Twelfth Night ritual of burning all the greenery I have used to decorate the house for Christmas and New Year.) In Ottery St Mary, in Devon, men, women and children still run through the streets with barrels of flaming tar on their shoulders on 5 November.

Most of us nowadays content ourselves with making New Year resolutions. But the instinct is the same: cleansing, making a fresh start. My New Year resolution is to go on a diet and take myself back to the gym: the midwinter flab is spreading. But my resolve has been undermined already. Shovelling a fermenting heap of hot resinous evergreens into the maw of the bonfire this week, I uncovered what I thought were grass snake's eggs – I often find them in the compost, like bunches of off-white slightly rubbery grapes, each with a neat slit where its occupant has escaped. On closer inspection they proved to be new potatoes, forced, I suppose, from the discarded haulm of the crop dug up in September, by the heat of the fermenting evergreens.

I'm going to eat them with a lake of hollandaise sauce. To hell with the diet. I'll start tomorrow.

1 January 2005

Chiltern Seeds

Rain today, rain yesterday and rain tomorrow. Rain standing in the hoof prints of the bedraggled cattle on the Church Meadow. Rain lying in the furrows of the ploughed fields down in the Corve Dale. Rain dripping from the iron railings in front of the Hall. The brook is the colour of weak cocoa, great spinning castles of foam in the slack water below the weir. Flood warnings out for the River Severn, the Wye, the Avon and further afield: the Trent, the Thames, the Ouse.

It seems as if early January has usurped February's role as 'February fill-dyke'. The ground squelches underfoot. The grass paths are rapidly turning to mud. I am doing no good outside. And I know that inside, gleaming through its plastic shrink-wrapping, is the latest Chiltern Seeds catalogue.

It has been waiting for me since Christmas. Mr Bowden always arranges for the catalogues to arrive then, so that the Rev. X can settle down to it with a glass of sherry after taking the service on Christmas morning. (It goes without saying that the Rev. X must be a man.) It is unlike any other seed catalogue – in shape, content, style or tone. It reminds me more than anything of an antiquarian bookseller's catalogue, one of those enormous printed lists which booksellers used to send out in the days before websites and email, when every item was a rarity or a choice old favourite, something disinterred from an old lady's attic or snatched from under the noses of competing booksellers at the local auction, something long sought-after or something you didn't know you needed until now – and now that you know, you've just got to have it.

Mr Bowden founded the firm twenty-eight years ago, and the catalogue is still an intensely personal affair. No photographs of plants, just him telling you where he found it, why you should grow it, what the Latin name means. Reminding you of the difference between spadix and spathe in the entry for *Zantedeschia*, and how 'the writer has grown it entirely, seed to flower, in the sitting-room'. Reassuring you that the spelling of the Windamere palm (*Trachycarpus latisectus*) is not a misprint for Lake Windermere but an allusion to the Windamere Hotel in Darjeeling, handy for the famous narrow-gauge railway. (Mr Bowden is a railway buff.) Recommending that you have a go with his hardy *Echium* hybrids (*E. wildpretii* x *E. pininana*) – 'eventually producing a noble and spectacular stem up to 14 ft. in length with the thickness at its base of a man's leg and bearing countless thousands of pale Wedgwood-blue flowers'. (He grows them himself in his own garden on a windswept hilltop high above the Furness peninsula in Cumbria.)

This is a catalogue to read, not just a way of shopping. Look up one thing and you find yourself seduced by the entries for a dozen others. *Lychnis* leads you to *Lycium*, the Chinese matrimony vine, 'one of the best of all shrubs for seaside planting'. *Lathyrus* leads on to lion's ear (*Leonotis ocymifolia*, from South Africa), lion's claw (*Leontochir ovallei*, from the Atacama Desert of Chile) and lion's foot (*Leontopodium alpinum*, the edelweiss). More than 4,500 items from suppliers all over the world. Everything from trees to Japanese vegetables.

Exotics have always been Mr Bowden's strong suit. There are eight species of banana in this year's catalogue, five species of tree ferns, seven species of cycads (with a long note on the habits of the Australian ones), and he is always on the lookout for new forms likely to prove hardy in the British Isles. Like the Windamere palm, new this year, which he says is likely to prove hardier even than *T. fortunei*. Or *Cycas panzhihuaensis*, the hardy sago palm, so new that it appears in the addendum, only discovered in 1981 and named after the mining town of Panzhihua in Szechwan Province of China, where it survives severe frost and snow, prolonged periods of drought and the odd fire, as well as tolerating damp and wet conditions.

I shake the raindrops from my hat, pile my wet gloves and muddy boots by the kitchen door, and slide the catalogue from its plastic wrapping. Now where's the entry for that cycad? After Szechwan, life in Shropshire would be a breeze . . .

4 January 2003

Weathervanes

As Bob Dylan famously observed, you don't need a weatherman to know which way the wind blows. (And weathermen can in any case be fallible, as we all know and Michael Fish learned to his cost.) But when after sixteen weeks under scaffolding and blue plastic wraps our weathervanes finally re-emerged – repaired, re-gilded and hoisted back into position by a mobile crane, just in time for Christmas – it was a cause for general rejoicing.

I had forgotten how much I missed them. That glint of gold against the black and white of the hanging wood on a cold winter's morning. The airy filigree of the wrought ironwork spiralling up into the shimmering blue of a midsummer sky. The flash of the arrow as the wind changes direction, backing and veering as the weatherfronts roar over the garden in spring. There are two of them, tall narrow tapering structures, graceful as a pair of ballet dancers, facing one another on top of the two gate lodges across the lawn in front of the Hall.

Forecasting the weather has always been crucial for farmers and gardeners alike, and in the days before barometers, predictions were almost entirely dependent upon accurate observations of the direction of the wind. Weathervanes date back at least as far as the first century BC, when the astronomer Andronicus of Cyrrhus placed a weathervane in the shape of a bronze Triton on the top of his observatory, the Tower of the Winds, in Athens. Nowadays you can buy weathervanes in the shape of boats, planes, trains, cars, motorbikes, dogs, cats, gardeners, anything you like – you name it, they'll make it. The weathercock, however – a weathervane in the shape of a cockerel – is a much older device, dating back as far as the ninth century AD, when it was decreed that the figure of a cockerel be set up on every church tower and steeple as an emblem of St Peter, to remind the congregation not to deny Christ as Peter had done.

Much of the old weather-forecasting lore was encapsulated in verse to make it easier to remember, such as 'If the wind is nor'east three days without rain, Eight days will pass before south wind again' – an allusion to the stability of anticyclonic weather. Most of these rhymes were derived from a set of maxims known as *The Rules of the Shepherd of Banbury*, first published in 1670. The Rules (subtitled 'To judge of the changes of the weather, grounded on forty years' experience; by which you may know the weather for several days to come, and in some cases for months') were still being reprinted well into the twentieth century, and cheap second-hand copies are not difficult to find on the internet.

The weather in the first few days of January was always reckoned to set the pattern for the next three months. For example, if the wind on New Year's Eve was in the west, it betokened 'much milk and fish in the sea; If North, much cold and stormes there'll be' – the milk presumably because the west wind was usually a bringer of rain, and hence of lush grass. The rhyme goes on, 'If East, the trees will bear much fruit', presumably because the east wind is dry, but 'If North-east, flee it man and brute.' I can testify to that. I don't need a weatherman to tell me when the wind is in the north-east. For a whole week before Christmas the cat flap in the back door stood out horizontally and the carpets lifted on the floor, while the bananas and I shivered in our shoes.

There's no such thing as bad weather, only bad clothes, and if you're going to work out of doors all winter, you need to keep warm and dry: thermal underwear, gloves, hat, boots, jacket, the works. So my Christmas present to myself this year was a new waxed jacket. The old jacket had served me well for nearly twenty years, but it was so tattered that I was beginning to look like M. R. James's terrifying raggedy ghost in 'Oh, Whistle and I'll Come to You, My Lad' in *Ghost Stories of an Antiquary*. The new one cost me nearly £150, but divide that by twenty years and it comes out at sixty-two pence a month. Not bad, I say.

11 January 2003

In Praise of Winter

Winter is the time for thinking and planning, for imagining the garden as someday it may be, for remembering those other gardens that continue to haunt us like unsatisfied ghosts until we reincarnate them in our own gardens – a little bit of Sissinghurst here, a little bit of Barnsley there. How much of our gardening is done in the mind!

In 1988, when I took a twenty-year lease from the National Trust, the garden consisted of a few overgrown flower-beds around the house and an old orchard beyond, full of cow parsley and nettles. That first winter, I read and dreamed and cross-referred and made lists, until by March my imaginary garden was so real that I could walk about in it and smell the flowers.

But the National Trust needed to be convinced. They wanted detailed plans before they would give the go-ahead. An outline plan I could just about manage, but I can't draw, and I couldn't do planting plans. So instead I sent them a description, a sort of conducted tour of the garden as it existed inside my own head – 'If you look to the left you will see . . . and turning to the right . . . ', pointing out a vista here, an arbour there, the smell of the honeysuckle, the sound of water – written (to their amusement) in the present tense. Years later, I was still being introduced as the person who wrote the guidebook before the first sod had even been turned.

Winter lays bare the bones of the garden. It is the time when one can appreciate the curve of a hedge, the siting of a path or walk, the relative volumes of the various spaces, without the distraction of flowers. In the hectic days of summer, we gardeners become so preoccupied by the daily round of grass-cutting, weeding, staking, tying-in, pinching-out, that we barely have time to lift our heads and look around us. Gardeners' suntans never extend to their faces: whey-faced, we peer over shoulders bronzed from stooping in the sun. Winter gives us time to *look*. We should treasure it for that.

It is not only the body that needs a rest: the eye does, too. After the sensuality of summer, with its heady perfumes and rich diet of colour, I need the sobriety of winter before I can face the clear bright colours of spring with any appetite. I don't want 'Universal' pansies. Not for me the idea of 'winter colour'. I don't want red-stemmed dogwoods that look like sealing-wax, or yellow-stemmed willows, however wonderful I am told they are with the winter sun behind them.

I love my empty winter garden, with its subdued colours – black earth, white frost, the evergreen hedges of dark yew and shining green holly and box. I love the effect of the low sun across the winding paths of the Turf Maze; the nights of starshine and moonshine when the shadows of the obelisks are as crisp as noonday, and the full moon floats in the Canal in the naked arms of the old pear tree; the days of fog when the yew hedges disappear into the distance and the garden becomes again the mysterious place of my imagination.

I shall gorge myself instead on the brightly coloured illustrations of seed catalogues and plant lists as I sit in the warmth of the kitchen, my back to the open door of the Rayburn, surrounded by cats and the smell of airing linen, dreaming of scarlet poppies and red hot pokers, flame-coloured cannas and sulphurous crocosmias.

This rhythm of the seasons is what gardening is all about. Why try to disguise it with everlasting flowers?

19 January 2002

Glamour

What makes a garden glamorous? Conspicuous expenditure of money? The latest, most fashionable flowers? The blackest of black hellebores, the most expensive of snowdrops?

Some things come for free. There's nothing like a touch of frost to add glamour to the winter garden. Like hard white icing on a dark fruit cake, it transforms the stuff of everyday life into something special – a birthday or a christening instead of the usual Saturday teatime in front of the telly. Like white chalk highlighting a pencil drawing. It makes you take notice. It emphasises the horizontals and the verticals, the edges of things, the structure of it all. And it focuses attention on the details: the veins on the back of a fallen leaf, the sword-edge on a blade of grass, the slight unevenness of a stone slab.

The other week I whiled away that whole first morning of frost, captivated, wandering around the garden, just looking. But alas! When the frost finally melted I found that my every move had been recorded in a trail of yellow footprints along the grass paths – how I had lingered here, half-turned there, turned up into the Wild Garden and back down through the Cloister Garden, peered at the frost on the red berries of the *Iris foetidissima*, stopped to admire the long shadows across the frosted grass of the Turf Maze. My careless feet had crushed the frozen grass, fracturing the tissue walls and killing the leaf blades. The roots are unharmed, and the paths will eventually recover. But meanwhile I follow myself around the garden each day like a penitent ghost.

For summer glamour there's nothing to beat lilies. I have a friend who filled his garden with hundreds of pot-grown lilies specially timed for his adored daughter's June wedding. In principle you could do this for a special occasion at any time of the year, if you have a greenhouse, as lilies are easily retarded or triggered into growth by manipulation of the temperature at which the bulbs are stored. The chilling process itself is best left to the experts – a degree or two either way can spell disaster – so order your bulbs from a reputable firm, having first told them the date you want the lilies to flower. Bear in mind too that chilling the bulbs will result in accelerated growth: according to grower Andy Devine (who specialises in the Oriental group of lilies), a spell in the deep freeze will coax Orientals into flower in eight to ten weeks instead of the usual sixteen.

Prepared bulbs will flower at the natural time in subsequent years, but you can have a succession of lilies in flower in the garden from May to September if you choose your varieties carefully. Recently voted the nation's favourite flower (ahead of all the old garden favourites like roses, fuschias and sweet peas), lilies are statuesque, self-conscious, look-at-me sorts of flowers, with a sheen on them like heavy satin and a perfume to stop you in your tracks at ten paces. And they are, as the Stella Artois advert says, reassuringly expensive enough for a clutch of them in the garden to make you feel truly glamorous.

But back to muddy reality. I've still got all the roses to prune first.

25 January 2003

A Little Vase of Flowers

Just before Christmas I was lucky enough to be taken to Stratford to see Judi Dench as the Countess of Rossillion in *All's Well That Ends Well*. It was a delight: superlative performances, exquisite lighting effects, and period costumes to die for – all black and white and rustling grey silk – played out in front of a silvery backdrop of bare leafless trees representing both the wintry isolation of the Countess of Rossillion's country estate and the Countess's own bleak frame of mind at the start of the play.

But what chiefly lingers in my mind is a small bunch of flowers on the Countess's little writing table in the middle of the bare stage – a gleam of colour and hope in a wintry grey world.

It reminded me of a photograph I once saw of Vita Sackville-West's writing-room in the tower at Sissinghurst: on her

writing-table, among the litter of books and photographs, pen
and pencils, was a little vase of flowers. She always had flowers
on her writing-table, picked every day from the garden. I believe
the National Trust still keeps up the tradition, forty years after
her death.

There is something very touching about flowers seen like this:
just two or three blooms, picked at random, not 'arranged'. They
still seem part of the garden. And having the flowers close at
hand, at eye-level, you can see them properly – get to know them
in a way which we rarely do when they are growing in the garden.
As the painter Georgia O'Keeffe famously said in the catalogue
of an exhibition at the New York gallery, An American Place:

> Still – in a way – nobody sees a flower – really – it is so small – we
> haven't time – and to see takes time, like to have a friend takes
> time.

There is something especially magical about midwinter flowers.
I remember my mother used to cut the bare stems of flowering
currant (*Ribes sanguineum*) and bring them indoors into the warm,
where the flowers would open white instead of the usual dark pink
– to me, as a small child, a piece of magic quite as clever as any
conjuring trick.

I don't pick many flowers from my own garden. On the whole
I prefer to see them growing. But prompted by the thought of the
Countess's little vase of flowers, I walked up into the garden the
other day to see what I could find. The first snowdrops. The last
sprays of fragrant pink *Viburnum* x *bodnantense*. A stray hellebore
or two – greeny white and pinkish green – hanging their heads
with their backs to the wind. Not much else. Except for the tangle
of yellow winter jasmine by the front door. I had overlooked that:

it's too ordinary, I suppose, or so near the door that I see it too often and it becomes invisible.

It was planted as a host for the much nicer (to my mind) summer-flowering jasmine, the fragrant white *Jasminum officinale*, which scrambles through it. The winter jasmine is the hardier of the two, and protects the summer jasmine from the worst of the winter cold. Summer jasmine is a native of Iran and Afghanistan, and has been grown in this country since the time of Henry VIII. Winter jasmine was introduced from western China in 1844 by the plant-hunter Robert Fortune. Fortune was also responsible for introducing two other stalwarts of the winter garden, gathered on the same trip, *Mahonia japonica* and *Forsythia viridissima*. I confess to having grubbed up my forsythia. And the mahonia in the garden was only just coming into bud, so I picked three little sprays of winter jasmine instead and brought them into the house.

They are sitting on the table now as I write, and on a dreary January afternoon they light up the room with their long trumpet-shaped sulphur-yellow flowers, wrapped in overlapping pale-green bracts like fish scales. Their square, ribbed stems are a darker green, and bare of leaves (hence the Latin name *Jasminum nudiflorum*), and they gracefully arch over, as if admiring their reflection in the polished surface of the table. The more I look, the more I like them.

17 January 2004

Traveller's Joy

There are some images you never forget, like my first sight of *Clematis vitalba*. It was January 1979, and I was driving in freezing fog – an undifferentiated world of grey: road, sky, air, all one

– the only colour the fluorescent orange and yellow warning strip across the back of the lorry I was following. I was in my old Riley, my breath freezing on the split windscreen as I peered through it, trying to find the right turning. It was then that I saw, beside the road, a little wood drowned in hoar frost so deep and wreathed with old man's beard – the country name for *Clematis vitalba* – so thick, its vine-like trunks and trailing sheets of silver seed-heads draping the trees and the surrounding hedges, knitting them all together into one ghostly billowing shape, that it looked as if it had been asleep for a thousand years.

I was at that time compiling entries for a directory of rare book collections outside the major institutions. My patch was Oxford-shire, and the library of the house I was trying to find was believed to include papers of the poet and satirist John Wilmot, Earl of Rochester, the infamous seventeenth-century rake recently portrayed on screen in the film *The Libertine*, with Johnny Depp as Rochester and John Malkovich as Charles II.

Rochester was no respecter of persons, though Charles was a match for him when it came to trading witticisms. In reply to Rochester's mocking epitaph – *Here lies our sovereign lord the King / Whose promise none relies on;/ He never said a foolish thing,/ Nor ever did a wise one* – Charles replied, 'That is very true: for my words are my own, and my actions are my ministers.' But eventually Rochester went too far and he was banished from court, returning to Oxfordshire where, his health ruined by his excesses, he died in 1680 at the age of thirty-three.

The house was closed up for the winter, and I was led down dark shuttered passages and heavily curtained rooms, electric lights being alternately switched on and off as we passed, to the library where I sat in my overcoat with my gloves on, turning the pages and making notes on the books, the shutters open a little to let the pale winter light into the icy room, the vast park outside white with the hoar frost. But the manuscripts – if ever they were here – were long gone.

I have never forgotten that old man's beard. Its other name is traveller's joy, apparently coined by the herbalist John Gerard in 1597, on account of its habit of 'decking and adorning waies and hedges, where people travel'. That was also the soubriquet adopted by one of the characters in Julia Horatia Ewing's charming tale 'Mary's Meadow', in which a family of children, prevented from playing in the eponymous meadow as a result of a quarrel (which sounds eerily modern) between their father and the Old Squire next door about footpath rights, devise a game called the Game of the Earthly Paradise, based on an old botanical book which they find in their father's library. The book is John Parkinson's *Paradisi in Sole, Paradisus Terrestris*, published in 1629. Delighted by the book with its woodcuts of old-fashioned flowers such as primroses and hose-in-hose cowslips and daffodils, the children start in secret to plant flowers by the hedge alongside the footpath, turning the meadow into a real 'Earthly Paradise' and softening the Old Squire's heart into the bargain.

The story appeared as a serial over the winter of 1883/4 in the children's paper *Aunt Judy's Magazine*, and readers were so captivated by the tale that many of them wrote to ask Mrs Ewing about the plants she described, which at that time were much neglected in favour of showier hothouse plants and bedding-out. She answered their queries in the columns of the paper, and this led in July 1884 to the formation of the Parkinson Society. The aims of the society included 'to search out and cultivate old garden flowers which have become scarce', 'to exchange seeds and plants', and 'to try to prevent the extermination of rare wild flowers, as well as garden treasures'. This was the beginning of the revival of interest in hardy plants which ultimately led in 1956 to the founding of the Hardy Plant Society. The Hardy Plant Society now has branches all over this country and in North America, and hundreds of thousands of members.

Clematis vitalba is only really suitable for the biggest and wildest of gardens, rapidly growing to forty feet and more in all directions. But if you have the space, the effect in winter is incomparable. The flowers are small and greeny white, produced in large clusters in late summer. Smaller alternatives would be the orientalis group of clematis, with nodding yellow flowers and good seed-heads in winter, including *C. tangutica, C. tibetana* and related hybrids such as 'Bill MacKenzie' and 'Lambton Park'.

22 January 2005

A Different Perspective

One photograph showed a flat terrain strewed with what seemed to be boulders. Another appeared to show a network of channels cut through the surface crust as if by water or some other liquid. A third showed a surface pockmarked with craters. Not Titan, the largest of Saturn's moons, but *Protoblastenia rupestris*, *Aspicilia calcarea* and *Lecanora campestris*, three commonly occuring British lichens.

As the Cassini-Huygens space probe started to beam back the first photographs of the surface of Titan I happened to have open on my desk a page of photographs in Frank Dobson's *Field Key to Common Churchyard Lichens*. Looking from the television to the book and from the book to the television, I had a sudden sense of vertigo, conflating the image of this enormous planetary object, beamed across the immensity of outer space, with these tiny brilliantly coloured organisms viewed down the lens of a microscope, each with a surface like that of a miniature moon, rugged, cratered, fissured – unique – a place rather than a plant. Some have craters, as if from extinct volcanoes. Others ripple outwards into lobed protruberances, like ancient solidified lava flows. One even has the name *Rhizocarpon geographicum* – the 'map lichen' – its thallus (the body of the lichen) intersected with wavering black lines like those on an ink-drawn map.

And if the world of Titan is weird – its surface bathed in a strange orange glow caused by frozen particles floating in its upper atmosphere; the network of channels in its surface cut not by water but perhaps by liquid methane – the biology of a lichen is hardly less so. A lichen consists of not one but two organisms living in symbiosis: a fungus, capable of withstanding extremes of temperature and drought but unable to photosynthesise, and an alga, which – Dalek-like – inhabits the protective structure provided by the fungus and in return manufactures enough food for its own needs and those of the fungus. Every lichen partnership is unique, and neither partner can survive without the other.

There are some seventeen hundred British lichens. Many churchyards have well over a hundred, cohabiting on individual gravestones in what lichenologist Dr Vanessa Winchester calls 'miniature, self-maintaining gardens'. Churches and churchyards are important havens for lichen, even where stone is common, because the churchyard may include gravestones made from different sorts of stone, not necessarily native to the area, each of which will support a different population of lichens. My local church, for example, is built from sandstone, whereas many of the gravestones are of limestone from nearby Wenlock Edge. Alkaline stone such as limestone typically supports vivid orange and yellow crustose species (flat, crust-like lichens) such as *Caloplaca flavescens*, together with other pale-grey and white alkaline-loving species. Acid stone such as granite, slate or sandstone often has foliose (leafy, more three-dimensional) lichens, which may be tinted green (such as the mint-coloured *Flavoparmelia caperata*) or even pale pink.

Any stone will do, as long as it is not too smooth: modern polished gravestones are anathema to lichens. And any tiny variation in the environment will be reflected in the lichen population. Different lichens will grow in the shelter of recessed lettering, compared with those on exposed surfaces; and those growing at the damper, shadier bottom will differ from those on the sunlit top – especially where the top is 'nutrient-enriched' with bird droppings or pollen from overhanging trees. The front and back of a gravestone, and the different parts of the church itself, will also have different lichens, according to their orientation towards the sun. And in an area of acid stone the old lime mortar used in building the church may support an entirely different population from the stone of the walls or the slate of the roof.

Lichens are extremely sensitive indicators of environmental pollution: a rich bloom of lichen means clean air. They also grow infinitesimally slowly – half a millimetre a year is fast – so lichen growth is also an indicator of age. Many lichens will be as old as the tombstones on which they live. So don't scrub them off (it is a misconception that they destroy the stone) but do keep the surrounding undergrowth cut, as lichens need sunlight in order to thrive. And when choosing a gravestone for a loved one (or for oneself), consider choosing natural stone rather than the highly polished surfaces seen in so many graveyards nowadays. That way, as the centuries roll on, you can be sure of your own miniaturised memorial garden.

29 January 2005

Tax Return

I sit at the kitchen table, adrift in a sea of paper, my past flashing before my eyes like a drowning man. Train tickets, petrol receipts, bills for hotels, sheafs of incriminating white receipts from amazon. com, muddy lists from tree nurseries, packing slips from bulb merchants, subscriptions to the Royal Horticultural Society, the Garden History Society, the NCCPG. What on earth was I doing in Stevenage in October? Whatever did I buy at Birmingham Botanic Garden in July? Why did I need wood from the Burwarton Timber Yard in March? After twenty months it is not always easy to remember.

Some things of course you don't forget. The P&O Scottish Ferries ticket dated 11 September 2001: I was returning from researching a book about gardens in Orkney, and was re-crossing the Pentland Firth when the news came through. And the crumpled receipt from a taxi-driver in Alnwick three days later. I was there to interview the Duchess of Northumberland about her new garden. Our appointment was for eleven o'clock. I was a little early, and as I waited for her by the Portacabin offices at the foot of the slope I watched the work in progress – the huge central crane swinging in a great arc above the half-built cascade, the dump trucks dwarfed by the crane's central pillar grinding away at its foot, the toing and froing of suppliers' lorries, the roar of the JCBs – deafened by the shouts of the men, the noise of the machines. But then, as I watched, the whole immense building site gradually came to a standstill, and each of the men, standing a little apart from each other in their yellow reflective safety jackets, all over the site, took off their hard hats and stood in silence. Slowly the sounds of an ordinary autumn morning reasserted themselves: the twitter of small birds, a solitary black crow flapping its way across the site, the clock of Alnwick parish church striking the hour in the distance.

18 January 2003

February

February, fill dyke
Weather either black or white

Snowdrops

Candlemas Day

Today is Candlemas Day, 2 February. We're beginning the long countdown to Easter now, and the days are drawing out again – every day a little longer than the last, the arc of the sun appreciably wider as it swings from horizon to horizon. I can work outside until five o'clock, half past on a good day. The temperature is a balmy 52°F (11°C). In the Nuttery the bright green shoots of the leucojums, emerging from the litter of dry brown leaves, are already six inches high. Pollen from the yellow catkins of the hazels brushes on to my sleeve as I pass. The grass is growing: I might even be tempted to give it a gentle trim.

Candlemas is the feast of the presentation of the child Jesus in the Temple, and it was traditionally the day on which people brought candles to be blessed in church. The custom arose from the opening words of old Simeon's canticle when he recognised the child as the Messiah – *'Lumen ad revelationem'* – a light to lighten the darkness of the world. Candlemas was always seen (at any rate in these northern lands) as a time of renewal and rebirth, a celebration of the returning light, of the beginning of spring. Each parishioner brought his or her own candle, and after the candles had been blessed they were lit and carried in procession around the church.

Candlemaking is one of the incidental pleasures of bee-keeping. I make them every year at Christmas, and now that the number of hives in the garden has grown to four (and a half – a late swarm I caught last year) there are one or two extra candles left over to burn at Candlemas. They are a deep golden-brown colour, and burn with a smell richly redolent of the hive – a combination of flowers, honey, and the pungent smell of the antiseptic orange-red propolis which the bees use to glue the hive together and make it secure against draughts and intruders.

It's always an anxious time, watching for the re-emergence of the bees from their hives after the winter. Today it was warm enough to be out in the garden without a coat, so I walked up into the Wild Garden to see if the bees were flying. And there they were! In the weak winter sunshine, a few brave souls were testing the air on the landing board of each hive. Any day now the queen will be starting to lay again, raising a new army of workers who will sally forth in spring to pollinate my pears and apples and broad beans and all the other crops, and in return harvest the pollen and nectar to make the honey which will keep them fed next winter. I exact a modest toll of honey for myself. We eat it straight from the comb, the perfumed honey oozing from the cut surface of the papery white wax. Each comb tastes different, depending on the crop the bees have been working – pale green lime-flower honey, tasting of mint, from the trees of the avenue up to the Hall; bright yellow dandelion honey from the roadside verges; dark viscous heather honey from my neighbour's rockery: the distilled essence of flowers.

2 February 2002

Madonna of the Pinks

Is it possible to paint a perfume? Last weekend I went to see Raphael's *The Madonna of the Pinks* at the National Gallery. It was painted in Florence in about 1507–8. The first thing that strikes you is how tiny it is, barely nine inches by twelve. The young Madonna, hardly more than a child herself, sits in a shadowy stone chamber – a small turret room, perhaps – with the child on her lap. In her left hand she holds a small bunch of pinks. With her right she offers one of them to the child, who pulls the flowers towards himself as if to smell them. Everything about the picture – from its small size and the delicacy of its colouring, to the transparent veil of gauze wound round the Madonna's head and the long pale fingers with which she grasps the flowers – composes a sort of allegory of the flowers themselves, with their nodding heads, their pale grey-blue foliage, their fragile fringed petals, and that smell, that wonderful lingering scent, which as you gaze seems to expand to fill the whole of that small cool room.

Pinks have been grown in gardens since Roman times. Their English name comes not from the colour (in fact the reverse is true) but from the 'pinks' or ornamental openings cut or punched in Elizabethan dress to show a contrasting colour beneath. This is in reference perhaps to the streaks and splashes of colour found on some pinks, or more probably to the outline of the open flower, which seems to be pierced by five gaps in the centre, between the bases of the petals. Not, at any rate, in reference to their fringed edges: the verb 'to pink', in the sense of to cut an ornamental scallop on the edge of a piece of fabric, was apparently a nineteenth-century coinage. 'Pink' as a colour word arose in the early eighteenth century as a shortened form of 'pink-coloured', i.e. coloured like the flower: before that, people would have referred to 'light red' or pale 'murrey' – a purply red, mulberry sort of colour.

The principal ancestor of the garden pinks is the wild *Dianthus plumarius*, a species with an enormously wide distribution, from south and eastern Europe right up to Siberia. Its beauty and apparent fragility are belied by its toughness – it's certainly the only one that thrives on my heavy soil. Named pinks are not all that easy to grow, and are even harder to keep. It's about this time of year that I start to count the cost of all the varieties I have lost over the winter. Many of them seem to be naturally short-lived, but a heavy soil and a damp winter will do for most of them. *Dianthus plumarius*, however, seems indestructible, spreading in sheets of blue-grey foliage, crossing with all its neighbours, and setting copious amounts of seed. So I console myself with the thought that even though the named sorts perish, their progeny live on with a transfusion of tougher genes from their wild neighbour. Nameless, but just as beautiful in their way.

1 February 2003

Make Yourself at Home

From the very grandest gardens like Anglesey Abbey in Cambridgeshire to the smallest cottage garden or urban window-box, snowdrops are an essential part of winter. They line woodland edge, country lane and motorway verge with equal grace. And no churchyard is complete without them. In fact snowdrops are so ubiquitous that it's sometimes rather easy to take them for granted.

So it comes as something of a surprise to realise that they are not native at all. Gerard, the great Elizabethan herbalist and plants-man, knew them only as garden plants. The first wild colonies were not recorded until as late as the 1770s. The snowdrop originally comes from Italy and Switzerland and parts of France, including Brittany. It's no coincidence that there are particularly strong colonies in the neighbourhood of medieval religious foundations, from whose gardens the snowdrops seem to have spread into the neighbouring villages and thence out into the countryside. Tradition has it that they may even originally have been introduced by the Romans.

So how long does a plant have to live here before it is classified as indigenous? Some introductions date back as far as neolithic times, arable weeds spread by the first farmers among their crop seed. This is a process which is still continuing: it is by no means unknown for strange plants to appear by the wayside at sea ports where crop seed is imported. Technically these are known as archaeophytes if introduced before 1500, and neophytes if introduced after 1500. A naturalised plant is a non-native plant which sets seed or spreads in other ways, thereby colonising new territory, like the snowdrop. The vast majority of alien plants, however, are 'casuals', in that they may survive for a time, but tend not to persist unless reintroduced. A truly wild plant is considered to be one which has existed here since pre-neolithic times.

Most early introductions were brought here as food or medicine. Even the snowdrop had its uses: an old glossary of 1465 classifies it as an emmenagogue (a plant used to regulate the female reproductive system.) The great bulk of more recent introductions, however, are garden escapes, brought into this country to satisfy our insatiable desire for beauty and novelty. And they are not all as innocuous as the snowdrop. Take the infamous Japanese knotweed (*Fallopia japonica*), which is not only virtually impossible to eradicate but has been known to undermine flood defences. Or the giant hogweed (*Heracleum mantegazzianum*), which can cause severe phytophotodermatitis in people who come into contact with it. Or *Rhododendron ponticum*, which has reduced biodiversity in some Western counties to a fraction of what it was a hundred years ago.

The irony is that these plants all appeared perfectly well-behaved in gardens. Such plagues as these always follow fashion

– in the case of giant hogweed, the nineteenth-century taste for shrubberies and wild gardening. One product of the late twentieth-century fashion for water-gardening is the release into the wild of *Crassula helmsii* from New Zealand, a highly invasive aquatic plant which can totally displace the native vegetation in infected water systems.

So think carefully how you dispose of your unwanted garden refuse. If it contains something you don't want to compost, and you are not in a position to burn it, make sure you dispose of it safely. You never know what you might be releasing. It might be something lovely like the snowdrop. But then again, it might be a new Japanese knotweed.

8 February 2003

February

We should have known, of course. 'If Candlemas Day be fair and bright, / Winter will have another flight: / If Candlemas Day it be shower and rain, / Winter is gone and will not come again.' Is it the natural caution of the countryman which teaches us to distrust a mild February, or just a feeling that winter can't be over until we have suffered a bit? At least we can't say we weren't warned: the weather forecasters were trailing the cold snap all the previous week, and I spent the time wrapping emerging shoots in fleece, covering tender plants in the cold frames with bubble wrap, lugging the big pots back into shelter and feeling rather smug that I hadn't yet pruned the roses: much better to delay pruning until March than to prune early, as I used to, and risk the new growth being blasted by a late cold spell.

By the time the first flakes came whirling down I was well

prepared. But before I retreated to the house I couldn't resist going back up into the garden, to watch the snow filling the crevices on either side of the path, smoothing out the unevennesses in the dug earth, weighing down the long unpruned shoots of the roses – turning the green garden into a place of black and white.

The electricity was already off when I got back to the house, but with the Rayburn and candles and a pile of logs, who cares? The garden was safe.

But next time we may get caught out. It's a good plan to keep an eye on the weather: a sky clearing of clouds at evening, the smoke of neighbouring cottages rising straight up – both signs of imminent frost. But it's also a good idea to check the local five-day weather forecast on the internet (go to www.bbc.co.uk/weather and type in your postcode). I use this to try to plan ahead: wet days for working in the polytunnel, repotting lilies and agapanthus; dry days for working outside, trying to finish pruning the roses.

Lilies don't need repotting every year, only every second or third. I'll separate out the smaller daughter bulbs for potting on at the same time – that way they'll get more nourishment and will grow to flowering size more quickly. As for the agapanthus, I won't be potting them all on, just some of the big overcrowded clumps which need dividing. Agapanthus are not bulbs at all but herbaceous perennials with rhizome-like root systems, a bit like iris. In order not to damage the terminal buds I'll carefully tease the clumps apart, working from the outside rather than slicing through the middle. According to agapanthus expert Dick Fulcher, horticulturally agapanthus fall into two categories: those which come from parts of South Africa where rain falls in winter (the evergreen sorts), and those which come from areas where summer rainfall predominates (the deciduous sorts). The evergreen ones tend to be more resistant to drought and therefore perform better

in containers. So I'll add a bit more organic matter when repotting
the deciduous ones, to compensate for any shortfall in my summer
watering regime.

Indoors, the kitchen table is littered with lists and reminders:
sweet peas and dahlias still to be ordered, potatoes to be put up
for chitting, the plan for the new little blue and yellow borders
still to be finalised. The fridge is bursting with envelopes of seed
collected from the garden last autumn – shrubby blue-flowered
hyssop, with its sharp penetrating smell, white-flowered *Lychnis
coronaria* 'Alba', with its felty grey leaves – all the colours and
smells and tastes of summer, waiting to be sown.

14 February 2004

A Winter's Tale

As the first snowflakes spiralled down last week, I felt I could take
a day off with a clear conscience. The garden at Castle Bromwich
Hall, on the outskirts of Birmingham, is a repository of all that is
old and rare and interesting, and I rarely visit it without having to
write down the name of something I simply must have for my
own garden. This time it was *Hermodactylus tuberosa*, a splendidly
sombre plant, both in name and appearance. The flowers, like
small neat irises, have three inky black falls with rolled green edges,
and three paler green forked standards like the fangs of a snake
poised to attack. One of its common names is snake's head, though
not, I think, from the flowers, but from the large oval seed-head
which bends its neck and droops down as it ripens. The first part
of the Latin name refers to Hermes, trickster and messenger of
the gods, and the second element, 'dactylus', to its knobbly, hand-
shaped tubers with their sinister swollen roots, thought to

resemble dead men's fingers. *Hermodactylus tuberosa* was formerly classified with the irises, as *Iris tuberosa*, and its other common name is the widow iris, from its funereal colouring.

It was the foliage which first attracted my attention: a big patch of slender, rush-like, rather dark sea-green foliage, quite tall – about eighteen inches – and looking unexpectedly luxuriant in the wintry border. At Castle Bromwich it grows at the foot of a south-facing wall, but it is not fussy about aspect nor, I gather, about soil, and it is perfectly hardy – and indeed is naturalised in parts of Britain and Ireland. It looks startlingly modern, but has been known in this country since the late sixteenth century. Parkinson, writing in 1629, called it the 'Velvet Flowerdeluce' and was very complimentary. Gerard, on the other hand, writing in 1597, described it as 'goose-turd green'. It's all a matter of taste. Either way, it has a delicate honeyed scent.

Iris graminea, known as the plum-tart iris, is a true iris, and is another covetable miniature which dates from the same period. It flowers a little later in spring and early summer, and is even more deliciously scented, smelling of sun-warmed greengages. It has violet-purple falls, marbled with white, but the flowers are hidden deep in the foliage and you really need to pick one or two and bring them indoors, in order to snuffle up their intriguing fragrance without having to get on to your hands and knees.

Scent for me is a much more immediate link with the past than taste. For Proust, it was a madeleine dipped in tea. For me, it is the smell of balsam poplars. Just a few twigs in a vase on my friends' kitchen table, and instantly I am back in my navy-blue uniform, cycling to school. The poplars used to stand all along one side of a steep little track, about a dozen of them. I remember the sound of them in summer, a rustling tunnel of shade as I pedalled uphill, late as always, at twenty to nine; the feel of them in autumn, about my feet, when their heart-shaped leaves, leathery and butter-yellow, carpeted the track as I dawdled home at four; and – best of all – the scent of them in early spring, when their unfolding leaves filled the air with incense for hundreds of yards around.

The twigs on the kitchen table had that gleaming, slightly crumpled look of the newborn. My friends had pressed them, dripping, into my hands. Placed in water, they told me, the stems would soon make root. They did. Now, two years on, they are already twice as big as me. And one day soon, when the snow has melted, and the sun has warmed the air, their leaves will start to unfurl and I will smell again that never-to-be-forgotten smell.

26 February 2005

Springwatch

They are worried down in Shelsley Walsh. I was there the other night to give a talk to the Gardening Club, and the conversation was all of daffodils flowering before Christmas, primroses flowering in January, and a ceanothus which had been flowering all winter. Lent started early this year (Ash Wednesday was 8 February), but the Lenten roses (*Helleborus orientalis*) were even earlier: mine were in bloom on New Year's Day. And as for the summer snowflake (*Leucojum aestivum*), one clump in my garden was in flower almost before the snowdrops were out.

But while many plants, birds and insects are breeding, flowering or coming into leaf earlier, some spring events quixotically seem to be getting later. A gap seems to be opening up between the oak and the ash, with oak coming into leaf earlier and earlier, and ash lagging behind. Hawthorn and horse chestnut are racing

First frost: a corner of the Cloister Garden in winter

Frost outlines the paths through the Fruit and Vegetable Garden (*above*)
The Wild Garden in winter (*below*)

Fallen apples in the Wild Garden provide food for the birds

The Fruit and Vegetable Garden and Apple Tunnel in winter (*overleaf*)

Low winter sun shines through the entrance to the Maze

Wintry weather: clockwise from top left, the last rose of summer ('Nathalie Nypels'), frost on *Helleborus orientalis* leaves, *Eryngium giganteum* seedheads, 'What will the robin do then, poor thing?'

The Canal Garden in winter

away, but the time when beech comes into leaf seems to be getting later and later, and not just in relative terms. So what's going on?

I spoke first to Tim Sparks of the Centre for Ecology and Hydrology. It seems that we are in for longer and increasingly chaotic springs. Instead of everything straightforwardly happening earlier in response to the warming of the climate, the picture is much more complicated, as phenologists like Tim are now beginning to realise. Phenology (the study of periodic biological phenomena like flowering or migration, especially in relation to climate) officially began in Britain in 1875, when the Royal Meteorological Society established a national network of recorders. Annual reports were published up until 1948, but then lapsed until Tim revived the network in 1998. By linking the earlier records with those of the last seven years, Tim is now able to go beyond mere anecdotal evidence and to discern some pattern in all of this.

Most plants have a period of dormancy in order to protect themselves from adverse weather conditions: tropical plants, for example, become dormant in dry or cool spells, sending up new shoots when the rains return. In our higher latitudes, dormancy – and the breaking of dormancy – is a product of complicated responses to a number of different factors, such as day length and the temperature of soil and air, which are not yet all competely understood. Oak, for example, responds to higher temperatures in spring by coming into leaf eight days earlier for every degree of warming, whereas ash responds by coming into leaf only four days earlier – as if some other mechanism were putting a brake on the ash's response to the rise in temperature. That mechanism might be sensitivity to day length, or it might be a combination of other factors. According to Dr Phil Gates of the University of Durham, beech buds contain a hormone which acts as a chemical inhibitor of bud-burst. The hormone needs cold to break it down, so if there is no cold spell the buds take longer to wake from dormancy.

Naturalist Richard Fitter recorded the date of flowering of more than five hundred plant species over a period of nearly fifty years. His data have now been analysed by his son Alastair Fitter, Professor of Biology at the University of York, and he too has discovered anomalies. He told me that insect-pollinated plants (which would include many garden flowers) have responded to warming more than wind-pollinated ones such as grasses and trees. Annuals have responded more than perennials. And while one in six species is flowering significantly earlier than it did a decade ago – about two weeks earlier in many cases – others (such as buddleia, coltsfoot and whitebeam) are flowering later. In any given habitat this may alter the balance between species, so that some species die out as a result of increased competition. New hybrids may also emerge between species which have not previously flowered at the same time, such as water mint and field mint. Red and white campion already do this, and in some parts of the country the hybrid is more common than either of its parents.

So things are going to be interesting in gardens, where plants from all over the world live cheek by jowl. But this may have more serious consequences in the wild, if the links in the food chain start to come apart and a gap opens up between the time a species starts producing its young and the times when its preferred food source is available. Species which have a single food source are particularly at risk, such as the larvae of some fritillary butterflies which eat only violets. Birds on the whole are likely to fare better: earlier breeding may mean that they miss out on the caterpillars they are used to, but, being more omnivorous than butterflies, they should find plenty of different ones with which to feed their chicks.

19 February 2005

Treasure

I came to gardening rather late in life. Until then, my days were spent not with pitchfork in hand but with pencil and magnifying glass among rare books and manuscripts. So it was with a feeling of being back on home territory that I went to see the exhibition of illuminated manuscripts at the Royal Academy in London the other day.

There, in reverential gloom, were some of the most precious books in the world – Books of Hours and other manuscripts created mainly for the medieval dukes of Burgundy and their successors the Habsburgs, rulers of Spain, Germany and Flanders – each laid out as if on its own life-support machine, in temperature-controlled, humidity-controlled bubbles, the air filtered of all impurities, light levels kept low to protect the delicate pigments, each supported on its own transparent cradle. The pages gleamed with gold leaf and lapis lazuli. The subjects are crucifixions, martyrdoms, Last Judgements, the lives of the Blessed Virgin and the saints, each exquisite miniature surrounded with wide, luxuriously patterned borders of stylised entwined foliage and flowers.

But what I had especially come to see were the miniatures painted in the new style, a style of great psychological realism unique to the Flemish miniaturists of the late fifteenth and early sixteenth centuries, where the surrounding borders are of the utmost simplicity – a scattering of simple flowerheads on a ground of plain beaten gold: blue cornflowers, daisies, a handful of tiny violets, a purple columbine, little yellow-and-purple heartsease, red roses, irises with freckled throats, the curling tendrils of strawberry plants – each painted in three dimensions with such astonishing naturalism that they rise up from the vellum page as if freshly picked. Simple garden flowers, as familiar to us today as to the artists who painted them five centuries ago.

Later the same day I went to see a much smaller exhibition about the work of the Herbarium at Wisley, the Royal Horticultural Society's garden in Surrey. Dried plants, pressed flat on sheets of ordinary paper. But what romance, what clouds of glory! A small brown insignificant-looking plant with a creeping rootstock and trailing thread-like hair roots proved to be *Polygonum forrestii*, dug up at thirteen thousand feet on the Mekong–Salween divide in the mountains between Burma and China by the plant-hunter George Forrest in July 1917. The label recording its finding was written in spidery brown ink – by George Forrest, perhaps, as he crouched in a tent on that stony slope in Burma while, half a world away, the rest of the world was at war? The creamy white flowers are discoloured now to dark ochre, and the sheen of the leaves is dulled to a dingy khaki, but that moment and the plant's conformation and DNA are captured for ever.

Am I alone in finding herbarium specimens exciting? The oldest herbarium in Britain is at Oxford University, and dates from the founding of the Botanic Garden there in 1621. Here you can see a three-hundred-year-old specimen of *Senecio squalidus*, now known as Oxford ragwort, brought back from the slopes of Mount Etna in Sicily. The plant subsequently colonised the waste places of the city, and then set off down the Great Western Railway line (where no doubt the smoke and sparks reminded it of home) to colonise the rest of the country. In the herbarium at the Natural History Museum in London you will find the type specimen of cocoa (*Theobroma cacao*) brought back from Jamaica by Sir Hans Sloane at the beginning of the eighteenth century. Sloane had been introduced to the drink while in Jamaica but, finding it 'nauseous',

mixed it with hot milk in order to make it palatable – the recipe
still in use today.

These specimens and millions more like them, housed in
herbaria around the world, are preserved as the ultimate author-
ities in the identification and naming of plants – treasures as
precious as any illuminated manuscript. But they are also part
of working collections, and there's a fine balance to be maintained
between accessibility and preservation. New media can help:
many herbaria are beginning to make their specimens available
as digital images over the internet in order to reduce damage
from handling. On the Natural History Museum's website, for
example, you can now view not only Sloane's specimens, but
specimens of some of the first magnolias, asters and acers ever
to be seen in Europe, sent back by John Clayton of Virginia in
the 1730s; or George Clifford's specimens of cannas and canna-
bis from the East Indies, mounted in eighteenth-century style as
if growing out of ornamental urns; or Paul Hermann's specimens
from Ceylon, sent back in the 1670s. The past, as they say, is a
different country. But with treasures like these it is possible to
bring it vividly to life.

21 February 2004

Et In Arcadia Ego

Arcadia is a remote mountainous region in the central Pelopon-
nese, synonymous since classical times with the delights of the
pastoral life. It is also the origin of the name Cajun, for the inhabitants of the French seventeenth-century settlement of Acadia in
Nova Scotia who were dispossessed by the British in 1755 and
resettled in what was then the Spanish colony of Louisiana. But

we remember Arcadia chiefly nowadays for an inscription carved on tombs in the paintings of Poussin and others, 'Et in Arcadia ego' – usually translated as 'I too [meaning Death] am in Arcadia'.

I thought of this last weekend, as the tanks surrounded Heathrow airport and anti-war demonstrators thronged the streets of London, when I found myself in Trebah Garden in Cornwall, looking at a memorial to the men of the 29th US Infantry who embarked from the garden on the first day of June, 1944, bound for the D-Day landings in Normandy. It is hard now to imagine the noise of the tanks and the trucks lurching down through this serenely beautiful garden to the sea – the shouts of the men, the stink of diesel, the clank and rattle of the landing-craft. Harder still to imagine the scene which greeted them on the beaches of Normandy at the other end of their journey. Their destination was Omaha Beach, where nearly a thousand of them fell in two days.

Many of the men came from Virginia and Maryland. Did they look back up the garden as the boats drew away from Trebah? Did the magnolias remind them of home?

Today Trebah is a wild, romantic place of tumbling foliage and flowers, the only sounds birdsong and the gentle lapping of waves on the beach. The garden occupies a steep narrow ravine running down to the sea at the mouth of the Helston river in Cornwall. It was originally planted during the nineteenth century by the Fox family, Quakers from nearby Falmouth, who also created the garden at neighbouring Glendurgan (now owned by the National Trust). At its peak, Trebah was reckoned to be one of the eighty most beautiful gardens in the world, with pink flamingoes wading in the pool and a treasury of exotic plants. Later Trebah fell on hard times. It was rescued from dereliction in the 1980s by Major and Mrs Tony Hibbert, who bought the house and garden in 1981 and handed it over to the Trebah Garden Trust.

It is the iconic Cornish garden: a group of towering Chusan palms at the head of the ravine, great banks of rhododendrons cladding the sides, woodland walks lined with camellias and magnolias, groves of bamboos and tree ferns, a jungle of gunnera on the valley floor, and acres of blue and white hydrangeas between the garden and the sea.

22 February 2003

Welcoming the Wilderness

What would the world be, once bereft
Of wet and of wildness? Let them be left,
O let them be left, wildness and wet;
Long live the weeds and the wilderness yet.

Gerard Manley Hopkins

Wilderness is a lovely word. In a largely synthetic world we long for wildness. In a world we believe to be corrupt, we long for what is untouched. In a world weighed down by history we long for innocence. But it was not ever thus. Our taste for wildness goes back no further than the late eighteenth century. Medieval Cistercian abbots sited their monasteries at Fountains, Jervaulx or Buildwas not so that their monks could be inspired by the sublimity of God's creation, but because these were awful God-forsaken wildernesses where temptation would be absent: this was Nature as penance, Nature as mortification of the flesh. When Christ went into the wilderness, he wasn't anticipating a picnic: it was a test of his resolve.

It is a measure of our confidence (undoubtedly misplaced) in being able to control Nature that we are now on such comfortable terms with the idea of wilderness. People measure the success of their holidays by how deserted the beach was or how few people they saw. They climb Ben Nevis without taking even a minimum of equipment, secure in the knowledge that, should they get into trouble, help is only a mobile-phone call away. This is Nature as commodity, Nature as scenic wallpaper.

Even we gardeners have a tendency to trivialise and patronise Nature. We rescue rare or endangered plants from around the world and put them in our gardens as if they were animals in a zoo. We hang up a few bird-feeders, or plant a buddleia to attract butterflies while ignoring – or struggling against – our own native flora.

There is another way. Miriam Rothschild, who died last month at the age of ninety-six, called it 'the new sympathy' with Nature. In her garden at Ashton Wold, in Northamptonshire, lawns were replaced by long grass and native wild flowers – 'I do not much care for living on a snooker table,' she said. 'Weeds' (self-seeded foxgloves and poppies and ox-eye daisies) lapped right up to the window-sills of the house. The vegetable garden blazed with ragwort and harebells. This was more than just the horticultural equivalent of Jenny Joseph's poem 'When I am an old woman I shall wear purple / With a red hat which doesn't go' – though some people did profess themselves shocked by it. Her garden was the product of a passionate commitment to wild flowers and wild creatures of every sort. 'The battle with weeds, the conquest of Nature, is a thing of the past,' she said.

Few of us have the acres of Ashton Wold, or the nerve to go quite so far. But as an approach this has much to commend it, even in quite small gardens, and especially as one grows older and the work of maintaining a conventional garden starts to become less of a delight and more of a chore.

There are a few rules. You can't just stop cutting the lawn. And this is not a work-free regime. But you can stop cutting some of the lawn, and the work does tend to be concentrated in a short-ish period towards the end of the summer.

Transitions are important: most of us, I suspect, would prefer to let the wildness lap around the edges of the garden while contriving some sort of formality near the house. Try mowing the grass in two or three different lengths, one section mowed every week, an outer rim mowed every three or four weeks, and the rest left to grow long. Mow some paths through the longer grass, to give it shape and definition.

None of this will produce a wild-flower meadow, but longer grass can be a delight in itself, providing life and movement in place of the static expanse of the conventional lawn. It can also provide a basis on which you can do other things. Give up the flower-beds and tempt wild flowers into the grass instead by scarifying the wild areas in September and sowing yellow rattle (*Rhinanthus minor*); this will weaken the grass and allow the wild flowers to get a toehold. Plant plugs of strong-growing things directly into the grass, like ox-eye daisies and wild blue *Geranium pratense*. Add bulbs which flower in spring or early summer when the grass is relatively short. For other planting ideas refer to Christopher Lloyd's book, *Meadows* (Cassell, 2004). But whatever you do, it is essential to cut the long grass very short once a year in late summer and rake it all off. (A strimmer is perfectly adequate for this, unless you are converting acres of lawn, in which case you might consider hiring a power-scythe.)

And what about the areas beyond the long grass, at the edges of the garden? It helps if you can plan your garden with a view to retiring from it gracefully. In this respect, different 'rooms' are easier to manage than the sort of garden which can be seen all at one go. Divide the garden into separate areas by tall shrubs, hedges or trellises with climbers. Then you can gradually relax the regime in one area at a time.

So next spring, as you sit in the sun and watch the birds, forget about the hoe and the hand trowel. Remember Miriam Rothschild and Hopkins instead.

12 February 2005

and Spring again . . .

March

Spring has come when you can
put your foot on seven daisies at once

Daisy: 'the day's eye'

A Windy Day

There are some days which feel like the seaside, wherever you are. A big sky, with a big boisterous wind, and high scudding clouds, grey and white. A spatter of stinging rain, then patches of blue sky and glancing shafts of sunlight extinguished as rapidly as they came, the light dimming and the wind picking up again as the next front blows in over the garden. It's no coincidence that the poet George Mackay Brown could capture weather better than anyone else: he was born, bred, lived and died among the islands of Orkney, where the weather can change four times in the course of an hour.

I've just been recovering from 'flu, and sometimes it seemed as if my only contact with the garden was what Mackay Brown called 'the endless ballet of the weather', glimpsed from my bedroom window. Weather is an integral part of the experience of gardening. It is one of the things I miss most when confined to the house. I miss the feel of it on my skin. I miss the sound and the smell and the taste of it: how you can tell what's only going to be a shower from a real downpour simply by how it smells; how you sometimes know it's raining before you see it or feel it, just from the sound of the rain on the leaves where you're working. When I lived in Canada I longed for English weather – for drizzly, misty, half-and-half sort of weather, instead of everlasting sunshine. There is a short story by Carol Shields in which the weather simply stops happening, and instead a sort of dreary numbness sets in. 'To live frictionlessly in the world,' the narrator writes, 'is to understand the real grief of empty space' ('Weather', in *Collected Stories*, Fourth Estate, 2004).

Part of the delight of weather is not just its infinite subtlety and variability, but the challenge of working out what comes next. One need never be bored with the weather to look at, even out of a bedroom window. Never heard of the 'crossed winds rule'? Alan Watts's slim paperback *Instant Weather Forecasting* (Adlard Coles Nautical, 1968) will explain all.

It was just such a day which tempted me into the garden again, still snuffling and coughing but pleased to be outside at last. As I dodged the showers, intermittently running for cover under the rambling roses in the tunnel, I could see that the late-flowering clematis, still unpruned, were already breaking bud. These are the *viticella* varieties and the blue descendants of 'Jackmanii' such as 'Perle d'Azur', scrambling about among the roses. The newly opened buds are lovely – plumes of soft and silvery grey-green – but I will harden my heart and chop them down to two or three buds, nevertheless. It does no harm to leave late-flowering clematis unpruned now and again, but eventually this leads to an untidy tangle of bare stems at the bottom, with all the flowers way out of reach, just where you can't see them. (One eminent clematis-grower told me he prunes with a baseball cap on at this time of year – not to protect himself, but so that he can't see all the new growth he is cutting off.)

While I have been laid up, I see that the garden has provided me with a very neat example of chaos theory. This is the theory which famously expounds how the beat of a butterfly's wings in the Amazon can cause a typhoon in China – or, in less emotive terms, how the slightest uncertainty (however small) in any physical system can lead to vast and unforeseen consequences. I have an underwater pump, which pumps the water in my Canal out through a series of filters and then back again, via a smaller round pool. The smaller pool has two overflow pipes which connect it to the Canal, set just under the stone coping in such a way that as the water rises to the brim of the smaller pool it doesn't overflow but flows instead via the pipes into the Canal. So far so good.

To economise on electricity, the pump is automatically timed to switch itself off at night. Some time during the autumn, a fallen oak leaf floated down into the smaller pond and in due course lodged itself in one of the pipes. An oak leaf, as you will perceive, has irregularly shaped lobes – wavy edges. Every time the pump switched itself on or off, the flow of water in the pipes reversed direction and the oak leaf changed its position. Sometimes those irregularly shaped lobes impeded the flow more, sometimes less. But eventually the day came (while I was laid up in bed, naturally) when the oak leaf shifted position enough to cause the water in the smaller pool to back up, overflow, and start to drain the whole Canal – all two thousand gallons of it.

6 March 2005

It Must Be Spring

It must be spring. The tempo has suddenly quickened. The first daffodils, the first white *Prunus* blossom (*P. cerasifera*, clipped into shapes in the Cloister Garden), the first lipstick-red peony shoots in the Rose Border, the first pulmonaria, all following one another in quick succession. I don't know what the pulmonaria's name is, but it makes a pool of vivid blue which I pass every morning on my way up the garden. I just call it John Long's pulmonaria. John was the person who gave it to me years ago. I suspect it may be a form of *Pulmonaria longifolia*, which has the same long narrow dark green leaves, spotted with white – but pulmonarias are very promiscuous creatures and as a result there are lots of intermediate sorts between the various species.

Our own native pulmonaria is the paler blue *P. officinalis*. The old country name here is 'Jerusalem cowslips', though as a child in Somerset I knew them as 'soldiers and sailors' because of the way they changed in colour from pink to blue. The first bit of the Latin name, *Pulmonaria*, and the English name, lungwort, both refer to the spots on the leaves, which were supposed to look like lungs. According to the seventeenth-century Doctrine of Signatures, this was a sign from the Almighty that the plant would be good for the treatment of lung troubles – hence the second part of the name, *officinalis*, which means used in medicine. (It is not in fact particularly efficacious, though the viscous juice obtained from the leaves does no harm, and may even have a soothing effect.) In the same way, the wrinkled hemispheres of walnut kernels were taken as a sign that they would be good for diseases of the brain. Pickled walnuts, anyone?

I suppose every garden has one: an elephants' graveyard of discarded labels. Mine is an old clay pot which sits on the end of the draining-board in the kitchen, a tangle of yellowing plastic and paper tags which functions as a sort of *memento mori* of the plants I loved and lost last year.

There's a high proportion of crocus labels in my elephants' graveyard. There's one for *Crocus imperati*, buff-coloured without, but a rich rosy lavender within. There's another one for the lovely old 'Scotch Crocus', also known as 'Cloth of Silver' (*C. biflorus*), which I grew in the form 'Alexandri', which has luscious dark grape-purple outer segments, edged with white, and pearly white inner segments. And a third for the honey-scented *C. angustifolius* (syn. *susianus*), also known as 'Cloth of Gold'. This one has burnished bronze-striped outer segments, curling back like coiled springs to reveal shining golden-yellow interiors, and I mourn its passing most of all.

It may be that the fault lies with my heavy soil. Most crocuses, after all, come from the drier parts of southern Europe and the eastern Mediterranean. But one crocus which does do well for me is *C. tommasinianus*, which comes from slightly further north, in the south of Hungary. In the wild the flowers vary in colour from a shimmering silvery grey through pale lilac-blue to deep amethyst, borne on long slender white stalks. In the garden here it seeds itself in multicoloured drifts all down my Rose Border, flowering in late winter under the bare brown stems of the rose trees. With their long white stockings, the crocuses remind me of the slim white ankles and dainty feet of my cat Grace, picking her way fastidiously beneath the bare branches of the same roses, en route for some thrush or blackbird's nest. The crocuses have the same sort of elegance and natural insouciance to weather and the laws of man that she has.

But don't be seduced by the named sorts, such as *C. tommasinianus* 'Ruby Giant' or 'Whitewell Purple'. The named sorts have larger flowers than the species but (probably because derived from a single clone) they tend all to come out at once, and they have none of the subtle colour variations which you find from flower to flower in the so-called 'unimproved' ones. Some of the named sorts also seem distinctly less willing to seed themselves around ('Ruby Giant' is itself sterile). So stick to the plain species, if you can find it. In the case of crocuses, bigger and brighter is not always better.

22 March 2003

Beginning Again

There's something incredibly exciting about that first whiff of mown grass. It's like the overture to Mozart's *Marriage of Figaro* – all that suppressed excitement and fizz, just waiting to explode like a magnum of champagne. It gives me butterflies in my stomach just thinking about it. Gardening's like that: every year the chance to make a fresh start, take off in a different direction, be someone new. Maybe this year I'll sow brilliant annuals everywhere, get the Vegetable Garden going again, succeed at last with *Clematis flammula*, grow a dozen different varieties of beans just for the hell of it.

Lady Day, 25 March, is a good time to start. Until the reform of the calendar in 1752 this used to be the start of the new year. Much more sensible to begin the year at the beginning of the growing season instead of in the deep midwinter. Lady Day is the Feast of the Annunciation – placed where it is in the calendar because it's nine months before Christmas Day – and many leases and agricultural tenancies are still reckoned from it (including my own here at Morville). So forget about last year's catastrophes. Start again: gardening is all about second chances.

The smell of the first hyacinth, like the first whiff of mown grass, is for me one of the most evocative in the garden, pinpointing the start of the gardening year as precisely as any fanfare of trumpets. A blue hyacinth, just beginning to open, its florets still lightly washed with green, a violet lustre at the tips giving a hint of the colour to come, releasing that inimitable fragrance on to the cold air. I can quite see why in the early eighteenth century they inspired a collecting mania almost as fevered as the tulipomania which gripped Holland in the 1630s. For me it has to be a blue hyacinth, though the current craze is for blacker-than-black varieties. Three hundred years ago the most favoured sorts were doubles, especially double whites with differently coloured 'eyes'. They drove eighteenth-century gardeners to a frenzy.

Most famous of these was 'King of Great Britain', a fully double white hyacinth with inner petals of red. It was thought that this, like all the other old hyacinths which appear in the Dutch flower paintings of the period, was now lost, but 'King of Great Britain' sold in huge numbers over a long period and may well have been exported to eastern Europe, where gardeners remained passionate about hyacinths long after they had dwindled into obscurity in this country. The break-up of the former USSR has meant a steady trickling back into this country of old varieties previously unknown or thought to be lost to cultivation. More than thirty varieties have been added to Alan Shipp's National Hyacinth Collection from contacts in Lithuania alone, and the collection now contains more than 170 different varieties – a far cry from the dozen or so that used to be available. Could 'King of Great Britain' still be out there too, waiting to be rediscovered? Could bicoloured double hyacinths be the next big thing?

The older sorts are taller and more slender and altogether more elegant than the modern ones, and they come in a rain-washed haze of colours. They stand up to the weather better, too. So if all that hyacinths mean to you is a pot of dumpy cylindrical flowers in a lurid shade of pink, prepare to be converted.

23 March 2002

Cats & Cardoons

What could I do? Waiting to collect one of my cats from the vet, my eye was caught by one of those notices. You know: 'Good Home Wanted'. I can usually resist, having two cats of my own and a third as a lodger. But this was different. Two brothers, fifteen years old, who had lost their elderly owner nearly two years ago and so far failed to find a home. A month later the notice was still there. As I said, what could I do?

The next day, Billy and Jack were installed in the front drawing-room, both vast and calm and silent – one grey, the other black – unlike my own demanding, noisy pair. But one of Jack's first actions was to spray the two big dried-flower arrangements which stand on the floor in opposite corners of the room, scent-marking them with his urine. The next morning, I came down to find one of the arrangements sprawled on the floor: seven-foot stems of cardoons with their tiny thistle-heads, leeks like footballs on sticks, flat artichoke flowers like giant sunflowers, tall branching heads of angelica, spiky eryngiums, the seed capsules of poppies – broken bits everywhere. Clearly either the dried flowers or the cats had to go.

They had woodworm anyway. I dragged them out through the front door and slung them on to the bonfire. They are all easy to grow and require no special treatment for drying. By next autumn (by which time Billy and Jack will, I hope, have learned better manners), I can replace them.

I grow the cardoons (*Cynara cardunculus*) amongst pink and purple roses, in the Rose Border. Given their height, they are best at the back, but it is rather exciting to have one or two further forward. Cardoons are really vegetables, but they would also look good in a mixed shrub border. They are perennial, and come into leaf early, before most woody things are stirring. Mine are under-planted with late winter bulbs like the green-leafed snowdrop *Galanthus ikariae* – one of the very last to flower – and pale purple and silver *Crocus tommasinianus*, with thickets of dusky pink and purple *Helleborus orientalis* hybrids in front. Later, their huge, soft, arching grey leaves are the perfect counterpoint to the rather stolid effect you tend to get with a lot of roses grown together, and their matt texture makes a good contrast to the smaller, rounder, shinier leaves of the roses. And then at the end of summer, just when everything is beginning to look jaded, they produce their electrifying violet-blue thistle-heads. They are not the sort of plants you can ignore.

They have a reputation for being slightly tender – they came originally from Italy – but in my experience this applies only to seedlings and small plants, not to established clumps. Mine were well into leaf at the beginning of the recent cold snap, and have come through without batting an eyelid. If they have a fault, it is that as the flower stems rise the lower leaves yellow and droop and collapse, but this can to some extent be camouflaged by their companions. And you can easily pull off the leaves as they decay.

The fact that my cardoons are in the Rose Border is – as with so much else in my garden – a happy accident. When I was start-ing the garden, I used to make a new series of beds every year, planting them in the first season with potatoes and things like runner beans and cardoons, to break up the soil before putting in the permanent residents. (Runner beans on wigwams of canes are an excellent way of giving height and structure to new beds: in the seventeenth and eighteenth centuries they were grown for their flowers, as climbers, long before anyone ever thought of eating them.) The potatoes and beans were harvested in due course, but

I liked the cardoons so much that they have stayed there ever since, with the roses growing up around them.

They are easily raised from seed – if you want to eat your cardoons you will need to do this every year in any case – and this is the time of year to do it. Start them in gentle heat (I do it on the kitchen window-sill) in late March or April, aiming to plant them out at the end of May. By October they will have made a fountain of big, deeply serrated leaves with wide succulent midribs. Blanch them by wrapping each plant in corrugated cardboard or straw matting; they will be ready in about six weeks. Eat the midribs – either raw, like a giant celery, or cut in pieces and gently stewed in butter, with an anchovy or cheese sauce. The thistle-heads are produced in the following year, but they are not usually eaten, unlike the cardoon's near relative, *Cynara scolymus*, the artichoke.

19 March 2005

Simple Pleasures

I find myself getting up earlier and earlier each day, intoxicated by the colours and shapes and smells of the spring. Every year it's like seeing it for the first time: the vibrant yellows and blues of daffodils and scillas, here and there the brilliant red of an early tulip, overhead the white foam of plum and pear blossom. The air is a tantalising multi-layered compound of scents: hyacinths, grass, the foxy stench of crown imperials, the aroma of moist sun-warmed soil (like hot-cross buns straight from the oven – yeasty, spicy, full of promise), the smell of daffodils, too – the aniseed of the big doubles, the mossy 'green' smell of the little wild *pseudonarcissus*, the freesia-like perfume of the double campernelles. Somehow I never really believe it will happen again, and when it does, my dreary winter spirits rise like the bubbles in champagne.

But there are quieter pleasures, too, at this time of year: the pleasures of re-establishing that quiet intimacy with the garden sometimes lost in the hurly-burly of winter when fingers freeze and the weather is too cold to stand and stare; the pleasures of lingering about a not-too-onerous task, allowing one's thought to drift and eddy like leaves in a water butt; the simple pleasures, in short, of tending a garden.

Watering, for example, can be the most exquisite of pleasures. In a pearly dawn, with the hose snaking in the dew behind, and all the day before you. Or on a fine spring evening, standing up straight for the first time, and leaning over backwards to stretch tired muscles, admiring the neatness of the newly weeded border or the rows of seed sowed that day, gently pottering about, watering as the golden light floods the garden. Or, best of all, late on a summer night, when the water from the hose is warmed by the day's heat and the activity is reduced to a sound (the hiss of the water) and a smell (wet earth), the arc of water occasionally catching the light from a street lamp or a lighted window, scattering into a million sparkling droplets.

I like grass-cutting, too. Up and down, backwards and forwards, each time a different slice of the garden, each time a slightly different view. Time to look. Time to consider. Would that penstemon look better over there? Would it be fun to cut a window in the hedge over here? And all the time that wonderful smell rising. And when finally it's finished, and the shadows are lengthening, and you stand back to admire your handiwork, the swallows come skimming the smooth green surface of the newly cut lawn like skaters on a vast green ice-rink.

I even like weeding. I like the close-up focus, nose to nose with the emerging aquilegias, like small purple and green primroses. I like the fact that at this time of year I can sit back on my heels in the sunshine and see through the borders which in high summer will become mysterious shady places – the strip between the yew hedge and the backs of the tallest shrub roses, the ground beneath the naked stems of the philadelphus and the soon-to-be forest of towering Michaelmas daisies. I like the repetitiveness of it, systematically working through a bed on hands and knees (one hand clean, one hand dirty), filling the bucket, the buckets filling the wheelbarrow, quietly on until the task is completed.

And this is, after all, why we garden, isn't it? Not to show off, or make money for charity or have somewhere to put the marquee when the eldest daughter marries, not to have flowers for cutting or vegetables for the table – though all those things bring pleasures of their own – but simply because we like doing it.

12 April 2003

APPENDIX

Recipes

Cassis

The recipe I use comes from Jane Grigson's *Fruit Book* (Penguin, 1983).

> 2 lb blackcurrants
> scant 2 pints reasonably good red wine
> about 3 lb sugar
> about 1½ pints brandy, gin or vodka

Soak the fruit and wine in a bowl for 48 hours. Put through a food processor, then tip into a straining-cloth or an old sheet draped over a large basin. Pull the cloth together and twist so as to wring out the liquid. (I use an old tea-towel firmly tied at the corners with string, suspended from the four upturned legs of a kitchen chair, and put the bowl beneath, between the legs. Then I leave it to drip overnight first, before wringing out.)

Measure the liquid, put it into a heavy pan, and to each pint of liquid add 1 lb sugar. Note the level. Stand it over a moderate heat and stir until the sugar has dissolved. Then regulate the heat so that the temperature stays above blood heat but well below simmering. Check the temperature every 15 minutes or so, to make sure. In about 2 hours the level will have gone down slightly and the liquid will be slightly syrupy. Leave to cool.

Add the brandy or whatever you are using in the ratio three measures of liquid to one of brandy, and bottle in screw-top spirit bottles. Keeps for years – if you can keep your hands off it that long . . .

Membrillo (quince paste)

An easy method of making quince paste. (The fruit is so hard and the cooking so long that making quince paste is enough of a labour without complicating the recipe. But the results more than compensate.) This makes a lovely firm paste which can be used in a number of different ways.

Quarter the fruit without peeling, and cut out the hard, gritty cores (which can be used separately to make jelly). Wash in cold water to remove the fur. Weigh the fruit, cover with water, and simmer until soft enough to mash to a pulp with a potato-masher. Stir in an equal weight of sugar and warm gently until the sugar dissolves, then bring to a rolling boil (the sugar will rise quite high in the pan). Cook, stirring all the time, until the paste changes colour from pale custard to dark red. Do not let it stick to the bottom or it will burn. Continue cooking until the paste is thick enough to come away from the sides of the pan. (This can take a couple of hours, so you may want to do it in relays with other members of the family.) Take care to wear long sleeves and cover your hand with a cloth to prevent burns, because the thicker the paste gets, the more likely it is to burp violently over you like hot porridge.

Pot up into warmed jam-jars and cover while still hot. Serve with sharp white cheese such as Wensleydale, or in place of redcurrant jelly with lamb or game, or stir into any dish containing apples. A teaspoon also makes a splendid addition to gravies.

For a special treat, go on cooking the paste until very thick: you should be able to pull it away from the bottom as well as the sides of the pan. Turn it out into a shallow straight-sided dish, making a layer about one inch thick; when cold, put in a very low oven (the plate-warming compartment of the cooker is ideal, or failing that, the airing cupboard) for several hours until quite solid. Cut into squares and store in an airtight container in the fridge. Keeps for years. Serve with dessert or as a sweetmeat.

Scones

A foolproof recipe for garden openings, guaranteed to rise even though your mind may be on other things.

Makes about a dozen scones.

1 lb plain flour
2 teaspoons bicarbonate of soda
4 teaspoons cream of tartar
2 teaspoons sugar
4 oz soft margarine
a scant half-pint of milk
sultanas (if liked)

Sift the flour with the bicarbonate of soda and cream of tartar. Add the sugar and cut in the margarine. (Having rather warm hands, I do it with a steel pastry-blender, which keeps the mixture light.) Add a few sultanas if liked. The amount of liquid rather depends on the flour you are using: if you keep the mixture on the dry side, the scones will keep their shape better; if you use a wetter mixture, the scones will bubble up delightfully like miniature summer thunder-clouds, but they won't be so easy to slice. Gather the mixture on to a pastry board and roughly pat into shape. Cut into thick rounds (an inch and a half or two inches thick) with a pastry-cutter, and brush the tops with milk. Arrange on a greased baking tray and bake at 425°F (220°C) for about ten minutes, until beginning to colour.

Allow to cool. Cut in half horizontally and spread with clotted cream, then add a dollop of home-made jam (or do it the other way round if you prefer).

These scones are so delicious that you are unlikely to have any left over, but if you do, you can freeze them (though they are so much more delicious freshly baked, and so easy to make, that it scarcely seems worthwhile).

Hints on home-made jam

For the most luscious home-made jam with the most intense flavour, pick a combination of ripe and less-ripe fruit and add as little water as possible. Soft fruit like raspberries, which need no cooking, can be made into jam with no water at all: simply fold the sugar into the fruit and gently warm until the juice starts to run. If you have had a glut of fruit such as blackcurrants or damsons and have frozen some of it, you can also often get away without using any water at all, as the freezing process will have tenderised the fruit. Adding the sugar right at the beginning helps to preserve the shape of very soft fruit such as raspberries or strawberries. As a rule of thumb, for fruits which set well (acid fruits such as blackcurrants, damsons, etc.) add 3 lb sugar to each 2¼ or 2½ lb prepared fruit, depending on ripeness. The acid in slightly unripe fruit combines with the pectin (the setting agent present in varying amounts in all fruit, but especially in acid ones) to set more sugar than ripe or over-ripe fruit. For fruits which set less well (such as raspberries), the proportion is about a pound per pound; and if the jam obstinately refuses to set, the addition of a little lemon juice often helps. I find strawberry jam almost impossible to get right: the best taste (simply strawberries and sugar – no water – in the proportion of 3¼ lb fruit to 3 lb sugar) often produces a runny (though delicious) result – more a conserve than a jam – which tends to drip down your chin as you eat. You can make strawberry jam set by adding home-made apple pectin (a good use for windfall apples) or the juice from a quarter-pound of cooked redcurrants or gooseberries, but I feel it never quite tastes the same. I prefer to eat my strawberries straight from the garden – usually standing in the strawberry patch.

Summer pudding

Not really cooking at all, but what summer is complete without at least one summer pudding?

Line a large pudding basin with overlapping slices of day-old white bread minus the crusts, keeping a few pieces back to make the lid. Mix together whatever soft fruit you have – traditionally raspberries, blackcurrants and redcurrants (the idea is to have a sparkling jewel-like mixture of red and black fruits which will contrast with the white of the bread) – add sugar to taste, then gently warm until the juice starts to run. Fill the pudding bowl with the fruit, reserving some of the juice to pour over the pudding when you serve it. Place the remaining pieces of bread on top as a lid. Chill overnight. Turn out on to a deep plate, and pour the reserved juice over – or use cassis instead (see above). Serve with double cream.

Addresses

Seed & Plant Suppliers

Louisa Arbuthnott Stone House Cottage Nursery, Stone, nr Kidderminster, Worcestershire DY10 4BY
www.shcn.co.uk

Barnhaven Primroses 11 rue du Pont Blanc, 22310 Plestin Les Grèves, France
www.barnhavenprimroses.com

Pat & Nick Bean Springfields Fresh Produce (Manorbier) Ltd., Manorbier, Tenby, Pembrokeshire SA70 7SL
www.springfieldsdaffodils.co.uk

Chiltern Seeds Bortree Stile, Ulverston, Cumbria LA12 7PB

The Eckford Sweet Pea Society of Wem Lyndale, Nook Lane, Weston-under-Redcastle, Shropshire SY4 5LP

Thompson & Morgan Poplar Lane, Ipswich, Suffolk IP8 3BU
www.thompson-morgan.com

Wakefield and North of England Tulip Society Priory Lodge, Leeds Road, Harrogate, North Yorkshire HG2 8AA

National Plant Collections

Agapanthus

Mr & Mrs Dick Fulcher, Pine Cottage, Fourways, Eggesford, nr Chumleigh, Devon EX18 7QZ. Tel. 01769 580076. Open mid July to end August, Monday to Saturday, other times by appointment.

Hyacinthus orientalis

Mr A. K. Shipp, 9 Rosemary Road, Waterbeach, Cambridge CB25 9NB. Tel. 01223 571064. Open day: last weekend in March, and by appointment.

Lupinus

(Russell introductions): Mrs P. Edwards, Swallow Hayes, Rectory Road, Albrighton, Wolverhampton, West Midlands, WV7 3EP. Tel. 01902 372624. Open by appointment.

(Westcountry Lupin cvs): Mrs S. Conibear, Westcountry Nurseries, Donkey Meadow, Woolsery, Bideford, Devon EX39 5QH. Tel. 01237 431111. Open daily March to end July.

Primula

(British floral variants). Dr M. Webster, 18 Lye Mead, Winford, Bristol, Somerset BS40 8AU. Tel. 01275 472818. Open by appointment.

Others

Contact Plant Heritage (the working title for the National Council for the Conservation of Plants and Gardens)
12 Home Farm, Loseley Park, Guildford, Surrey GU3 1HS. Tel. 01483 44754. *www.plantheritage.com*
email: info@plantheritage.org.uk

Acknowledgements

Thanks first of all to Mirabel Osler, for her gaiety and good friendship, and for her example as both gardener and writer. Also to my agent Felicity Bryan for suggesting my name to Jane Wheatley of *The Times*, and to Jane for taking on a completely new and untried columnist; I learned a very great deal from both of them. Also to Annie Gatti, then Gardens Editor of *The Times*, for her unfailing kindness and tact; Sandy Saunders for accompanying me on many of the trips described here and for gardening while I wrote; and Ken Swift, as always, for his encouragement and for making the initial selection of columns upon which this book is based. Thanks too to all the neighbours and friends at Morville who appear in the column: in particular John, Mary & Jamie Begg, Elizabeth Bacon, Bridget Chappuis, Chris & Sara Douglas, Alison Foxall, the late Natalie Hodgson, Barry & Joy Jenkinson, John & Brenda Lane, the late John Long, the late Joyce Needham, and Pat, Ian & Arthur Rowe. Thanks also to Graham Morris, Mike Suter and Julia Williamson. Also to John & Merrilyn Coutouvidis, Rosemary Duffy, John James, Andrew Lawson, Harriet & Iris Strachan, Jim Partridge & Liz Walmsley, Charlotte Petherick, David Vincent, Jean Wallace and David Wassell. For technical help, thanks to Louisa Arbuthnott for information on climbing plants, Crawford

Balch and Roger Norman on willows, Avril Cliff on cut flowers, Andy Devine on lilies, Alan Shipp on hyacinths, Steve Thompson on tulips, Dr Jonathan Briggs & Stanley Yapp on mistletoe, Margaret Webster on anomalous primulas, and Dr Phil Gates, Prof. Alastair Fitter and Tim Sparks for explaining about phenology. Thanks also to Jane Sebire for a year of photographs, Dawn Burford for the plant portraits and Reginald Piggott for the maps. Finally, thanks to the team at Bloomsbury, especially Bill Swainson, Emily Sweet and Anna Simpson, for making this book happen.

Index

Acadia, 273
Aesop, 126–7
aestivation, 185
Aethelflaed, Lady of the Mercians, 44
Afghanistan, 248
agapanthus, 35, 37–8, 117–19, 176, 213–14, 265, 304
Albrighton, 95
Aldebaran, 154
alder, 225
alexanders, 53, 169
Alison (Foxall) *see* Foxall, Alison
alliums, 86, 182–3, 208
allotments, 144
Alma-Tadema, Sir Lawrence, 38
almonds, 223
Alnwick, 254–5
alstromerias, 117
amelanchiers, 64, 223
American Declaration of Independence, 196
Andromeda, 154
Andronicus of Cyrrhus, 241
anemones, 28–9
angelica, 53
Anglesey Abbey, 262
Anson, George, Lord Anson, 16
Anthemis punctata, 177
Apollo, 84, 191–2
apple orchards, 157–8, 222–3
apple wood, 225
apples, 22, 124–5, 143, 180–2, 194, 260
 'Lord Derby', 181–2
 windfalls, 186, 194, 218, 221, 301
aquilegias, 34, 66, 111, 294
Arbuthnott, Louisa, 129–30, 303
Arcadia, 273–4
archaeophytes, 263
argyranthemums, 213
artemisias, 66
artichokes, 169, 292
ash, 112, 268–9
Ashton Wold, 276
Astley Abbots, 132

Athens, Tower of the Winds, 241
Atkinsons perfumiers, 179
Aunt Judy's Magazine, 250
auriculas, 41–3
Aurora Borealis, 232
Austin, David, 81, 87
Avon, river, 183, 238

back gardens, 143–4
Bacon, Elizabeth, 229–31
badgers, 126, 220–1
balm, 105
bamboos, 275
bananas, 214, 239
Banks, Sir Joseph, 76–8
Barnard Castle, 172
Barnsley house Garden, 242
Barrow-in-Furness, 179
Barry (Jenkinson) *see* Jenkinson, Barry
bats, 74, 147
Bean, Nick and Pat, 7, 303
beans, 66, 144, 197, 288
 broad beans, 81, 260
 runner beans, 291
bee candy, 226–7
bees, 50, 71, 74, 105, 131–3, 146–8, 160–1, 185–6, 259–60
Begg, John, 180
Begg, Mary, 64
Bellême, Robert de, 44
Belloc, Hilaire, 62, 187
Belmont Abbey, 120
Beltane, 236
Ben Nevis, 276
bergenia, 229
Bernhardt, Sarah, 215
Bible, 177
Billingsly, Colonel, 44
birch, 112, 225
 silver birch, 199
bittercress, 32, 82
black fruit salad, 123
black lovage, 53

black spot, 10, 73, 80, 90
blackberries, 167
blackbirds, 120, 129, 167, 186, 220–1
blackcurrants, 105–6, 122–4
blackthorn, 30–1, 49
'blackthorn winter', 49
blue cedar, 230
bluebells, 51–3, 60, 136
Bodnant, 59
bonfires, 235–7
Books of Hours, 271
Bowden, Mr, 238–9
box, 167, 207, 244
Box of Delights, The, 224
'bread and roses', 177–8
Bridget (Chappuis) *see* Chappuis, Bridget
Briggs, Jonathan, 222–3
Bristol Channel, 85
British Colour Council, 174
Brittany, 262
Brown Clee, 49
Brussels sprouts, 144, 168
Buchan, Alexander, 78
buddleia, 270, 276
Buildwas Abbey, 275
bullfinches, 11
Buscot Park, 59–60
Bute, 171
butterflies, 185–6, 213, 276
    fritillaries, 38–9, 270
    gatekeepers, 137
    peacock, **141**, 185
red admirals, 150, 152, 186

cabbages, 144, 197
Caersws, 55
Cajun, 273
calendar, reform of, 51
camassias, 53, 137, 208
Cambrai, battle of, 145
camellias, 143, 230–1, 275
campanulas, 33, 97, 109
campions, 270
cancer drugs, 162–3, 223
Candlemas, 259–60, 264
candles, 259–60
cannas, 118
Capra, Frank, 225
cardoons, 99, 148, 290–2
carnations, 29, 108, 219, 230
Cassini-Huygens space probe, 251
Cassiopeia, 154
cassis, 123, 297–8
Castle Bromwich Hall, 266–7
cats, 17–18, 94, 105, 124, 152, 180, 213, 225,
    244, 287, 290
ceanothus, 268

celandines, 32–3, 98
Cephalaria gigantea, 109
Cepheus, 154
Ceylon, 273
chaos theory, 284–5
Chappuis, Bridget, 13, 97, 124
Charles I, King, 44
Charles II, King, 249
Chaucer, Geoffrey, 55, 169
Chelsea Flower Show, 62, 64, 95
cherries, 54–6, 157, 174
    cherry blossom, 30, 54–5, 64
Chiltern Seeds catalogue, 238–40, 303
Chris (Douglas) *see* Douglas, Chris
Christmas box, 231
Christmas Carol, A, 225
Christmas roses, **211**, 230
chrysanthemums, 28–9, 219
Clayton, John, 273
Cleese, John, 95
clematis, 97, 147, 251, 288
    Clematis vitalba, **233**, 248–51
    'Lady Betty Balfour', 149–50
    pruning, 284
Clifford, George, 273
cloud types, 155
cobnuts, 167
cockspur thorn, 185, 199
cocoa, 272
Cocteau, Jean, 170
coffee, 50
coltsfoot, 270
columbine, 33–4, 271
Common Ground, 158
Conibear, Sarah, 96, 304
Constable, John, 155
Cook, Captain James, 76–7
coppicing, 27
Corinth, 123
cornflowers, 161, 271
Cornford, Frances, 144
Corsica, 168
Corve Dale, 238
Cosmos astrosanguineus, 152
cottage gardens, 104–6
couch grass, 32
courgettes, 132
cow parsley, 82
cowslips, 12–13, 66
crab apples, 97
cranesbills, 137
Crassula helmsii, 264
crocuses, 133, 194, 286–7, 291
crown imperials, **23**, 40–1, 208, 292
Cumberland, 31
Cunnery, the, 67
Cupressocyparis leylandii, 230

currants, 123–4, 247
cycads, 239

daffodils, 6–9, 136, 208, 268, 285, 292
  Narcissus obvallaris (Tenby daffodil), 6–8
  Narcissus poeticus, 137
  Narcissus pseudonarcissus, 8
dahlias, 29, 64, 118–19, 148, 152, 174, 185, 194, 266
daisies, 271, **281**
  ox-eye daisies, 276–7
  see also Michaelmas daisies
damsons, 31–2, 54, 122, 157
dandelions, 215, 260
Dark Is Rising, The, 225
Day, Doris, 95
D-Day landings, 274
Dee, river, 96
Delaney, Mrs, 58
delphiniums, 176
Dench, Judi, 246
Depp, Johnny, 249
depression, 83, 90
Derby, Lord, 181–2
Devine, Andy, 245
dianthus, 106, 261–2
diaries, 227–8
Dillon, Helen, 177
Dobson, Frank, 251
Dobson, Zuleika, 121, 123
Doctrine of Signatures, 286
dogwoods, 243
dormancy, 269
Douglas, Chris, 43
Douglas, Sara, 43, 64
Dower House garden
  Canal Garden, 9, 36, 75, 86, 120, 135, 148, 152, 199, 202, 207–8, 217, 244, 285
  Cloister Garden, 10, 12, 14, 56, 245, 285
  Ivy Garden, 5, 17
  Kitchen Border, 86
  Knot Garden, 49, 67, 86, 185
  Lammas Meadow, 97, 137
  Nuttery, 12, 136, 152, 194, 199, 259
  Orchard, 218
  Plat, 38, 152
  plates-bandes, 38, 75, 207–8
  Plum Walk, 136, 152
  Rose Border, 32, 38, 74, 97–9, 110, 184, 285, 287, 290–1
  Snowdrop Walk, 136
  Temple, 64, 202–3
  Turf Maze, 61, 64, 66, 163, 217, 244–5
  Vegetable Garden, 65–6, 75, 288
  Wild Garden, 10, 20, 36, 80–2, 98, 109–10, 136–7, 152, 183–4, 208, 245
dragonflies, 152

dried flowers, 107, 183
dried fruit, 123–4
Druids, 164, 223
Dunnett, Nigel, 160
Duthie, Ruth, 18
Dylan, Bob, 240

earthworms, 220–1
earwigs, 148
East Indies, 197, 273
Ebley, 158
echiums, 143, 239
Eckford, Henry, 103
edelweiss, 239
Edinburgh, 191
Edward I, King, 50
Edwards, Pat, 95, 304
eglantines, 79–81, 87, 200
elder, 112, 220
Elizabeth I, Queen, 79–80
elm, 157–8
emmenagogues, 263
Endeavour, 76–8
English Heritage, 151
Epicurus, 193
eryngiums, **91**, 94–5, 99
escallonias, 231
estrades, 32
eucryphias, 35
euonymus, 43
euphorbias, 52–3, 86, 110
Evelyn, John, 169
Ewing, Julia Horatia, 250

false acacia, 223
false bishop's weed, 161
Fanthorpe, U. A., 89
Faringdon, Lord, 59
Farrer, Reginald, 84
fascicularia, 213
Fawkes, Guy, 235–6
fences, willow, 26
feverfew, 34, 106, 111, 176
fiddleneck, 161
filberts, 167, 183
Finlay, Ian Hamilton, 113, 191–3
Fish, Margery, 127
Fish, Michael, 240
Fitter, Alastair, 270
Fitter, Richard, 270
flamingoes, 274
florist's feasts, 58
'florist's flowers', 18, 29
flower-arranging, 178–9
Floyd, William H. M., 100
footbridges, 169–72
Forrest, George, 272

Forster, E. M., 227, 229
forsythia, 248
Fortune, Robert, 248
Fountains Abbey, 151, 275
fox-and-cubs, 97
Foxall, Alison, 64
foxes, 126–7, 220
foxgloves, 33, 74–6, 98, 109, 111, 117, 276
French lilac, 105
Friedrich, Caspar David, 155
fritillaries, 39–41, 137
    crown imperials, 23, 40–1, 208, 292
    snake's head fritillaries, 39–40, 64
frost, 244–5
fruit trees, pruning, 124–5
fuchsias, 28, 143, 246
Fulcher, Dick, 265, 303
fungi, 149

Galega, 105, 176
gallygaskins, 13
Gansu, 84
Garbo, Greta, 59
Garden of Eden, 120–1
Garden of Paradise, The, 85–6
garlic, 168
Gates, Phil, 269
gentians, 35
George I, King of the Hellenes, 201–2
George IV, King, 19
geraniums, 111, 174, 176, 207, 277
Gerard, John, 39, 250, 262, 267
germander, 86
Gilbert, W. S., 26
Gildas, 85
gillyflowers, 108
ginger lily, 213–14
Giraldus Cambrensis, 7
Girnigoe, 231
gladdons, 195
gladioli, 195
Glastonbury, 93
Glastonbury thorn, 51
Glendurgan, 274
Goethe, Johann Wolfgang von, 155
goldenrod, 109
gooseberries, 115, 126
Gowbarrow Park, 8
Graham (Morris) see Morris, Graham
grapes, 122, 126–7
grass-cutting, 136–7, 277, 293
grasses, 109, 270
gravestones, 252–3
Grayling, Anthony, 81
Great Dixter, 118
Green, Charles, 77–8
Greenwich Mean Time, 62

Grolier, Jean, 99
ground elder, 32–3
groundsel, 32
guelder roses, 174, 200
guinea fowl, 39
gunnera, 275
Gunning, John, 62

Hadrian's Wall, 14
Halley, Edmond, 77
Hallowe'en, 89, 236
Hampton Court, Herefordshire, 161
Hampton Park, 224
Harber, David, 62
Hardenpont, Abbé Nicolas, 159
Hardy, Thomas, 145
Hardy Plant Society, 251
harebells, 276
Harrison, John, 16
hawk moths, 185–6
hawkweed, 137
hawthorn, 31, 112, 223, 268
hazels, 165, 168, 199, 220, 259
heartsease, 271
heathers, 133
hedge hebes, 231
hedgehogs, 220–1
hellebores, 33, 81, 133, 211, 230, 244, 247, 291
Helston, river, 274
Henry I, King, 44
Henry VII, King, 79
Henry VIII, King, 248
herbaceous borders, 109
herbaria, 272–3
Hermann, Paul 273
Hermodactylus tuberosa, 266–7
Herne the Hunter, 225
Herrick, Robert, 54
Heywood, John, 25
Hibbert, Major and Mrs Tony, 274
hibernation, 185–6
Hodgson, Natalie, 49, 132–3
Hogg's Fruit Manual, 204
hogweeds, 98–9, 109–10
    giant hogweed, 110, 263–4
holly, 174, 220, 222, 226, 230, 244
hollyhocks, 122
Holy Saturday, 20
Homer, 182
honey, 50, 167, 260
honeysuckles, 130, 135, 174, 220
Hopkins, Gerard Manley, 52, 275, 278
Horace, 54
horehound 13–14
hornets, 186
horse chestnut, 58, 199, 268

horseradish, 105
Horticultural Colour Chart, 174
hose-in-hose, 13
house martins, 113, 129, 154
houseleeks, 74
Housman, A. E., 54–5
Howard, Luke, 155
Hudson's Bay, 96
hyacinths, 35, 208, 219, 288–9, 292, 304
   'King of Great Britain', 289
hydrangeas, 143, 148, 275
hyssop, 14, 266

Ian (Rowe) *see* Rowe, Ian
Igarka, 100
immune system, 148–9
indigenous plants, 263
Inula hookeri, 137
irises, 27, 137, 194–6, 245, 267, 271
   Iris foetidissima, **189**, 194–6
ivy, 102, 226, 229

jackanapes, 13
jackdaws, 32, 213
jack-in-the-green, 13
Jackson, Maria Margaretta, 101
Jamaica, 272
James, John, 44, 46
James, M. R., 242
jam-making, 134–5, 300–1
Japanese knotweed, 263–4
Japanese moss gardens, 20–1
japonica, 223
jasmine, 120, 129, 146, 154, 248
   winter jasmine, 231, 247–8
Jebb, Eglantyne, 81
Jefferson, Thomas, 196–8
Jekyll, Gertrude, 177, 216
Jenkinson, Barry, 43,64
Jenkinson, Joy, 43
Jerusalem cowslips, 286
Jerusalem sage, 230
Jervaulx Abbey, 275
John (Begg) *see* Begg, John
John (Lane) *see* Lane, John
Joseph, Jenny, 276
Joy (Jenkinson) *see* Jenkinson, Joy
Julia (Williamson) *see* Williamson, Julia
juniper, 226, 237
Juvenal, 177

Kent, 55
Kerrachar, 36
Kew Gardens, 78
Kipling, Rudyard, 215

laburnums, 110, 223

Ladies' Companion to the Flower Garden, The, 101
Lady Day, 288
lady's lace, 60, 136
landscape gardens, 151, 170
larch, 225
Lane, John, 49
lavender, 86, 120, 131–3, 146–8, 154, 176,
   182, 185
Lawrence, Felicity, 168
Lawrence, Massachusetts, 177
Lawson, Andrew, 174, 193
leeks, 8–9, 168, 182
Leigh Hunt, James Henry, 99–100
Lenten roses, 230, 268
leopard's bane, 110–11
Lerwick, 236
leucojums, 64, 136, 259, 268
Levens, 59
Library of Congress, 196
lichens, 251–3
lightning, 73–4
lilies, 35, 57, 102, 106, 120, 176, 208, 213–14,
   219
   Lilium longiflorum, 5–6, 122, 184
   preparing bulbs, 245–6
   repotting, 265
   Turk's-cap lily, 86
   white lilies, 122
lily beetles, 81, 184
lily of the valley, 216
lime, 223–4, 260
limestone, 252
Linaria, 161, 176
Linnaeus, Carl, 76, 78, 155
lion's claw and lion's ear, 239
lisianthus, 102
Lithuania, 289
Little Sparta, 191–3
Lloyd, Christopher, 118, 277
Loach, Ken, 178
lobelias, 38, 118, 152
Logue, Christopher, 182
London
   cherry stones, 55
   forgotten rivers, 89
   mistletoe populations, 223–4
Long, John, 286
longitude, 16–17
Louisiana, 273
love-lies-bleeding, 102
Lucknow, siege of, 98
lupins, 95–6, 304
Lychnis, 33, 266
Lycium, 239

Mackay Brown, George, 283

Madonna and Child paintings, 10, 86, 260–1
magnolias, 64, 273–5
mahonia, 248
Malkovich, John, 249
mallows, 33
Malory, Thomas, 170
Malvern, 158
Manchester College, Oxford, 104
mandrakes, 85, 110
Manila galleon, 16
Manorbier, 7
maples, 112, 199–200, 219, 223, 273
Maplett, John, 25
marigolds, 38, 75, 219
   corn marigolds, 161
marjoram, 86, 106
Mark (Walker) see Walker, Mark
marrows, 104
Mars, 154
Marshall, John, 46
Marvell, Andrew, 54, 56
Mary (Begg) see Begg, Mary
Mary Magdalene, 20
'Mary's tears', 41
May, Reg, 13
mazzard, 55
meconopsis, 35
medlars, 199
Mekong–Salween divide, 272
melancholy thistle, 112
membrillo, see quince paste
Merlin, 7
Michaelmas daisies, 27, 109, 117, **141**, 154,
   185, 194, 273, 294
Midsummer, 61, 88–90, 235–6
migration, 269
Mikado, The, 26
Milky Way, 135
Milne, A. A., 170
mistletoe, 219–20, 222–4, 226, 230, 237
moats, 67
mock orange, 103
Molyneux, Robert, 76, 78
Monet, Claude, 227
monkshood, 110
Montes de Toledo, 7
Monticello, 196–8
moon, phases of, 229
morello cherries, 129
Morris, Graham, 219
Morville Flower Festival, 43, 63–5
mosaic viruses, 57, 95
mosses, 20–2
moths, 148, 185–6
Mount Etna, 272
mountain avens, 35
Mozart, Wolfgang Amadeus, 288

mulberries, 9, 202–4
mushrooms, 167
myrobalan, 30–1, 54
myrtles, 150, 207, 213–14

Napoleon Bonaparte, 51
nasturtiums, 38, 75, 207
National Trust, 73–4, 151, 242–3, 247, 274
Natural History Museum, 272–3
Nemophila, 101
neophytes, 263
newts, 213
Nicholas I, Tsar, 202
Nicholson, William, 215–17
Nick (Watkins) see Watkins, Nick
nicotianas, 38, 122, 147–8, 184
Nootka Sound, 96
Normandy, 274
Northumberland, Duchess of, 254
Nova Scotia, 273

oak, 172, 223, 268–9
oilseed rape, 50
O'Keeffe, Georgia, 247
old man's beard, 249–50
Old Red Sandstone, 175
Olearia, 231
Olga, Queen, 201–2
olive trees, 27, 197
onions, 168
open field agriculture, 11
Oppenheim, James, 178
orache, 161
oranges, 49–50, 86, 120, 207, 213–14
orchards, 157–8
orchids, 35
Orkney, 96, 231–2, 254, 283
Ottery St Mary, 237
Ouse, river, 238
Oxford University, 272
oxlips, 12, 19

Paeon, 84
Painswick Rococo Garden, 205–6
Palm Sunday, 25
palm trees, 143, 275
   sago palm, 239–40
   Windamere palm, 239
pansies, 243
papavers, 122
paper-clips, 227
Parkinson, John, 44, 250, 267
Parkinson, Sydney, 76, 78
Partridge, Jim, 170–2
Pat (Rowe) see Rowe, Pat
pear orchards, 157–8
pearlwort, 21

pears, 49, 124–5, 156–9, 199, 221, 223, 260
  pear blossom, 49, 54, 64, 292
  perry pears, 159
  warden pears, 158
peas, 66, 197, 217
pelargoniums, 106
penstemons, 127–8
Pentland Firth, 254
Penzance, Lord, 80–1
peonies, 27, 84–5, 285
perry, 159
Perseids, 135
Petherick, Charlotte, 230
Peto, Harold, 59
petunias, 148–9
Pevsner, Sir Nikolaus, 164
Phacelia tanacetifolia, 161
pheasants, 220
phenology, 269
philadelphus, 294
Philip, Prince, 202
phillyrea, 207, 213
'Pictorial Meadows', 160–1
pine, 226
pinks, 182, 260–2
Plant*for*Life, 83
plums, 30–2, 148, 150, 157, 184, 223, 292
  plum blossom, 30–2, 54, 64, 156, 285, 292
pollarding, 27
pollination, 132, 260
pollution, 253
polyanthus, 3, 12, 18–19
Polygonum forrestii, 272
poplars, 223, 267–8
poppies, 34, 122, 174, 217, 276
Porthpean, 230
Post Transcriptional Gene Silencing, 149
potatoes, 121, 237, 266, 291
Potter, Beatrix, 65
Poussin, Nicolas, 274
Pre-Raphaelites, 79
Prichard, George, 101
primroses, 12–13, 19, 49, 106, 136, 268, 294, 304
Prior, Maddy, 25
Proust, Marcel, 267
prunes, 124
pruning
  clematis, 284
  fruit trees, 124–5
  myrtles, 150
  roses, 14–16, 37, 150, 264–5
  wisterias, 10–11
pulmonarias, 133, 285–6

quince paste (membrillo), 214–15, 298–9

rabbits, 65–7
ragwort, 272, 276
raisins, 123
ramsons, 86
ranunculus, 28–30
Raphael, 260
raspberries, 120, 134, 207
Reg (May) *see* May, Reg
rhododendrons, 263, 275
rice, 197
robins, 220
Robinson, William, 109–10
Rock, Joseph, 84
Romans, 14, 55, 157, 177, 181, 261, 263
rose of Sharon, 90
rose-hips, 135, 152, 174, 184
roses, 9–10, 35, 96–8, 103–4, 106, 111, 146, 154, 207, 246, 271, 294
  Bourbon roses, 102
  eglantines (*Rosa rubiginosa*) 79–81, 87
  English Roses, 88
  moss roses, 87, 120
  musk roses (*Rosa moschata*), 79, 130, 185, 207
  old roses, 15, 103–4, 122, 173–4
  pegging down, 15
  Portland roses, 15, 174, 207
  pruning, 14–16, 37, 150, 264–5
  rambling roses, 15, 194
  Rosa banksiae, 43, 64, 150
  Scarmanising, 93–4
  scents, 87–8
  tea roses, 88, 149–50
roses (varieties)
  'Adélaïde d'Orléans', 9, 98, 103
  'Baltimore Belle', 15
  'Blush Noisette', 106, 174
  'Climbing Lady Hillingdon', 149–50
  'Eglantyne', 81
  'Jacques Cartier', 174
  'Königin von Dänemark' ('Queen of Denmark'), 14, 207
  'New Dawn', 71
  'Paul's Himalayan Musk', 36–7
  'Princesse de Nassau', 130
  'Rambling Rector', 36–7, 98, 130
  'Russelliana', 9–10
  St Mark's rose ('Rose D'Amour'), 112
  'William Lobb', 15
Rothschild, Miriam, 276, 278
Rousseau, Jean-Jacques, 193
rowan, 97, 112, 126, 223
Rowe, Ian, 42, 63
Rowe, Pat, 64, 109
Royal Horticultural Society, 76, 125, 174, 228, 254, 272
Royal Meteorological Society, 269

Royal Society, 77
Rozel, 172
rue, 110
Rules of the Shepherd of Banbury, The, 241
Russell, George, 95
Ryton Organic Gardens, 62

Sackville-West, Vita, 52, 117, 127, 156
    her writing-table, 246–7
SAD syndrome, 185
Saiho-ji temple, 20–2
'saining', 89–90, 223, 236–7
St Aelred of Hexham, 228
St David's Day, 7–8
St Gervais' Day, 153
St John the Baptist, 89, 236
St John's wort, 90
Saint-Just, Louis Antoine de, 191–2
St Mary Magdalene's Day, 153
St Peter, 241
St Petersburg, 202
St Swithun's Day, 153
St Thomas Aquinas, 228
salsify, 97, 169
Samhain, 236
sandstone, 252–3
Santayana, George, 182
Sara (Douglas) *see* Douglas, Sara
Sarcococca humilis, 231
Sargent, John Singer, 86
Save the Children Fund, 81
Scarman, John, 93–4
Schongauer, Martin, 86
Schwartz, Delmore, 41
scillas, 292
Scilly Isles, 17, 35, 36, 143
scones, 299–300
scorpion weed, 161
scorzonera, 169
Scott, Sir Walter, 80
sea holly, 109
senecio, 102, 231, 272
Severn, river, 158, 238
Shakespeare, William
    All's Well That Ends Well, 246
    Hamlet, 26
    Henry V, 8–9
    A Midsummer Night's Dream, 79, 89
    Othello, 26
Sheeler, Jessie, 193
Shelley, Percy Bysshe, 79, 155
Shelsey Walsh, 268
Shenstone, William, 193
shepherd's purse, 82
Shields, Carol, 283
Shipp, Alan, 289, 304
shooting stars, 208

Shovell, Sir Cloudesley, 17
Siberia, 83, 100, 261
silage, 132
Silesia, 51
Sirius, the Dog Star, 117
Sissinghurst, 156, 242, 246
Skimmia japonica, 230
Sloane, Sir Hans, 272–3
sloes, 30–1, 54, 64, 122, 167
slugs, 184, 201
snails, 148, 184
snake's head, 266
snake's head fritillaries, 39–40, 64
snowdrops, 201–2, 244, 247, **257**, 262–4, 291
Sobel, Dava, 17
Solander, Daniel, 76
soldiers and sailors, 286
Sparks, Tim, 269
Spicer, Harold, 104
spindle, 200, 220
Spöring, Herman, 78
spruce, 226
Spry, Constance, 178–9
Stauntonia hexaphylla, 129–30
Steep Holm, 85
stephanotis, 102
stocks, 106–9, 216
Stone House Cottage, 129
stonecrop, 74
Stonehenge, 89
Strait of Magellan, 16
strawberries, 105, 120, 132, 271
streptocarpus, 207, 213
Studley Royal, 151, 153
Stukeley, Rev. William, 223
sugar, 50–1
sultanas, 123
sumachs, 143
summer pudding, 122–4, 301–2
summer snowflake, 64, 268
sundials, 61–3
sunflowers, 109, 143, 219
sweet briars, 79–81
sweet chestnuts, 167–8, 183
sweet cicely, 51
sweet peas, 27, 35, 66, 106, 112, 120, 124, 185,
    246, 266, 303
    grandiflora varieties, 102–3
    'Lord Anson's Pea' (*Lathyrus nervosus*),
    16–17
sweet rocket, 33, 108
sweet williams, 106–7
Szechwan, 240

Tahiti, 77–8
Taurus, 154
Taxotere, 162–3

Tay, river, 96
tea, 50
Tenbury Wells, 222–3
textile workers' strike, 177–8
Thames, river, 77, 238
Theobalds, 80
Thomas, Edward, 145–6
Thomas, Graham Stuart, 79
Thompson, Steve, 201
thrushes, 120, 154, 220–1
thyme, 86
tickseed, 161
Titan, 251–2
Titterstone Clee, 6
toadflax, 161
tomatoes, 132, 143
traveller's joy, 250
Trebah Garden, 274–5
tree ferns, 275
Trent, river, 238
Tresco Abbey, 36
trilliums, 35
Trinity College, Dublin, 58
Tropic of Cancer, 88–9
tulip fire, 81
tulip wood, 225
tulipomania, 288
tulips, 29, 33, 35, 38, 45, **47**, 54, 64, 121–2, 137, 161, 208, 292
    growing in pots, 175–6
    planting, 200–1
    'rectified', 56–8
Turner, J. M. W., 155
turnips, 144, 169
Tyne, river, 77

Ullswater, 8
Up-Helly-Aa, 236

Vancouver, Captain George, 78
Vancouver Island, 96
Varroa mite, 132
Vaughan, Henry, 193
Venus, transits of, 77–8
Veratrum nigrum, 122
verbascums, 33
Vermeer, Johannes, 121
viburnum, 136, 231, 247
Victoria, Queen, 216
violets, 38, 270–1
viper's bugloss, 111
viper's grass, 169
Virgil, 191–3
Virginia, 197, 273–4

Wakefield and North of England Tulip Society, 57–8, 303

Walker, Mark, 13
Wallace, Jean, 231–2
wallflowers, 43–6, 106–9
Walmsley, Liz, 171–2
walnuts, 37, 152–3, 167–8, 183–4, 223, 286
Warden Abbey, 158
Warren, Joseph Loxdale, 98–9
Warren, Miss Juliana, 98–9
Wars of the Roses, 79
Wassell, David, 160–1
water-boatmen, 135, 152
Waterend, 158
water-gardening, 264
watering, 293
Waterloo, battle of, 36
Watkins, Nick, 13
Watts, Alan, 284
weather-forecasting, 240–2, 284
weathervanes, 240–1
wedding flowers, 101–2
weeding, 32–3, 293–4
Weir Green, 158
Wellington, Duke of, 36
Wenlock Edge, 252
Whitby, 76–7
whitebeam, 97, 270
wild heliotrope, 161
wild service trees, 199–200
Williamson, Julia, 124, 180–1, 219
Willmot, Ellen, 94–5
    'Miss Willmott's Ghost', **91**, 95
willows, 25–7, 112, 223, 243
    pussy willows, 27, 133
Wilmot, John, Earl of Rochester, 249
Winchester, Vanessa, 252
wintersweet, 130
Wisley, 272
wisterias, 10–11, 129–30, 183
witch-hazel, 129
wolf's bane, 111
Woodland Trust, 158
Wordsworth, William and Dorothy, 8
Wu Zetian, Empress, 84
Wye, river, 238

Yapp, Stanley, 222–3
yellow rattle, 137, 277
Yenisei, river, 100
yew, 136, 146, 162–4, 174–5, 203, 207, 230, 244, 294
    yew wood, 225–6
yucca, 213

Zantedeschia, 239
zinnias, 217

ALSO AVAILABLE BY KATHERINE SWIFT

THE MORVILLE HOURS

A BBC Radio Four Book of the Week

In 1988 Katherine Swift arrived at the Dower House at Morville to create a garden of her own. This beautifully written, utterly absorbing book is the history of the many people who have lived in the same Shropshire house, tending the same soil, passing down stories over the generations. Spanning thousands of years, *The Morville Hours* takes the form of the medieval Books of Hours. It is a meditative journey through the seasons, but also a journey of self-exploration. It is a book about finding one's place in the world and putting down roots.

'A magical book. I have read it twice now. I love the richness of Katherine Swift's prose; the flashes of her family's story that are scattered through the deliciously written text; the gorgeous detail. *The Morville Hours* is the most beautiful book I have read in years'
NIGEL SLATER

'This is gardening writing at its best. Swift's prose brings the garden alive in all its details, scents and meaning . . . Evocative, heartfelt and magical'
GUARDIAN

'A truly remarkable book that is both intimate and universal. We are left with a renewed sense of what it is to be human, and of how we make our place in a world that is intricate, unpredictable and filled with quotidian mysteries'
DAILY TELEGRAPH

ORDER BY PHONE: +44 (0)1256 302 699; BY EMAIL: DIRECT@MACMILLAN.CO.UK

DELIVERY IS USUALLY 3–5 WORKING DAYS. FREE POSTAGE AND PACKAGING FOR ORDERS OVER £20.

ONLINE: WWW.BLOOMSBURY.COM/BOOKSHOP

PRICES AND AVAILABILITY SUBJECT TO CHANGE WITHOUT NOTICE.

WWW.BLOOMSBURY.COM/KATHERINESWIFT

B L O O M S B U R Y